JANE AUSTEN

Critical Issues

Published

Mary Shelley	*Graham Allen*
Jane Austen	*Darryl Jones*
George Eliot	*Pauline Nestor*
Virginia Woolf	*Linden Peach*
Charlotte Brontë	*Carl Plasa*
Charles Dickens	*Lyn Pykett*
Joseph Conrad	*Allan H. Simmons*
John Donne	*Richard Sugg*
Henry James	*Jeremy Tambling*
John Keats	*John Whale*
William Wordsworth	*John Williams*
Thomas Hardy	*Julian Wolfreys*

In preparation

D. H. Lawrence	*Rick Rylance*
Thomas Hardy	*Julian Wolfreys*

Critical Issues Series
Series Standing Order
ISBN 1–4039–2158–X hardcover
ISBN 1–4039–2159–8 paperback
(outside North America only)

You can receive future titles in this series as they are published by placing a standing order. Please contact your bookseller or, in case of difficulty, write to us at the address below with your name and address, the title of the series and the ISBN quoted above.

Customer Services Department, Macmillan Distribution Ltd
Houndmills, Basingstoke, Hampshire RG21 6XS, England

Critical Issues

Jane Austen

Darryl Jones

palgrave
macmillan

First published 2004 by
PALGRAVE MACMILLAN

Palgrave Macmillan in the UK is an imprint of Macmillan Publishers Limited, registered in England, company number 785998, of Houndmills, Basingstoke, Hampshire RG21 6XS.

Palgrave Macmillan in the US is a division of St Martin's Press LLC, 175 Fifth Avenue, New York, NY 10010.

Palgrave Macmillan is the global academic imprint of the above companies and has companies and representatives throughout the world.

Palgrave ® and Macmillan ® are registered trademarks in the United States, the United Kingdom, Europe and other countries.

ISBN-13: 978-0-333-72743-0 hardback
ISBN-13: 978-0-333-72744-7 paperback

This book is printed on paper suitable for recycling and made from fully managed and sustained forest sources. Logging, pulping and manufacturing processes are expected to conform to the environmental regulations of the country of origin.

A catalogue record for this book is available from the British Library.

Library of Congress Cataloging-in-Publication Data
Jones, Darryl, 1967–
    Jane Austen / Darryl Jones.
        p.   cm.
    Includes bibliographical references and index.
    ISBN 0–333–72743–6
    1. Austen, Jane, 1775–1817—Criticism and interpretation.   2. Women and literature—England—History—19th century.   3. Love stories, English—History and criticism.   I. Title.

PR4037.J66 2004
823'.92—dc22

                                                            2004041592

Printed and bound in Great Britain by
CPI Antony Rowe, Chippenham and Eastbourne

For Margaret Robson and
Miss Morgan Elizabeth Hannah Jones, age 8,
With Love

Contents

Acknowledgements

This book has very deep roots going back many years. Therefore, I should firstly like to thank Melynda Jones, Nerys Jones, and Anne Tilley, teachers of English, who got me off to the best possible start. Without them, I would be doing something much less interesting (though possibly more lucrative).

R. T. Jones, formerly of the Department of English and Related Literature, University of York, long ago supervised my PhD thesis on Austen (traces of which are still visible, palimpsest-like, beneath the surface of this book), and remains a model of engaged critical intelligence to which I can only aspire.

At Trinity College Dublin my esteemed and truly amiable colleagues Aileen Douglas and Ian Campbell Ross were characteristically generous with advice, suggestions and encouragement. My friend, ideological ally, and former colleague Stephanie Newell invited me to give a talk entitled 'Jane Austen's Knickers' which metamorphosed into Chapter 1 (but lost something in translation), and was a constant source of support and enthusiasm.

At Palgrave Macmillan I should like to thank Anna Sandeman and Sonya Barker for their tolerance and patience in the face of my repeated requests for Just a Little More Time... Especial thanks to the General Editors of the 'Critical Issues' series, John Peck and Martin Coyle, for responding so keenly to my original proposal. Their comments on the original manuscript invariably improved it.

Of all the conceivable books on Jane Austen, Robert Clark suggested I might want to write *this* one. I hope he likes it.

For a long and illuminating discussion about Jane Austen at, most appropriately, a home-counties wedding, my thanks to Diz Bernal and Cathy Bernal Lintott, both of the Jane Austen Society.

For past and continuing support – moral, intellectual, alcoholic and other – I would like to thank Graham Allen, Alistair Austin, Barbara Benedict, Brenda Brooks, Steve Cadman, Nick Curwin, Nick Daly, Helen Briggsy Docking, Jack Donovan, Dara Downey, Elisabeth Ellington, Euros Jones Evans, John Exshaw, Malcolm Fox, Pauline Gallagher, Nicholas Grene, Isabel Grimshaw, Kate Hebblethwaite, Ernie Hebert, Kate Hunt, Paul Jackson, Chris James, Celia Hilton Jones, Jarlath Killeen, Mary Lawlor, Jim Livesey, Lizzy McCarthy, Jenny McDonnell, P. J. Mathews, Stephen Matterson, Margaret Matthews, Jim Mays, Frances Namba, John Nash, Helen O'Connell, Jean O'Mahony, Graham Parry, Maria Parsons, Eve Patten, Jim Phelps, Amanda Piesse, Brin Price, Joanne Quirke, Marilyn Robitaille, Diane Sadler, Ben Sealy, Brenda Silver, Joanna Stephens, Neil Sutcliffe, Janet Todd, Mike Waites, Tim Webb, Grant Williams, Judith Woolf, and Philippa Woolnough.

I consider myself privileged in having taught so many extraordinarily fine students at Trinity College Dublin over the years. Some of them are mentioned above, but all of them have my thanks.

To my parents, Yvonne and Dewi Jones, my parents-in-law, Tom and Kathleen Robson, my sister, Nerys Brown, and my late grandparents Daisy and Charles Keats I owe a great debt of thanks, now and always.

Finally, and deepest of all, is my love and thanks to my wife Margaret and my daughter Morgan, to whom, for what it's worth and if they'll have it, this book is dedicated.

Darryl Jones
Trinity College Dublin

Texts and Abbreviations

References to Jane Austen's works are to these editions:
The Novels of Jane Austen, ed. R. W. Chapman, 6 vols, 3rd edn
(London: Oxford University Press, 1969).
Jane Austen's Letters, collected and edited by Deirdre Le Faye
(Oxford: Oxford University Press,1995).

Abbreviations:

E	*Emma*
L	*Letters*
MP	*Mansfield Park*
MW	*Minor Works*
NA	*Northanger Abbey*
P	*Persuasion*
PP	*Pride and Prejudice*
SS	*Sense and Sensibility*

Introduction

'What is all this about Jane Austen? What is there *in* her? What is it all *about*?' (Joseph Conrad, to H. G. Wells[1])

I. WHO OWNS JANE AUSTEN?

In David Lodge's novel *Changing Places* (1975), two Jane Austen scholars, the American Morris Zapp and the British Philip Swallow, take part in an exchange scheme in which they swap jobs, lives and (this being a campus novel, and thus an opportunity for vicarious fantasy versions of academics' actually rather stolid lives) wives. Zapp, who likes to think of himself as '*the* Austen man', is an academic superstar, 'the man who had published articles in *PMLA* while still at graduate school...who had published five fiendishly clever books (four of them on Jane Austen) by the time he was thirty',[2] and provides a fictional vehicle for the dissemination of Lodge's more daring Austen criticism by another means. To underline, once and for all, his supremacy in the field, Zapp dreams of producing a 'total reading' of Austen's work. His dreams are megalomaniacal and apocalyptic: he wishes both to end and to become Austen studies, 'saying everything there was to be said about Jane Austen. The idea was to be utterly exhaustive, to examine the novels from every conceivable angle...so that when each commentary was written, there would be simply *nothing further to say* about the novel in question.'[3] Lodge's novel is set in 1969, across thinly disguised versions of Birmingham and San Francisco, and partakes powerfully of its recreated times in its depictions of political upheaval both globally and, microcosmically, on university campuses. By this contextualising, Zapp's total reading is rendered neither intrinsically foolish (it is *not* just the megalomaniac dream of a narcissist, though Zapp is that too), nor, on the terms given, ultimately realisable.

Indeed, in 1967, one such 'total reading' of Jane Austen had already been attempted, Avrom Fleishman's remarkable *A Reading of Mansfield Park*, which synthesised more-or-less every critical

1

methodology at Fleishman's disposal in 1967 – Formalism and New Criticism, Historicism, Myth Criticism – to produce a formidable synoptic account of the novel, and one which, several decades later, no serious critic of *Mansfield Park* can afford to ignore.[4] However, as Fleishman (if not Zapp) recognises, there can be no *authentically* totalising readings, no *absolute* last words, since paradigms of reading and of criticism are not themselves absolute, though they may seem so to many of their less historically conscious or self-aware practitioners, both inside and outside the academy.

Tellingly, this is demonstrated even in the relatively short timelapse of six years between the setting of *Changing Places* in 1969 and its publication in 1975, an historical gap which Lodge exploits to intelligent effect. On his transatlantic flight to the UK, Zapp finds himself seated next to a pregnant woman, who makes what will turn out for Zapp to be a disturbing prophecy: ' "Women's liberation, what's that?" says Morris Zapp, not liking the sound of it at all. "I never heard of it." (Few people have on this first day of 1969.)' 'You will, Professor, you will,' his companion replies, portentously.[5] As feminist criticism, its academic arm within the humanities, the 'women's liberation movement' was to effect a paradigm shift in readings not just of Austen but of all women writers – more, was to effect a paradigm shift in *reading* – which would render Zapp's dreams of 'total readings', at least as they were articulable in 1969, redundant, although by the sequel, *Small World: An Academic Romance*, published in 1984 but mostly set in 1979, Zapp has more than caught up, transforming himself – rather opportunistically, it is implied – into a prominent poststructuralist literary theorist along the lines of Roland Barthes, and by the final leg of the trilogy, *Nice Work* (1988), he has (to use the word advisedly) mastered his subject completely:

> The names of prominent feminist theorists crackled between them like machine-gun fire: Elaine Showalter, Sandra Gilbert, Susan Gubar, Shoshana Feldman, Luce Irigaray, Catherine Clement, Susan Suleiman, Mieke Bal – Morris Zapp had read them all.[6]

Feminism brilliantly revolutionised the discipline of literary criticism; its effects were entirely beneficial, in opening up the canon, and in exposing the gender-biases that seemingly underwrote our very reading practices. As perhaps the most prominent, and certainly the most 'popular' (that is, widely read, for a number of different reasons, and by a number of very different interpretive communities) of all canonical women writers, Jane Austen was a natural subject for feminist criticism. Thus it was that, from the early 1970s, the dominant critical methodology for the study of Jane Austen was feminist, or more precisely feminist-historicist. Outside of this discourse it seemed that, with very few exceptions, there really was very little that could be said. The parameters within which critical discourse was conducted were effectively established by the two great books of their era on Jane Austen, Marilyn Butler's *Jane Austen and the War of Ideas* (1975) and Claudia L. Johnson's *Jane Austen: Women, Politics and the Novel* (1988), both of which used identical critical methodologies – an attempt to situate Austen historically, most particularly within the post-revolutionary political debates of the 1790s, and with especial reference to an economy of other contemporary texts, most notably (though not exclusively) other novels by women writers who were approximate contemporaries.[7] Butler's and Johnson's critical-theoretical approaches may have been identical, but the conclusions to which their books came were diametrically opposed: either Austen was a post-1789 Burkean Tory, asserting (or shoring up) a traditional conservative sense of national and familial identity in direct reaction to the spread of Enlightenment and Jacobin thinking into English political discourse (Butler); or, Austen's writing, provided we know how properly to contextualise (and thus to read) it, displays undeniable marks of sympathy, if not actually of overt affiliation, with the Enlightenment-feminist tenets of 1790s Jacobin thinking as notably embodied by Mary Wollstonecraft, and thus offers variously powerful or bitter critiques of contemporary English social and political institutions (Johnson). Positioned somewhere between these two poles were a number of influential critical studies, by Margaret Kirkham, Alison G. Sulloway, Deborah Kaplan and others.[8] It is worth noting that this latter position of Johnson's – one which I broadly share – gained especial currency during the 1980s, when the dread figure of Margaret Thatcher provided an unavoidable embodiment of contemporary conservative womanhood. Most academics within the humanities – and particularly here feminist critics – being of broadly liberal political sympathies consequently found themselves positioned somewhere between unsympathetic and implacably opposed to Margaret Thatcher (or in my own case, personally affronted and morally outraged each and every day of that decade). Consequently, we would sooner have died than have our beloved Jane Austen associated with *her!* Like Austen herself, these feminist studies tended to stake their ideological claims by acts of indirectness and implication: only one work on Austen from the 1980s takes an *overt* anti-Thatcher(ite) stance, Mary Evans's bracing polemic *Jane Austen and the State*.[9]

But, inconceivable though it seemed *in medias res*, the era of Margaret Thatcher, too, was bound to pass, and Thatcher's presence (though not her influence) in government came to a formal end in 1990. And so it was, too, that the 1990s witnessed yet another paradigm shift in versions of Austen. Feminist historicism had provided the most compelling interpretive methodology for reading Austen that we are likely to get, but its permutations were not infinite, after all, and there was always more that needed to be said. Even Leavisite and New Critical theorising, which had served to secure Austen's place at or near the centre of a literary canon, the object of that great rolling subject within the twentieth-century academy, the discipline of English studies, had served its purpose and had its day. The world of Austen studies which we currently (2004) inhabit, to which this book, in a small way, contributes, but which inevitably contains its own built-in obsolescence, is one which seems to me primarily to be concerned with Austen's extra-textual status and existence, in the ways in which the novels and their author have been adopted, adapted or appropriated, either within the academy itself (as part of an interestingly self-reflexive or self-absorbed turn within current critical discourse, keen to examine its own foundations and methods, and to historicise 'English Literature's' own existence and practices), or, more frequently, as part of a broader appropriation within popular culture. For this, we need witness the many film and TV versions of Austen, plus the innumerable updatings, spin-offs and sequels to her work produced during the 1990s – not to mention the rash of biographies of this superficially uneventful life, and, perhaps most importantly in the long term, Jane Austen's new and energetic life online, in fan-based websites, chatgroups and listservers, perhaps best exemplified by the extraordinary 'Republic of Pemberley' (www.pemberley.com).

All of a sudden, in the 1990s, then, Jane Austen seemed, if not up for grabs, then at least open for debate in a way that she had not been for at least a generation. The 1990s phenomenon of 'Austenmania' was itself examined and historicised in a series of important studies by Claudia L. Johnson, John Wiltshire, and

Roger Sales, and by the scholars working under the editorships of Linda Troost and Sayre Greenfield, of Deirdre Lynch, and a number of others.[10] Perhaps Austen *was* (is?) indeed 'up for grabs', after all, since what these studies, and the practices of, for example, websites, tended to show was that *ownership* of Austen had been claimed, often in absolute terms, by a number of powerfully conflicting interpretive communities, from fans to scholars.

II. THE NOVEL, THE LITERARY MARKETPLACE, AND THE MARRIAGE MARKET

I want to begin this section of the introduction with some apparently simple questions. Who wrote novels during Austen's lifetime? What did it mean to write a novel? Who read novels? Whom were novels written about? Why should so many writers, such as Austen's contemporaries and acknowledged influences, Frances (Fanny) Burney and Maria Edgeworth, be so reluctant to use the word 'novel' to describe their own work? These are important questions because it is within a contemporary economy of literary production that we should first of all attempt to situate Jane Austen's novels.

The novel is the literary form *par excellence* of modernity. It is, as Mikhail Bakhtin suggested, the *only* major literary form not already fully theorised in classical antiquity.[11] Thus, the major studies of the novel's provenance, though they may disagree on specifics, all situate its 'rise' or 'origins' in and around the eighteenth century.[12] Samuel Richardson and Henry Fielding, two of the novel's great progenitors in English, both thought that they had hit upon something genuinely new and distinctive in their work. Richardson believed that *Pamela* (1740) 'might possibly introduce a new species of writing',[13] while in the Preface to *Joseph Andrews* (1742), a novel which passed itself off as the history of Pamela's brother (Fielding, clearly preoccupied by the subject, had already written *Shamela*, a crude spoof of *Pamela*, in 1740), Fielding writes:

As it is possible the mere English reader may have a different idea of romance with the author of these little volumes, and may consequently expect a kind of entertainment not to be found, nor which was even intended, in the following pages, it may not be improper to premise a few words concerning this kind of writing, which I do not remember to have seen hitherto attempted in our language.[14]

Certainly, some novelists, such as Fielding, considered themselves engaged, if not precisely in a high cultural exercise, then certainly working within a form able to accommodate such a cultural agenda. Thus, Fielding's own disquisitions at the beginnings of each book of his masterpiece, *Tom Jones*, consist precisely of the kind of learned classical and cultural allusions which would traditionally have separated the literate (that is, to all intents and purposes, the formally educated) from the rest. One such excursus, at the beginning of Book 9, is tellingly called 'Of those who lawfully may, and of those who may not write such histories as this', and contains passages such as the following:

> To invent good stories, and to tell them well, are possibly very rare talents, and yet I have observed few persons who have scrupled to aim at both; and if we examine the romances and novels with which the world abounds, I think we may fairly conclude, that most of the authors would not have attempted to shew their teeth (if the expression may be allowed me) in any other way of writing; nor could indeed have strung together a dozen sentences on any other subject whatever. *Scriblimus indocti doctique passim* ['Each desperate blockhead dares to write'] may be more truly said of the historian and biographer, than of any other species of writing: for all the arts and sciences (even criticism itself) require some little degree of learning and knowledge. Poetry indeed may perhaps be thought an exception; but then it demands numbers, or something like numbers; whereas to the composition of novels and romances, nothing is necessary but paper, pens, and ink, with the manual capacity of using them. This, I conceive, their productions shew to be the opinions of the authors themselves; and this must be the opinion of their readers, if indeed there be any such.[15]

Obviously, Fielding is assuming a constituency here – an implied readership composed of well-educated, classically literate, witty men of the world very much like himself. Accordingly, Fielding's narrator keeps up an ironic, and highly intellectual, comment on his own novel throughout, suggesting at all times a learned, gentlemanly distance from his occasionally sordid material: a self-consciously highbrow treatment of his self-consciously lowbrow subject-matter.

Nevertheless, as Fielding implies here, albeit with some disdain, the novel, requiring no classical education, and in principle no education at all beyond the ability to read (or to know someone who did, for they were often read aloud), was potentially the greatest force for democracy in the history of letters (for, as Fielding argues, even poetry presupposes some familiarity with metrics, which require some form of numeracy), which is one reason why it tended to be treated with hostility by a cultural-political establishment fearful of compromising its hegemonic power. This led to the numerous attacks on the novel on the grounds of culture, class or gender across the eighteenth century, where it was figured as a prime example of disreputable and possibly harmful popular culture. Thus, the *Critical Review* could describe the anonymous *Frailties of Fashion, or The Adventures of an Irish Smock* (1782) as:

> One of those pernicious incentives to vice that are a scandal to decency. A common pander, who confines his infamous occupation to the services of the stews, is less injurious to society than such prostituted miscreants as devote their time and attention to corrupt the imaginations of youth. The most ignominious punishment prescribed by our laws is infinitely too slight for offences of so heinous a nature.[16]

'Entertainment alone,' write Peter Garside, James Raven and Rainer Schöwerling, 'was no proper manifesto for the novelist; only when this was combined with useful instruction might the novel escape charges of insignificance or depravity.'[17] This hegemonic position was internalised by many of the novelists themselves, who could go to great lengths in their denials that the text in question is a novel at all: rather, it is a 'Moral Tale', like Maria Edgeworth's *Belinda* – its 'author not wishing to acknowledge a Novel' – or simply a 'little Work' like Frances Burney's *Camilla*.[18] It is to Austen's great credit that she is willing to buck this trend of public reticence and denial, recognising as she does that it is predicated on grounds of gender:

> Yes, novels; – for I will not adopt that ungenerous and impolitic custom so common with novel writers, of degrading by their contemptuous censure the very performances, to the number of which they are themselves adding – joining with their greatest enemies in bestowing the harshest epithets on such works, and scarcely ever permitting them to be read by their own heroine, who, if she accidentally take up a novel, is sure to turn over its insipid pages with disgust. Alas! if the heroine of one novel be not patronized by the heroine of another, from whom can she expect protection and regard?...Let us not desert one another; we are an injured body. (NA, 37)

It is significant that a novelist of the marriage market, in which women were so often positioned as the victims of predatory men, should describe the novel, its heroines and practitioners – women all in Austen's configuration – as 'an injured body'. Significant, too, that two of the novels she singles out for praise as examples of 'work in which the greatest powers of the mind are displayed, in which the most thorough knowledge of human nature, the happiest delineation of its varieties, the liveliest effusions of wit and humour are conveyed to the world in the best chosen language' (NA, 58) should be the generically self-denying *Camilla* and *Belinda*.

The history of eighteenth-century publishing legislation also effected a broadening of the reading public, though not necessarily in ways which cut across traditional class and economic boundaries. The Copyright Act of 1710 limited copyright to 21 years for books already in print and 14 years for new books (with the possibility of an extension of a further 14 years). This act was contested under Common Law, primarily by the booksellers, who argued for a system of effective perpetual copyright, thus keeping book prices high. In 1768, a restraining injunction by the Court of Chancery against the publisher Alexander Donaldson, who was producing cheap reprints, further confirmed the booksellers' monopoly. However, the injunction was overturned by the House of Lords in 1774, which led to the 1710 Act finally being properly enforced. This led to a publishing boom, with cheap reprint editions flooding the market, particularly outside London (Dublin especially became the centre of a vigorous trade in reprint publication).[19]

This in turn led to a proliferation of book clubs and especially circulating libraries, whose demands, we shall see, were in some ways to control the production and even the content of fiction over the next decades. The first circulating library was established in Bath in 1725, followed by one in London in 1739; by the 1780s, most major English market towns had a circulating library.[20] This certainly effected a change in the economics of reading practices, usually to the financial detriment of authors – Austen herself remarked in a letter of 1814 to Fanny Knight that readers were 'more ready to borrow & praise, than to buy' (L, 287), though she herself was, with Cassandra, a subscriber to Mrs Martin's new circulating library in Basingstoke in 1798: 'she tells us that her collection is not to consist only of novels, but of every kind of literature &c &c. She might have spared this pretension to *our* family, who are great novel-readers and not ashamed of being so; but it was necessary

I suppose to the self-consequence of half her subscribers' (L, 26) (this reminds us again of the dominant cultural view of novels as disreputable, and of Austen's dissent from this position). However, it would be a mistake to think that of itself this proliferation of circulating libraries democratised reading across the class system, as the annual subscription rates for these libraries certainly put them beyond the reach of the poorer sections of society (whose literary needs tended to be served by the extraordinarily flourishing chapbook market): in 1773, the *Critical Review* estimated 10s 6d as the average annual subscription for a circulating library, and by 1800 the cost could be as much as a guinea (these tended to be the rates for larger metropolitan libraries: their smaller provincial counterparts were certainly cheaper, though still comfortably beyond the means of many, if not most, readers).[21] Furthermore, as Edward Copeland argues, even within the libraries themselves, novels were aimed at different readerships divided on traditional class grounds and signalled according to choice of publisher: 'Genteel readers would be comfortable with something from one of the established publishers – Longman, Hookham and Carpenter, the Robinsons, Cadell, Johnson, or Noble. Readers from trade or from the lesser professions, though they could find pleasure in the genteel books, would discover that the Minerva Press addressed them specifically and as a matter of policy.'[22]

Nevertheless, the circulating libraries did provide access to novels at a fraction of the cost of purchasing them. In *Pride and Prejudice*, Mr Bennet's library, to which he constantly retreats, has a metonymic function, acting as guarantor of his social status as a member of the gentry; while Darcy's lament that he 'cannot comprehend the neglect of a family library in days such as these' (38) signals not only his cultural guardianship but also his wealth – he need not concern himself with the economics of maintaining a great library, which he can comfortably afford. Similarly, in *Sense and Sensibility*, Colonel Brandon maintains a library well stocked with works of 'modern production' (343), ideally suited to Marianne, 'the bulk of [whose] fortune would be laid out in annuities on the authors or their heirs' (93).[23] Furthermore, as Lee Erickson has noted, the circulating libraries came to accrue an extra-literary social function: 'In the resorts the circulating libraries became fashionable daytime lounges where ladies could see others and be seen, where raffles were held and games were played, and where expensive merchandise could be purchased.'[24] Thus, when Walter Scott reviewed *Emma* after its publication in 1815, he adjudged it, along with Austen's other works, 'far superior to ... the ephemeral productions which supply the regular demand of watering-holes and bathing-places.'[25] While, in *Sanditon*, the foolish Sir Edward Denham professes that 'I am no indiscriminate Novel-Reader. The mere Trash of the common Circulating Library I hold in the highest contempt' (403), the novel's aspiring resort nevertheless has a circulating library positioned right at its centre. Even Clarke's, Meryton's very own circulating library in *Pride and Prejudice*, operates as a modest version of the fashionable resort circulating library: Kitty and Lydia Bennet certainly don't go there primarily to borrow books, but to ogle soldiers.

It is a generalisation, though not inaccurate, to say that during Jane Austen's productive years as a writer, from the 1790s to the 1810s, the novel was a literary form written by, for and about women. In their magisterial bibliographical survey of English fiction 1770–1829, whose findings (like all serious students of the fiction of the period), I draw heavily upon in this section of the Introduction, Peter Garside, James Raven, Rainer Schöwerling and their collaborators have produced a meticulously realised map of the gender-distribution of authorship across the period.[26] While in the years to 1800, the number of published male and female novelists is roughly the same (this allowing for the very large numbers of novels published anonymously, whose authorship is often impossible to attribute according to gender), nevertheless there are considerably more *novels* being written by women than by men. In the 1810s, the decade, lest we forget, in which *all* of Austen's novels were originally published, the domestic or sentimental novel (structured, as Austen's novels are, around the marriage plot) really was the dominant form of fiction, with 344 new titles published by named, identified or implied women writers, as against 191 by authors named, identified or implied as male. It is in the 1820s, in the wake of the phenomenal success of Walter Scott, who set out quite explicitly to masculinise what he clearly figured as the feminine gender of the novel, that the male writers definitively overtake their female counterparts, with 419 men as against 273 women. Scott himself understood and appreciated Austen's genius as a novelist, at the same time recognising that the two of them stood as the opposing gendered poles of the contemporary novel. Musing on *Pride and Prejudice* in his journal of 14 March 1826, Scott wrote: 'The Big Bow-Wow strain I can do myself like any now going, but the exquisite touch which renders ordinary commonplace things and characters interesting from the truth and description of the sentiment is denied to me. What a pity such a gifted creature died so early!'[27]

All of these facts – copyright law, circulating libraries, the cost of books, the gender-history of publication – have a significant bearing on Austen's novels, which have generally been viewed as high-order aesthetic artefacts, above or beyond such grubby concerns, rather than as material productions embedded in the literary marketplace of the time. In his influential account of the Victorian literary marketplace, John Sutherland has stressed the importance of publishers in dictating, often at the level of plot and character (who lives or who dies, for example), the substance of the novels they published, so that frequently it behoves us to treat author and publisher alike as an amalgam of creative writer and cultural businessman working together to produce what we now think of as stable, canonical, authored major novels.[28] Similarly, during Austen's writing years, the publishing market was controlled by a relatively small number of influential concerns, notably William Lane's Minerva Press, which effectively cornered the market in the Gothic novel, and the publishing firm of Thomas Norton Longman and his various partners. It was also, as we have seen, heavily under the influence of the circulating libraries which, in Erickson's words, 'dominated the market for fiction throughout the nineteenth century' – so much so that when Austen was writing the majority (in some cases, the great majority) of copies of any given novel were sold to circulating libraries rather than to private consumers.[29] This directly affected the *kinds* of novels published to meet the specific demands of the libraries, which in turn provides an explanation for some of the features of Austen's writing which many readers find puzzling or in some cases irritating: specifically, her constant reliance on the marriage plot for her novels which makes them all, on a structural level, identical.

Compared with the power of publishers and libraries, the power of individual authors – and thus, in extreme cases, the degree of control they could exercise over their own texts – could be negligible. While a number of high-profile novelists – such as Ann Radcliffe and, later, Walter Scott – could command high prices for their work, this was rarely the case. The high instance of anonymity amongst the authors of novels is a telling factor here, and we should of course remember that *every one* of Austen's novels was initially published anonymously, from *Sense and Sensibility*, 'By a Lady', to the posthumous edition of *Northanger Abbey* and *Persuasion*, 'By the Author of "Pride and Prejudice," "Mansfield Park,", &c.' Similarly, Frances Burney, probably the most celebrated woman novelist of her generation, published all her works anonymously – their prefaces record, across a time-span from the 1770s to the 1810s, a consistent anxiety about issues of naming, authorship, identity and legitimacy which feeds quite clearly into the novels themselves. What this tells us is that Romantic theories of authorship, which stress the primacy of the individual creative self, are at best post-facto concerns when it comes to the study of the majority of the period's fiction: contemporary readers of fiction are far more interested in authorship than our counterparts of two centuries ago would have been.

What this also tells us is that the novel was a *generic* as opposed to an individualistic medium. Scott was quite right to talk about circulating library fiction as 'ephemeral' – transient, designed for speedy reading, designed to be read once. Consequently, as Barbara Benedict notes, library catalogues often classed books together according to length – what was important was how long a given work would take you to read. In her brilliant account of Austen's novels as 'Regency Popular Fiction', Benedict, indeed, goes so far as to conclude that:

> Austen structures her fiction according to circulating novels' formulas and strategies. In libraries and their catalogs, these novels become part of a public literary collection featuring tales of love in elite settings, a happy ending in the form of a marriage, and the fulfillment of readerly expectations. In her plots, characterization, organization, and narrative strategies of intertextuality, tonal fluidity, and self-consciousness, Austen underscores her obedience to them. Libraries' practice of lending work by the volume required readers to read quickly. It also encouraged Austen to arrange for her plots to move rapidly to a climax at the end of each volume while continuing to provide dramatic beauties for her readers to remember after they had returned the book...Readers approached Austen's novels expecting to read quickly through all their volumes, closing the last with a sense of identificatory triumph with a familiar character, not with an extraordinary Romantic hero.[30]

Thus, we need to understand Austen's novels firstly as generic products, before we can appreciate precisely what it is that she does with her generic template that produces great art. The anonymous

reviewer of *Sense and Sensibility* from the *Critical Review*, 1
February 1812, in the first ever review of an Austen novel, commented on the novel's generic quality:

> The story may be thought trifling by the readers of novels, who are insati-
> able after *something new*. But the excellent lesson which it holds up to
> view, and the useful moral which may be derived from the perusal, are
> such essential requisites, that the want of *newness* may in this instance
> be readily overlooked.[31]

Even her novels' very titles are, for the most part, generic. When, in
Northanger Abbey, Henry Tilney explains to Catherine his love of
novel-reading, he says, 'Do not imagine that you can cope with me
in a knowledge of Julias and Louisas' (NA, 107), it may be that he
is referring to *Julia Benson; or, The Sufferings of Innocence* (Anon,
1775), Henry Mackenzie's *Julia De Roubigné* (1777), *Julia Stanley*
(Anon, 1780), Lady Cassandra Hawke's *Julia De Gramont* (1788),
Helen Maria Williams's *Julia: A Novel* (1790), Helen Craik's *Julia
De Saint Pierre* (1796), or any one of a number of others, or of the
seven various *Louisas* published before 1800. Emma Woodhouse
is one of nine titular Emmas to appear between 1770 and 1829.
Austen's most direct source for the title of *Pride and Prejudice* is
Burney's *Cecilia* (1783): ' "The whole of this unfortunate business"
said Dr. Lyster, "has been the result of PRIDE and PREJUDICE....Yet
this, however, remember; if to PRIDE and PREJUDICE you owe
your miseries, so wonderfully is good and evil balanced, that to
PRIDE and PREJUDICE you will owe also their termination.'[32]
The conjunction also appears in Charlotte Smith's *The Old Manor
House* (1793): ' "Nay, nay!" cried his father impatiently – "Why
has she invincible pride, and obstinate prejudice?" '[33]
    Benedict suggests that 'The titles of Austen's first two published
novels announce the novels' allegiance to one particular subgenre:
romances about the education of heroines. In titling these books,
Austen employs terms that were highly familiar to her audience
and would immediately signal the central plots of her novels:
"sense," "sensibility," "pride," and "prejudice." '[34] The success of
Mary Brunton's dour novels of socialised repression, *Self-Control*
(1811) and *Discipline* (1814) led, as Garside, Raven and Schöwerling
note, 'to a chain of similar morally charged domestic fictions, often
discernible through their deliberately unadorned titles, these sometimes consisting only of single words reflecting moral qualities.'[35]

These include novels duly (and perhaps dully) entitled *Duty, Self-Denial, Correction*, and *Decision* – and, of course, Jane Austen's own contribution to the subgenre, *Persuasion*.

Austen's habitual reliance on the marriage plot is, then, to a very great extent determined by the constraints of the publishing market of her day: it was, to offer a broad generalisation, virtually impossible for a woman writer of Austen's generation to publish any other kind of novel. (There are exceptions, but these tend to come from writers working within an explicit ideology of political radicalism – Mary Wollstonecraft, for example, works outside the confines of the marriage plot.) Inextricably interwoven with the gendering of publishing concerns here is a broader eighteenth-century theory of gender, the so-called 'separate spheres' argument which figured women's inherent sphere of activity as the domestic, the private, the internal, the familial, while the masculine sphere was external, public, political, historical. This ideology, which underpins virtually every conduct-book for young ladies, and which certainly informs Walter Scott's understanding of the essential difference between his own work and Austen's, has its classic formulation in George Savile, Marquis of Halifax's *The Lady's New Year's Gift: or, Advice to a Daughter* (1688, and reprinted at least 14 times during the eighteenth century). Halifax asserts 'That there is *Inequality* in the *Sexes*, and that for the better Oeconomy of the World, the *Men*, who were to be the Lawgivers, had the larger share of *Reason* bestow'd upon them.' It was not all bad for women, however:

> We are made of differing *Tempers*, that our *Defects* may the better be mutually supplied: Your *Sex* wanteth our *Reason* for your *Conduct*, and our *Strength* for your *Protection: Ours* wanteth your *Gentleness* to soften, and to entertain us. The first part of our Life is a good deal subjected to you in the *Nursery*, where you Reign without Competition, and by that means have the advantage of giving us the first *Impressions*. Afterwards you have stronger Influences, which, well manag'd, have more force in your behalf, than all our *Privileges* and *Jurisdictions* can pretend to have against you. You have more strength in your *Looks*, than we have in our *Laws*, and more power by your *Tears*, than we have by our *Arguments*.[36]

So, perhaps it was all bad, after all, as it need hardly be added that, far from being equal-but-different, this theory operates hierarchically, privileging the public above the private sphere at every turn in a manner which sought comprehensively to deny real political power to women, as Mary Wollstonecraft was to argue in the 1790s. And while Harriet Guest has recently (2000) argued that women insinuated themselves into the political mainstream nearer to sources of power than the 'separate spheres' theory had generally allowed for, it is nevertheless, in Guest's telling phrase, as the 'small change' in the cultural pocket that women tended to operate: always there, perhaps, and often necessary, but rarely afforded much real significance.[37]

The marriage plot also has a basis in the shifting configurations of marriage across the eighteenth and into the nineteenth century. The practice of marriage was not standardised in law until shortly before Austen's birth, with Lord Hardwicke's Marriage Act of 1753, under which all marriage ceremonies had to be undergone in church and entered into the parish register with the signatures of both parties for the contract to be legally binding, and enforced by the state rather than canon law; under this act, no marriage between persons under the age of 21 could be legally binding without the consent of parents or guardians.[38] As the Marriage Act did not apply under Scottish law, it could be circumvented by an elopement across the border, most frequently to Gretna Green. This is what the young Colonel Brandon had planned to do with his beloved Eliza in *Sense and Sensibility*, and what Lydia and Wickham do in *Pride and Prejudice*.

The historian of marriage Lawrence Stone has written of 'the development of a national marriage market in London and Bath [which] greatly widened the pool of potentially satisfactory spouses, from the parental point of view', by introducing young people from the same social class but disparate geographical regions, thus keeping property and power, if not localised by region, then certainly theoretically within the same hegemonic class.[39] That is to say, the marriage market ensured and reinforced *endogamy*, marital relations within the social group. The marriage market took place during the two social 'seasons', the late winter and spring season in London, and the summer season either in Bath, where much of *Northanger Abbey* is set, or, increasingly, in fashionable coastal resorts such as Lyme Regis, where much of *Persuasion* is set – and what we have of Austen's last, unfinished novel, *Sanditon*, is focused entirely around a fictional south-coast resort with aspirations to be the latest fashionable haunt. As David Spring has suggested, Austen's real social milieu is not precisely that of the upper classes, the aristocracy and landed gentry, but rather of the 'pseudo-gentry'.[40] These are members of the church and professions, military officers, successful businessmen of various kinds, all of whom intermingle and often aspire to intermarry with the old landed families. Austen's novels, we shall see, chart the progressive taking-over of social control by this 'pseudo-gentry', symbolically played out across the Napoleonic Wars. Nevertheless, it is unquestionably the case, as many of the following chapters will explore, that Austen's young women are, to varying extents, reified into 'heroines', consumer products on the marriage market. This is the real significance of Catherine Morland's being taken off to Bath, as soon as she is of age: she is there to find a husband, which she in fact does almost immediately. This is also the real significance of the famous opening sentence of *Pride and Prejudice*: 'It is a truth universally acknowledged that a single man in possession of a good fortune, must be in want of a wife' (PP, 3). The fact that Mr Collins, sleazebag though he is, sees himself able to command such power in the marriage market is because he, with a war on, is a marketable commodity: 'gentlemen were scarce' (PP, 175). The capitalist *realpolitik* of the marriage market, with its clear mercenary overtones in Austen, has certainly proven too much for some readers, perhaps particularly those with socialist political leanings. W. H. Auden famously wrote of Austen that:

> You could not shock her more than she shocks me;
> Beside her Joyce seems innocent as grass.
> It makes me uncomfortable to see
> An English spinster of the middle class
> Describe the amorous effects of 'brass',
> Reveal so frankly and with such sobriety
> The economic basis of society.[41]

Which seems a reasonable position, and in the light of this it seems to me highly suggestive, at least to us as contemporary readers, that this great novelist of sex and money, 'the amorous effects of "brass" ', should name one of her heroines Fanny Price.[42] The bawdy or erotic overtones in this name seem implicit in the libidinous Henry Crawford's remark to his sister Mary that 'I cannot be satisfied without Fanny Price, without making a small hole in Fanny Price's heart' (MP, 229), a phrase which, as Jill Heydt-Stevenson notes, 'in itself suggests defloration'.[43]

Maria Edgeworth's *Belinda* (1801), which Austen cites with admiration in *Northanger Abbey*, opens unambiguously within the mercenary context of the marriage market:

Mrs Stanhope, a well-bred woman, accomplished in that branch of knowledge, which is called the art of rising in the world had, with but a small fortune, continued to live in the highest company. She prided herself on having established half a dozen nieces most happily; that is to say, of having married them to men of fortunes far superior to their own. . . . Mrs Stanhope lived at Bath, where she had opportunities of showing her niece [Belinda] off, as she thought, to advantage; but as her health began to decline, she could not go out with her as much as she wished. After manœuvring with more than her usual art, she succeeded in fastening Belinda upon the fashionable Lady Delacour for the season.[44]

Belinda is initially treated with suspicion by her potential suitors in Bath, tarred by her aunt's predatory reputation as a gold-digger. This is broadly the opinion of Elizabeth Bennet offered by Lady Catherine de Bourgh in *Pride and Prejudice*, and taken at face value this is understandable: Elizabeth, like all her sisters, *must* marry in order to be financially secure, as the entail upon her father's estate devolves it, on Mr Bennet's death, to the nearest male relative, Mr Collins. Indeed, a cynical interpretation of the novel might plausibly suggest that it is precisely only *after* Elizabeth visits Pemberley, and sees for herself the truly magnificent wealth Darcy is able to command, that she discovers herself in love with him: 'at that moment she felt, that to be mistress of Pemberley might be something!' (PP, 267). Nor should this *necessarily* be construed as cynical after all: Copeland notes that 'there is little economic rejoicing to be found in women's fiction of any sort in the 1790s', and that this concern, amounting on occasion to a paranoia, with women's financial status (with women's financial *survival*) unites Austen with her contemporary women writers in 'an unsettling sisterhood of loss'.[45]

Perhaps 'love', then, is a classic modern category mistake made by contemporary readers in approaching Austen's novels. Though the existence of the marriage plot does seem to us to presuppose a 'love story', the practice of the novels themselves, I shall argue throughout this study, serves desperately to complicate and muddy such conventionally romantic readings. Nancy Armstrong's influential theory of the provenance of domestic fiction argues, surely correctly, that 'the history of the novel cannot be understood apart from the history of sexuality'.[46] Drawing on the work of Michel Foucault, Armstrong argues that, far from articulating any pre-existing or constant emotional essence, the configurations of desire in domestic fiction and in the non-fictional prose-writings on gender, such as conduct-books, which surround and inform the novel (and from which, Armstrong insists, again correctly, it should not be disentangled), are semiotic systems, linguistic constructs whose ultimate purpose is to underpin middle-class notions of a stable, discrete family unit structured in accord with the 'separate spheres' theory around 'the opposition of complementary genders':

> As the heirs to a novelistic culture, we do not very likely question the whole enterprise. We are more likely to feel that the success of repeated pressures to coax and nudge sexual desire into conformity with the norms of heterosexual monogamy affords a fine way of closing and provides a satisfactory goal for the text to achieve. Novels do not encourage us to doubt whether sexual desire already existed before the strategies were devised to domesticate it. ... I know of no major criticism of the novel which does not at some point capitulate to the idea that sexual desire exists in some form prior to its representation and remains there as something for us to recover or liberate.[47]

A product of its own time, of the hard-line theoretical turn of much literary criticism emanating, in particular, from the American academy in the 1980s, Armstrong's work, in its absolute insistence that, in Jacques Derrida's famous phrase, 'there is nothing outside the text', now seems perhaps too rigorously poststructuralist, and she herself acknowledges having 'overstated [her] case'.[48] Certainly, many historicist critics, including myself, would now wish to argue for a greater fluidity in the relations between text and context, and for a less conspiratorial, more contingent vision of cultural praxis. Nevertheless, Armstrong's work still operates as a powerful reminder that the marriage plot, and the love-story it presupposes, are not given eternal verities but cultural and ideological constructs, and constructs which, I suggest, Jane Austen's novels do not simply accept passively. Rather, the novels interrogate and, within the strict parameters of publishing history described above, seek to deny or circumvent them, or, as Auden suggested, to expose their fundamental economic basis. Thus for me, at least, Jane Austen's novels rarely make comfortable reading.

In order to point up the disturbing element in Austen's use of the marriage plot, we should begin by considering the novels' heroines themselves. They are, with the obviously significant exception of Anne Elliot, very young. Younger, in fact, than we might imagine.

Catherine Morland and Marianne Dashwood are both 17, Elinor Dashwood 19, Elizabeth Bennet 20, Emma Woodhouse 21, Anne Elliot an initially creaking 27, while the action of *Mansfield Park* takes Fanny Price from young girlhood to late teens. Though today, 17 is well past the average age of female puberty, in Austen's day the average age at the menarche – the onset of first menstruation, or 'flowers' as it was then known – may, largely for reasons of relative dietary inadequacy, have been as high as 18 or even 20, though 16–17 seems a more reliable figure, compared to a constant of 13¼ since 1960.[49] What this means is that a good proportion of Austen's heroines (indeed of all the heroines of the time) were physically and very probably psychologically adolescent. One step towards modernising Catherine or Marianne, then, might be to envisage them as, say 13–14 rather than 17, though it has to be said that every modern version of Austen, in cinema and television, does the precise opposite, making them older – often much older. Thus, in Robert Z. Leonard's *Pride and Prejudice* (1940), the 20-year-old Elizabeth Bennet was played by the 37-year-old Greer Garson, while Ang Lee's *Sense and Sensibility* (1995) starred Emma Thompson as a 36-year-old Elinor Dashwood and, rather better but still slightly too old, the 20-year-old Kate Winslet as Marianne; Douglas McGrath's *Emma* (1996) featured 24-year-old Gwyneth Paltrow in the title role, the same age as Kate Beckinsale in Andrew Davies's 1997 TV adaptation; and Patricia Rozema's *Mansfield Park* (1999) starred Frances O'Connor as a (wonderful) 32-year-old Fanny Price. While some of these differences in age are quite startling, others represent only minor shifts; but nevertheless the adjustments are always upwards. While this can in part be explained by the economics and demographics of film casting and the star-system, they also, I think, signify a modern unease at the idea that Austen's sophisticated and sometimes quite heartless comedies of courtship, sexual rivalry, economic exchange and marriage are in fact played out by children.

The powerful ideological constraints of decorum and propriety also served to normalise and socialise what were fundamentally material, economic imperatives by inscribing them, in conduct books and domestic fiction, as moral or even ontological categories. This is of course most powerful in the ideologies surrounding female chastity: 'Consider,' Boswell records Dr Johnson as saying, 'of what importance to society, the chastity of women is. Upon that, all the property in the world depends.'[50] This view is reinforced by

Stone, who remarks of the sexual economy of the eighteenth century and earlier:

> Anthropologists tell us that the value attached to chastity is directly related to the degree of social hierarchy and the degree of property ownership. Pre-marital chastity is a bargaining-chip in the marriage game, to be set off against male property and status rights. Pre-marital female sexual repression is thus built in to the social system, since male and female are bargaining on the marriage market with different goods, the one social and economic, the other sexual. The withholding of sexual favours is a woman's only source of power over men. . . . The system serves the interests of both parties, since the male is guaranteed that he is purchasing new and not second-hand goods, while the female has a powerful lever to obtain marriage.[51]

In the marriage market, an unbroken hymen was a woman's only genuine marketable commodity. Chastity acted as guarantor of the smooth transfer of inheritance and property down the generations: while a husband could not, in the eighteenth century, *prove* that his children were his own, he could at least prove that his wife had not had pre-marital sexual relations, thus at least diminishing the likelihood of illegitimate children contesting and dissipating the inheritance of property. This brutal *economic* fact was translated into a strictly female *moral* lexicon – 'virtue', 'shame', 'ruin', the 'fallen woman' – which a tradition of writing for women in novels and conduct-books served to enforce and to naturalise, presenting them as inherent (and inherently desirable) qualities rather than ideological configurations.

The heroines of domestic novels, ideological constructs that they are, married slightly younger than their actual historical counterparts: the average age of marriage for women in the landed classes across the eighteenth century was around 22–23. Men tended to marry older, for reasons either of education (time spent at university; the Grand Tour) or, most often, of economics: older sons waiting to come into their inheritances upon the death of a parent or other relation; younger sons, the victims of primogeniture, having to make their way in the world before settling down in financial security.[52] Given this age difference, and given the fundamentally endogamous attitude to marriage encouraged by the marriage market, it is perhaps little wonder that so many of the period's novels, including Austen's, can present marriage symbolically in quasi-incestuous terms. The Gothic novel drew heavily upon incest in presenting a world where beautiful young women were the victims of predatory powerful men, frequently men violating some form of familial or pastoral role as fathers, father-figures, guardians or confessors. Thus, incestuous desire, as William Patrick Day suggests, 'parodies the values of the affective family, transforming emotional and spiritual bonds into sexual ones'.[53] Diane Long Hoeveler has argued persuasively that these Gothic conditions of victimhood have clear implications for the position of women within the marriage market who are likewise potentially the victims of powerful, predatory men, a circumstance Austen explores in her negotiations between the Gothic and domestic novels in *Northanger Abbey*.[54] The incestuous sexual relations of *Mansfield Park* have been much discussed, and will be analysed fully in Chapter 4. In *Sense and Sensibility*, the 17-year-old Marianne marries the 35-year-old Colonel Brandon, whom she initially describes as 'old enough to be *my* father' (SS, 37), while in *Persuasion* it is Sir Walter and Elizabeth Elliot whose actual father–daughter relationship has strongly incestuous overtones based on mutual narcissism. Emma Woodhouse, 21, marries Mr Knightley, 38, a man who quite clearly fulfils for her a paternal role given the hopelessness of her actual (or ostensible?) father, Mr Woodhouse. Emma and Mr Knightley constantly hint at a familial, consanguineal relationship. He tells Mrs Weston, 'I have a very sincere interest in Emma. Isabella does not seem more my sister' (E, 40) (Isabella, Emma's sister, has married John, Mr Knightley's brother, redoubling the symbolic incest here). Later, at the ball in the Crown, Emma and Mr Knightley dance:

'Whom are you going to dance with?' asked Mr Knightley.
   She hesitated a moment and then replied, 'With you, if you will ask me.'
   'Will you?' said he, offering his hand.
   'Indeed I will. You have shown that you can dance, and you know that we are not really so much brother and sister as to make it at all improper.'
   'Brother and sister! no indeed.'   (E, 331)

After proposing, Mr Knightley confesses all to Emma: 'I ... have been in love with you ever since you were thirteen at least. . . . How often, when you were a girl, have you said to me, with one of your saucy looks, "Mr Knightley, I am going to do so and so; papa says

I may, or, I have Miss Taylor's leave" – something which, you knew, I did not approve' (E, 462). We should, I think, be quite rightly troubled by the paedophiliac overtones of this passage, and perhaps of the novel as a whole: a man in his thirties 'in love' with a 13-year-old girl and her 'saucy looks'.

Glenda A. Hudson, who has examined the incestuous elements in Jane Austen's novels in more depth than anyone, suggests that Austen structures her social mechanics around the concept of 'sibships': 'an innovative social and moral power-base that closely resembles a fraternity or community of brothers and sisters, constituted either by actual blood relatives or by individuals having relationships that closely imitate those of blood relatives.'[55] Furthermore, Hudson suggests, these 'sibships' are vindicated by the novels' resolutions:

> Austen's creation at the close of all her novels of ideal family communities, built of core groups of sibling mentors and students of moral fibre, who, the author implies, will coexist harmoniously and guide each other through life, and who represent spiritual and moral hope for the future.... These marriages are meant to protect and fortify the home and consolidate the family residing in it. There is no suggestion in Austen's novels that the pool of eligible spouses be expanded or broadened. Hers was a conservative temperament.[56]

I find this pronouncement difficult to accept, since not only are the family units in Austen's novels figured variously as collapsing (collapsing, that is, in on themselves through incest), riven, or otherwise dysfunctional, but also, and profoundly, it is the case that Austen's novels, while they may habitually deploy the marriage plot, seem profoundly uninterested in the marriages themselves, the events which provide their ostensible climaxes. I discuss the closure of *Northanger Abbey* and its implications in Chapter 1, but here I just want to stress that the representation of that marriage is in fact risibly brief – it does not, indeed, even merit a whole sentence, but rather is given in a relative clause which is part of a much longer sentence which soon overwhelms it:

> The event which it authorized soon followed: Henry and Catherine were married, the bells rang and every body smiled; and, as this took place within a twelvemonth from the first day of their meeting, it will not appear, after all the dreadful delays occasioned by the General's cruelty, that they were essentially hurt by it.   (NA, 247)

Indeed, it is not only brief, it is dismissive: 'Henry and Catherine were married, the bells rang and every body smiled.'[57] In *Sense and Sensibility*, all we are told of Elinor and Edward's marriage is that 'the ceremony took place in Barton church early in the autumn' (SS, 374), while Marianne's marriage to Brandon is rendered obliquely and casts Marianne as entirely passive: 'With such a confederacy against her – with a knowledge so intimate of his goodness – with a conviction of his fond attachment to herself, which at last, though long after it was observable to everybody else – burst on her – what could she do?' (SS, 378). *Pride and Prejudice* represents Elizabeth and Darcy's marriage as primarily disemburdening Mrs Bennet – 'Happy for all her maternal feelings was the day on which Mrs Bennet got rid of her two most deserving daughters' (PP, 385) – while the novel itself closes not with the married couple, but with the Gardiners, signifying the novel's expanding social horizons. *Mansfield Park* closes with an act of denial, keeping the whole thing as vague and generalised as possible:

> I purposely abstain from dates on this occasion, that every one may be at liberty to fix their own, aware that the cure of unconquerable passions, and the transfer of unchanging attachments, must vary much as to time in different people. – I only intreat every body to believe that exactly at the time when it was quite natural that it should be so, and not a week earlier, Edmund did cease to care about Miss Crawford, and became as anxious to marry Fanny, as Fanny herself could desire. (MP, 470)

Emma is similarly vague and unindividuated, rendering the proposal as a knowing joke: 'What did she say? – Just what she ought, of course. A lady always does' (E, 431). Indeed, it is only at the end, with *Persuasion*, that Austen seems to me able to offer an unambiguous love-story between mutually desiring adults.

This shift of register at the novels' close is partly explicable in purely abstract terms, on a theoretical, narratological level. D. A. Miller, whose *Narrative and its Discontents: Problems of Closure in the Traditional Novel* is a full-length study of precisely the kinds of issues I am discussing here, suggests that:

> Each novelist ... motivates the narratable with different kinds of content. ... In general ... all the motivations refer us to two primary determinations: the drift of desire, continually wandering in a suggestive state of mediation, and the drift of the sign, producing other signs as it

moves toward – or away from – a full and settled meaning. Whether in its erotic or semiotic dimension, the narratable inherently lacks finality.

It is, as Miller more simply puts it, an inherent tendency in narrative simply 'to keep going'.[58] Thus, by Miller's reading, *all* acts of narrative closure, at least within the realist novel, perform an effective act of violence on the preceding text. However, overlaid onto this general theory I would suggest a quite specific reaction by Austen and some of her contemporaries to the enforced strictures of the marriage plot. We should ask as readers whether the endings of these novels do not in fact provide a commentary upon or a critique of that which has come before them by laying bare the absolute generic, formulaic nature of the material. In extreme cases, we might wonder whether these closures actually *invalidate* the narratives which precede them. If these novels, ostensibly of love and marriage, close by dismissing marriage, then do they not also dismiss love? I believe they do, at least in the terms laid down by the marriage plot.

Even more graphically than Austen, though perhaps less consciously, examples of this can be found in the novels of Frances Burney. Certainly her last three novels, *Cecilia, Camilla* and *The Wanderer*, weighing in at nearly a thousand pages each, present readers (present *this* reader, at least) with over 900 pages of genuinely unbearable, unrelieved misery (psychological trauma, victimisation, paranoia) which concludes with a pat ending where the heroine marries her true love (who has frequently been at the root of the troubles). Within a strictly realist economy, Burney's heroines would be traumatised beyond endurance by the events to which they are subjected – mad or dead. Are we really expected to believe that 5 pages of highly conventionalised resolution can counterbalance 900 pages of agony? I think not. What these endings do is to highlight Burney's profound conception of the condition of women (and let us not forget that *The Wanderer*'s subtitle is *Female Difficulties*) as, in Raymond Williams's figuration, social *subjects*:

> The *subject*, at whatever violence to himself, has to accept the way of life of his society, and his own indicated place in it, because there is no other way in which he can maintain himself at all; only by his obedience can he eat, sleep, shelter, or escape being destroyed by others. It is not *his* way of life, in any sense that matters, but he must conform to it to survive.[59]

This is very grim stuff, and Burney's novels *should* be tragedies. But tragedy was denied on gender and aesthetic grounds to women writers, having been theorised since Aristotle as an inherently aristocratic form, the form, in Northrop Frye's words, of 'the leader', one 'superior in degree to other men'.[60] As such, its aesthetic transcendence, its status as the most serious and exalted dramatic form, was underwritten by political power. Denied access to this power, Burney characteristically falls back on *melodrama* to articulate her grievances about the subject-ion of women. Defined by M. H. Abrams as 'any literary work or episode which relies on improbable events and sensational action', and generally understood as a debased cultural form, melodrama is theorised by Frye as 'comedy without humor', though it seems more proper to me to define it as 'tragedy without nobility', or, more simply and inclusively, 'tragedy without power'.[61] Frank Rahill has described the way in which melodrama, particularly in the theatre, could operate as a 'substitute franchise', and Copeland notes the ways in which melodrama 'is particularly well-adapted to interpreting the feelings of disenfranchised, disinherited groups'.[62] Certainly, Burney's heroines are all variously disinherited (*Cecilia*, subtitled *Memoirs of an Heiress*, intimately demonstrates the ways in which its heroine is progressively swindled out of her fortune) and disenfranchised, denied access to power, silenced.

More self-conscious than Austen, more open in its exposure of the ending as a purely fictional convention, is Edgeworth's *Belinda*. Here, Edgeworth elegantly demonstrates women writers' lack of access to tragedy, their enforced reliance upon a comic form, by having her heroine and her guardian, Lady Delacour, go to a masked ball dressed as the comic and tragic muse: 'you must be the comic muse;' Lady Delacour says, 'and I must be tragedy.'[63] This seems generically appropriate as Belinda, 'an heroine', is denied access to anything but comedy on ideological grounds, while Lady Delacour, a glamorous society queen dying, she believes, of breast cancer, comes very near to tragedy. Very near, without formally achieving it; and it is Edgeworth's point that these absolute generic categories are problematised and blurred: at the ball, the two switch masks, and a series of mistaken identities ensues. So startlingly formalised is *Belinda*'s denouement (which even takes place in a chapter called 'The Denouement'!) that it is worth studying at some length here.

Edgeworth closes the novel with a lengthy discussion amongst the main characters on how best to close a novel. Lady Delacour gathers the characters together and asks, 'And now, my good friends...shall I finish the novel for you?', and is reminded by Belinda that 'there is nothing in which novellists [sic] are so apt to err, as in hurrying things toward the conclusion'. 'Would you choose,' Lady Delacour asks, 'that I should draw out the story to five volumes more?' There then follows a discussion of Harriet Byron's marriage in Richardson's *Sir Charles Grandison*, after which Mrs Margaret Delacour opines that 'I like to hear something of the preparation for a marriage, as well as of the mere wedding. I like to hear *how* people became happy in a rational manner, better than to be told in the huddled style of an old fairy tale – *and so they were all married, and they lived happily all the rest of their days.*' Lady Delacour insists that 'Something must be left to the imagination. Positively I will not describe wedding dresses, or a procession to church.' Margaret suggests 'ending with a letter...for last speeches are always tiresome', after which Lady Delacour of course makes her last speech, in which she brings matters to an end as if the characters were actors in a play:

> 'Yes,' said her ladyship; 'it is so difficult, as the critic says, to get lovers off upon their knees. Now I think of it, let me place you all in the proper attitudes for stage effect. What signifies being happy, unless we appear so?...There! quite pretty and natural! Now, Lady Delacour, to show that she is reformed, comes forward to address the audience with a moral – a moral! – yes,
>   Our *tale* contains a *moral*, and, no doubt,
>   You all have wit enough to find it out.'
>   THE END[64]

By closing *Belinda* like this, Edgeworth reminds readers that the endings to domestic novels – and by extension the entire substance of these novels – is as ritualistically formalised as the close of a Shakespearean comedy, as rehearsed as the songs with which these plays close. But she is also articulating, wittily where Burney had done it melodramatically, a properly feminist dissent from the imposed formal strictures of the publishing market.

Belinda acknowledges that its heroine is inevitably a conventional construct, entirely circumscribed by the female sphere, the ideologies of decorum, propriety and passivity. 'I really was so provoked with the cold tameness of that stick or stone Belinda, that I could have torn the pages in pieces!' she was later to write.[65] What this means is that the novel's interest shifts away from the still, hollow centre of Belinda Portman herself and towards its margins, where Lady Delacour fights duels with women, and where her breast is kept in a state of suppuration by deliberate medical malpractice; where Virginia St. Pierre is brought up in isolation from society in a bizarre Rousseauan upbringing experiment which Edgeworth modelled on the activities of her father's friend Thomas Day; where the creole Mr Vincent comes over from the colonies and loses his entire fortune at the gaming-tables; and where Mrs Freke, an anarchic lesbian, rampages and terrorises. So disparate, indeed, do the novel's strands progressively grow, that Edgeworth is only able to tie up these strands as she does, effectively through magic. After all this it is, I think, Jane Austen's major contribution to feminist letters that she is able, albeit partially, to circumvent this ideology by presenting, at least in the figures of Marianne Dashwood, Elizabeth Bennet and Emma Woodhouse, confident, self-authorising, articulate, mouthy women who are placed right at the centres of her novels. This really was some achievement, and we should celebrate it.

III. CONTEXTUALISING AUSTEN'S NOVELS

During the decades in which the institutionalisation of English studies was completed, 'English Literature' was established as beyond question a valid (if not, according to many of the most influential voices within the academy, from Leavis to Trilling, *the central*) academic discipline. In Britain, certainly, a crucial generation of academic literary critics, emboldened by the expansion of the university sector in the 1960s, where they were to become the first cohort of recruits in the 'New University' sector, were trained in the dominant New Critical/Leavisite/Liberal Humanist methodologies of the mid-twentieth century. This generation imbibed and to a large extent internalised a set of key critical tenets which tended to view the literary text primarily and on occasion exclusively as if it were removed from its specific historical context, floating free from its temporal moorings into a transhistorical sea of art. This indeed was the mark of the truly major work, its transhistorical quality: far from being the product, albeit in complex ways, of a specific set of historical circumstances, the canonical literary text was a verbal icon, a well-wrought urn, transcending time. While only the most diehard cultural materialist would want to *deny* some quality of transhistoricity to the literary text, what this meant was that the history in which writers themselves were embedded tended, at the very least, to be downplayed. *A fortiori*, alas, this applied to Jane Austen, perhaps the most significant canonical woman writer in English Literature. Thus, F. R. Leavis began *The Great Tradition* (1948), still probably the most influential work yet written on the English novel, with this statement:

> The great English novelists are Jane Austen, George Eliot, Henry James, and Joseph Conrad – to stop for a moment at that comparatively safe point in history. Since Jane Austen, for special reasons, needs to be studied at considerable length, I confine myself in this book to the last three.[66]

Austen's exceptionalism required, then, either special treatment at considerably greater length than Leavis had at his disposal (though he never did get around to the full-length study which was to do her justice, more's the pity) or else simply went without saying. Unfortunately, post-Leavis critics up to the 1970s, while taking Austen's greatness for granted, seemed also to be working under the sway of eighteenth-century theories of gendered spheres of knowledge: if the greatest works of art are characteristically transhistorical, how much more would this be the case for Jane Austen, a woman writer of domestic comedies, removed by gender and genre from the masculine sphere of history? The examples of influential critical thinking from the mid-twentieth century adduced in the Afterword should stand as testimony to this.

As Linda Colley has argued, modern British identity was formed across the eighteenth century, in part through a series of wars with France, which became figured as the great national enemy and Other. From 1793 to 1815 (with a brief respite afforded by the treaty of Amiens in 1803), Britain and France were at war: this is a period which covers virtually the whole of Austen's writing career. It would be, I think, an act of intellectual irresponsibility to consider novels written in, for example, the years 1914–18 or 1939–45 as though the wars then raging had no bearing at all on them; yet this is precisely the way in which many chose to read Austen's work, as if it existed solely in some decorous parallel universe of moral discrimination and formal dances. This is certainly how Winston Churchill – perhaps understandably in his case – chose to read

Austen, as a balm for the mind, a blissful retreat from the pressures of history: 'What calm lives they had, those people! No worries about the French Revolution, or the crashing struggle of the Napoleonic Wars. Only manners controlling passion so far as they could, together with cultured explanations of any mischances.'[67]

This act of effective denial is further informed, as I have argued, by the suspicion, still current, that it is simply inconceivable that a genteel Regency lady should have any real concern with the politics of her day (or, worse, with the suspicion, never perhaps articulated, that no *woman* should concern herself with politics). Thus, the eighteenth-century separate spheres theory of gendered knowledge, which I discussed earlier, seems to be reinforced even now. Yet the interrelatedness of the personal and the political, as we would call them today, is there in Austen's writing from the very beginning. Her early fragment *The History of England from the reign of Henry the 4th to the death of Charles the 1st* (1791) is a very partial, pseudo-serious account of monarchical history which has little time for historiographical orthodoxy, offering instead a position of relative sympathy with Richard III while propounding a consistently anti-Tudor agenda: Henry VII is 'as great a Villain as ever lived' (MW, 141), and Elizabeth I, 'wicked as she herself was, could not have committed such extensive mischeif [sic], had not those vile and abandoned men [ministers] connived at, & encouraged her in her crimes' (MW, 145–6). *The History of England* reserves its greatest sympathy for Mary Queen of Scots:

> Abused, reproached & villified by all, what must not her noble mind have suffered when informed that Elizabeth had given orders for her Death! Yet she bore it with a most unshaken fortitude; firm in her Mind; Constant in her Religion; & prepared herself to meet the cruel fate to which she was doomed, with a magnanimity that could alone proceed from conscious Innocence. And yet could you Reader have believed it possible that some hardened & zealous Protestants have even abused her for that Steadfastness in the Catholic Religion which reflected on her so much credit? But this is a striking proof of *their* narrow souls and prejudiced judgements who accuse her. (MW, 145)

The Tudor dynasty ushered in modern British polity with the series of Acts of Union of England and Wales, 1532–36. Thus, on the evidence of the *History*, we have an Austen whose political sentiments are anti-Union and pro-Catholic: 'why', she asks of Henry VIII, 'should a Man who was of no Religion himself be at so much trouble to abolish one which had for Ages been established in the Kingdom?' (MW, 143). These were powerful and topical sentiments for the 1790s, and should cause us seriously to question received notions of an Austen who passively accepted the Tory orthodoxy in which she was apparently steeped. At the very least, *The History* suggests a writer profoundly engaged with the political history of her country.

Catharine, or The Bower (1792) follows on quite explicitly from *The History of England*, and is a work saturated with the political debates of its time. Catharine's aunt Mrs Percival warns her that 'the welfare of every Nation depends upon the virtue of it's individuals, and any one who offends in so gross a manner against decorum & propriety is certainly hastening it's ruin' (MW, 233). Such views would have been familiar during the 1790s, when conservative writers held up the Burkean concepts of 'private worth' and 'domestic confidence' (these particular terms are from Jane West's 1799 novel *A Tale of the Times*) as constituting in effect the home front of the post-revolutionary 'war of ideas'.[68] But Mrs Percival is herself a reactionary naysayer who gives Catharine copies of *Blair's Sermons* and Hannah More's *Coelebs in Search of a Wife* for her edification. *Pride and Prejudice* registers Austen's disapproval of conduct books and the anti-feminist virtues they sought to inculcate, while her letters demonstrate her dislike of More's Evangelically moralistic work (though the choice of *Coelebs* here is a later emendation of the manuscript – the original had the even more unpalatable-sounding 'Seccar's explanation of the Catechism'!). Nevertheless, Mrs Percival encourages women's 'Conversation...on the state of Affairs in the Political world', and her 'wish that she might live to see the Manners of the People in Queen Elizabeth's reign, restored again' is countered by Catharine in terms which reiterate *The History of England*: were Elizabeth to return, Catharine fears that 'She might do as much Mischief and last as long as she did before' (MW, 200–1). Mrs Percival also debates politics with Mr Stanley, a Tory MP, who 'resolutely maintained that the Kingdom had not for ages been in so flourishing & prosperous a state' (MW, 212); Mr Stanley's daughter Camilla complains that 'he never cares about anything but Politics. If I were Mr. Pitt or the Lord Chancellor, he would take care I should not be insulted, but he never thinks about *me*' (MW, 224). Catharine's childhood friend Mary Wynne is sent off to live with the Dowager

Lady Halifax, who, in what is surely a deliberate choice of nomenclature, is named for the most celebrated proponent of the separate sphere theory which sought to deny knowledge of politics to women. Catharine herself is 'well read in modern history' (MW, 198), and is left in surprised silence by Camilla's assertion, entirely proper for a young lady according to the separate spheres ideology, that 'I know nothing of Politics, and cannot bear to hear them mentioned' (MW, 201).

If history and politics are self-evident in Austen's early works, then the manner in which historical events insinuate themselves into her novels, I would suggest, may better be understood as analogous to the ways in which John Barrell has analysed the pervasive presence of the rural poor in eighteenth-century landscape painting:

> It is possible to look beneath the surface of the painting, and to discover there evidence of the very conflict it seems to deny. The painting, then, offers a mythical unity and – in its increasing concern to present an apparently more and more actualized image of rural life – attempts to pass itself off as an image of the actual unity of an English countryside innocent of division. But by examining the process by which that illusion is achieved – by studying the imagery of the paintings, the constraints upon it, and upon its organization in the picture-space – we may come to see that unity as artifice, as something made out of the actuality of division.[69]

Thus, while Austen's works are certainly themselves subject to the constraints of the literary marketplace, of genre and gender, which do attempt to impose a smooth unity, nevertheless this unity is often profoundly troubled, at times (in *Mansfield Park*, for example) to breaking-point, by the pressure of history. Even *Pride and Prejudice*, Austen's most consciously (and mythically) ameliorative, unifying work – and consequently, I argue, her most popular – has its harmony disturbed by 'the recent arrival of a militia regiment in the neighbourhood' (PP, 28). A garrison of militia (auxiliary forces, as distinct from regular army), on a war footing, move into Meryton, causing havoc amongst the locals. Lydia Bennet, for instance, whom the novel shows most directly affected by the war in her eventual marriage to Lieutenant George Wickham of (presumably) the Hertfordshire Militia, finds herself speculating about a visit to Brighton:

> She saw with the creative eye of fancy, the streets of that gay bathing-place covered with officers. She saw herself the object of attention,

to tens and scores of them at present unknown. She saw all the glories of the camp; its tents stretched forth in beauteous uniformity of lines, crowded with the young and the gay, and dazzling with scarlet; and to complete the view, she saw herself seated beneath a tent, tenderly flirting with at least six officers at once.   (PP, 232)

During the 1790s, when Austen began *Pride and Prejudice*, the military camps of Brighton had been, R. W. Chapman writes, 'important and notorious'.[70] As a response to the outbreak of war with France in 1793, Pitt's government had passed the Supplementary Militia Act (1796), creating a further 60,000 militiamen in England alone (making a total of 100,000) to boost national civil defence in the face of repeated threats of French invasions. The militias were to become the subject of sustained criticism with the suspicion that their purpose seemed primarily fashionable rather than military. Linda Colley writes:

As artists and cartoonists delighted in pointing out, it was their uniforms that gave many of these initial volunteer corps away. Very often, they were gorgeous, impractical and extremely expensive. Even a private's uniform in a fashionable London volunteer corps could set a man back £50, with a further £10 a year needed to maintain its smartness, and to provide ammunition.... [T]he wearing of uniform in this period was boosted with a heightened concern with heroism and virility.[71]

The celebrated military analyst C. W. Pasley, whom Austen read with great interest and admiration, certainly had his doubts about the military efficacy of the militias:

All that distinguishes a soldier in outward appearance from a citizen is so trifling; the military step, the exercise of the firelock, the words of command; every thing, in short, requisite for putting a battalion through the usual manœuvres of a review, is so simple, that any men, with good will and intelligence, may soon acquire them. Hence we have volunteer regiments all new, officers as well as men, who may appear to admiring multitudes almost as perfect under arms, as the oldest regiment in the line...But...an army, composed of such seemly officers and soldiers, would and must be [inferior], at their first outset in a severe campaign, to veteran troops.[72]

Early in the novel, when Elizabeth and Jane return from their stay at Netherfield, Kitty and Lydia, their young heads full of soldiers, fill them in on what they have missed: 'Much had been done, and much had been said in the regiment since the preceding Wednesday; several of the officers had dined lately with their uncle, a private had been flogged, and it had actually been hinted that Colonel Foster was going to be married' (PP, 60). Although subordinated to domestic concerns (which are here, at least, revealed as silly, if not callous), the historical veracity which the novels' surface seek to conceal or deny still nevertheless intrudes into the self-consciously stylised, artificial world of the romantic comedy. The private is still flogged; the streets of London are still perpetually threatened with mass protests and riots (*Northanger Abbey*); a gentleman's country estate may still depend on income from a West Indian sugar plantation worked by slaves, who may rise up against their masters (*Mansfield Park*); demobbed sailors from the Napoleonic wars still, after Waterloo, return home newly rich and in need of homes and wives (*Persuasion*).

But the idea of a political Austen amounts to more than a recognition of her novels' inclusion of external events. Jane Austen *remains* political. Her appeal rests partly on her status as an icon of Englishness. Indeed, I would contend that the heightened interest in Austen and her work during the 1990s was in part a response to the shifting configurations in the British political landscape during that decade, a shift both charted and steered by a number of important studies of the subject from a variety of different perspectives. Most influentially, Linda Colley, to whose work I return again and again in this study, has brilliantly demonstrated the ways in which a unified 'British' identity is an historico-political construct belonging fundamentally to the eighteenth century.[73] At the same time, as Katie Trumpener has shown, dissident nationalists from Ireland, Scotland and Wales (and some from England, such as William Blake) countered this unionising tendency by asserting or constructing their ancient, mystical or aboriginal identities in an ideological formation which Trumpener calls 'Bardic Nationalism'.[74] In turn, centralising or unionising tendencies called on Enlightenment progressivism to propound a 'doomed races' theory which figured marginal voices within British polity as colourful victims left high and dry by the dialectics of history: romantic, certainly, but belonging firmly to the past, that which we have left behind. Hence, as Fiona Stafford has shown, the outbreak of 'last man' or 'last of the race' works produced in and around Austen's lifetime.[75]

The Churchillian vision of British polity as an unbroken narrative unfolding down from King Arthur was powerfully debunked by

Norman Davies in his study *The Isles*.[76] Far from a continuous stream, Davies, quite correctly in my view, presented a vision of British geopolitics so fundamentally contingent and fragmented that we are unable even to find a name for these islands we inhabit, the islands which include England, Scotland, Wales, Northern Ireland and the Republic of Ireland. 'Britain' is simply confusing as few can agree where if anywhere it begins or ends; and anyway it is a word too often used synonymously with 'England', and is thus offensive to many inhabitants, nationalist or otherwise, in Wales, Scotland and Northern Ireland (which may not be in 'Britain' at all). 'Great Britain' is the name for the larger island which includes England, Scotland and Wales, but not Northern Ireland. 'The United Kingdom of Great Britain and Northern Ireland' is inclusive but imposes what is for many a false unity, as well as positing a monarchical 'subjecthood' which many republicans (including this one) reject. 'The British Isles' existed as an historical entity only between the Act of Union with Ireland in 1801 and the foundation of the Irish Free State in 1922; in no conceivable way can the Republic of Ireland be a part of the 'British Isles', except perhaps to an antediluvian imperialist mindset for which Britannia still Rules the Waves. The Scottish theorist of nationalism Tom Nairn, an enthusiastic prophet of the demise of Britain, suggests that 'in archipelagic terms, we ought now to try and perceive Archaic-British Sovereignty as an episode now approaching its end. It started with the late-feudal assimilation of Wales and ended (morally speaking, at least) amid the strident hysteria of Tory no-surrender Unionism between 1992 and 1997.... British Unionism was a short-lived pseudo-transcendence whose day is over.'[77]

One consequence of the breakdown of ideas of a stable British identity is that the English, it seems, are finally getting around to having their own identity crisis, undergoing a bracing period of national self-questioning which includes a recognition that, for a generation or more, symbols of patriotic identity such as the flag had been hijacked by the far right. For example, the Euro 96 football tournament saw, for the first time in my experience, the widespread display of the Cross of St George (as opposed to the Union Flag) as an assertion of a specifically *English* identity. The implications of this and of other displays of nationalism in popular cultural formations are very serious indeed, as Richard Weight suggests in *Patriots*, his account of national identity in Britain since 1940:

How did the English rediscover themselves? Not only had the institutions of Anglo-Britishness fallen into disrepute, vital elements of the national character had also been thrown in doubt. The belated acceptance that for half a century English society had been profoundly racist made it hard to celebrate tolerance as a virtue. Also, [the] greed of the Thatcher era made it harder to claim that they were a people with a social conscience. Pop music offered one sanctuary. In 1994 the Britpop group Blur explained that their songs were 'about Englishness rather than being British'.[78]

This sudden concern with English identity was the cause of wry amusement to many in Ireland, Wales and Scotland, where the national discourse had for a century or more been predicated entirely on identity politics – where for many years the only viable question had seemed to be, 'What does it mean to be Welsh/Irish/Scottish?' But if you are the imperial hegemon, the last question you need to ask is 'Who am I?' The answer is self-evident, visible for all to see in the outward symbols of your conquest: I am master of the world. 'National identity,' writes Norman Davies, 'is no trivial matter. It is the psychological cement which binds communities together. The Scots knew who they are. So, too, did the Welsh and the Irish. But a large part of the English were manifestly bewildered.'[79]

Such preoccupations might seem irrelevant or offensive to many readers – and perhaps particularly so to readers of Jane Austen. And yet I would contend that her continuing popularity is inextricably interwoven with her appeal to, or place within, an English national consciousness: this, at least, would seem to me both incontrovertible and uncontroversial. To look to Austen during a time of national crisis seems to me to be perfectly correct and reasonable, and while her novels may not necessarily reassure or comfort, they *will* enlighten. This is because they are, in their particular ways, every bit as much Condition of England novels (or, better, novels which continue to interrogate the Condition of the English) as anything written in the nineteenth century or since.

IV.   CRITICAL ISSUES

What kind of book is this? The admirable brief of the 'Critical Issues' series exhorts its contributors 'to take risks'. I have interpreted this as giving me the licence to take my argument in directions which may be seemingly inconsistent or even contradictory. The narrowness of focus which characterises the modern academic monograph can be inspiring in its limitations, and I am full of admiration for those works which, hedgehog-like, have one thing to say and say it brilliantly – in the field of Austen studies, I would cite recent work by, for example, John Wiltshire, Glenda A. Hudson, Edward Neill, or Barbara K. Seeber as examples of this kind of book[80] – so much more because, fox-like, I have never been able to confine myself to any one subject, always had too many different things to fit into the confines of one monograph. It is for this reason that I am most grateful to the editors of this series, Martin Coyle and John Peck, for giving me the opportunity to write this book, whose scope is, for better or worse, a little more capacious.

It is also at times unapologetically an eccentric book, and I have not curbed (very much) my own tendency for occasional jokes (which I only hope are funny), asides, tangential lines of inquiry, and the odd remark which certainly would not bear too much critical scrutiny, but which I feel may cast some light on something somewhere. In this age of the corporatisation of the academy, and consequently of literary studies and of academic publishing, in which individual scholars are increasingly expected to subordinate their own scholarship to a prepackaged corporate identity in the name of research assessment, on which state funding is increasingly based in the humanities (a condition in which some academics, alas, have colluded all too willingly), I thought it might be valuable to remember that there are such things as individual, specific readers, one of whom has written this book. That is to say, this book is not, or is not intended to be, a production-line work which could have been written by any competent scholar, but rather the product of many years of reading, thinking, teaching, researching, writing, conversation and debate by one specific (and hopefully competent) scholar. This is an unfashionable view, perhaps, not least because it is often evoked as an argument for academic freedom by cranks and old duffers who would resist any change. This view is also unfashionable because it presupposes a Romantic concept of authorship and selfhood, stable, inviolable, monologic, which virtually all poststructuralist and postmodernist theory rejects in its valorisation of the fragmentary, the plural, the shifting. Following on from Roland Barthes's hugely influential 'The Death of the Author' (1968),[81] Michel Foucault's 'What is an Author?' (1969) defined the author as 'a certain functional principle by which, in our culture, one limits, excludes, and chooses; in short, by which one impedes the free circulation, the free manipulation, the free composition, decomposition, and recomposition of fiction.'[82] But, as Terry Eagleton has written in one of his more recent books (I find it difficult to keep up):

> To historicize is indeed vital; but there is in vogue today a brand of left-historicism which seems more indebted to capitalist ideology than to socialist theory. In a world of short-term contracts, just-in-time deliveries, ceaseless downsizings and remodellings, overnight shifts of fashion and capital investment, multiple careers and multipurpose production, such theorists seem to imagine, astonishingly, that the main enemy is the naturalized, static and unchanging. Whereas the truth is that for millions of harassed workers around the globe, not many of them academics, a respite from dynamism, metamorphosis and multiple identities would come as a blessed release.[83]

Jane Austen is the most seductive of writers. What I mean by this is that readers are very often seduced into believing that they are in some way ahead of her game, cleverer than she is; that they, uniquely, are gifted with an understanding of her novels (and I certainly do not exclude myself from this tendency). I have lost count of the times when, on hearing that I work on Austen, virtual strangers have proceeded with great passion and certainty to explain to me their own ideas about the novels. We should be thankful for this, of course – that one great English novelist at least is able to inspire such enthusiasm in so many. Having said that, I would also have to say that the majority of these accounts resemble those of Winston Churchill in presenting a quietist, anti-historical, conservative Jane Austen. Perhaps one should be democratic about this and acknowledge that this may be the right reading after all; or perhaps, as the Afterword suggests, a great interpretive and ideological fissure has grown between the different communities of Austen readers, so much so that we now hardly read the same texts at all. I hope not.

This is my Austen, though. Chapter 1 focuses in on one thematic concern in *Northanger Abbey*, its preoccupation with dress, and uses that to illuminate the broader historical and political concerns of the novel. Chapter 2 examines *Sense and Sensibility*, often considered to be Austen's weakest novel, synoptically with its major intertexts, a series of novels from around 1795, when Austen began the ur-novel *Elinor and Marianne*, which deploy the double-heroine plot which also enfolds the histories of the Dashwood sisters. *Mansfield Park* is Austen's most explicitly ideological, Condition of England novel, and Chapter 4 offers an analysis of its many self-defeating contradictions. *Emma* is Austen's most claustrophobic novel, and the nearest her work comes to fulfilling the anti-historicism with which she is so often associated; Chapter 5 looks at the ways in which, nuisance that it is, historical reality still manages to insinuate its way into the novel. The final chapter considers *Persuasion* as qualitatively different from the other novels: it is a post-war novel, the novel of new kind of national identity politics; it is also, and unambiguously, a love story.

Which leaves *Pride and Prejudice*. The evidence adduced in Chapter 3 suggests that this is easily Austen's most popular novel, and that by a factor even greater than many assume. Yet it is a novel about which I have, relatively speaking, little to say, largely I think because its lack of rough edges makes it difficult for me to get a purchase on it. I consider this a critical position in itself, but also an acknowledgement of my own partiality and limitations as a reader. After all, Jane Austen herself reckoned Elizabeth Bennet 'as delightful a creature as ever appeared in print' (L, 201), and wrote sarcastically about readers like me:

> The work is rather too light & bright & sparkling; – it wants shade; – it wants to be stretched out here & there with a long Chapter – of sense if it could be had, if not of solemn specious nonsense – about something unconnected with the story; an Essay on Writing, a critique on Walter Scott, or the history of Buanaparte – or anything that would form a contrast & bring the reader with increased delight to the playfulness & Epigrammatism of the general stile. – I doubt your quite agreeing with me here – I know your starched Notions. (L, 203)

1

Northanger Abbey

I. LINEN

'To be burned.' So wrote Cassandra Austen in 1843 on a bundle of letters, many years of correspondence between herself and her sister Jane, who had become regarded, since her death in 1817, as one of the greatest of English novelists.[1] We will never know what was in those letters, but it is reasonable to assume that their content was in some way delicate – not necessarily libellous or lascivious, but private communication in the broadest sense, not intended for public consumption. Certainly, Jane Austen's niece Caroline recalled that 'Her letters to Aunt Cassandra (for they were *sometimes* separated) were, I dare say, open and confidential – My Aunt looked them over and burnt the greater part (as she told me), 2 or 3 years before her own death – She left, or *gave* some legacies to the Neices – but of those that *I* have seen, several had portions cut out.'[2] Certainly, too, the Austen family had always been understandably keen on presenting its most celebrated member in the best (that is to say, the most respectable) of all lights. Her brother Henry's 'Biographical Notice' appended to the posthumous edition of *Northanger Abbey* and *Persuasion* in 1818 closes with an affirmation of propriety:

> One trait only remains to be touched on. It makes all others unimportant. She was thoroughly religious and devout; fearful of giving offence to God, and incapable of feeling it towards any fellow creature. On serious subjects she was well-instructed, both by reading and meditation, and her opinions accorded strictly with those of our Established Church.[3]

Austen's great editor R. W. Chapman, in the introduction to his 1932 edition of Austen's letters, saw the need to defend the surviving correspondence against accusations of its perceived triviality: 'A familiar defence is that the letters have been robbed of their general interest by Cassandra Austen's pious destruction of all that she supposed might possibly excite general curiosity .... Doubtless this suppression has cost us much that we should value' (L, ix).[4] Given that Cassandra *did* burn 'the greater part' of their correspondence, then what is it that survived the flames? The overwhelming impression one gets, particularly from the Steventon years of the 1790s and early 1800s, is of a Jane Austen willing to write about almost nothing except clothing. 'You say nothing of the silk stockings; I flatter myself, therefore, that Charles has not purchased any, as I cannot very well afford to pay for them; all my money is spent in buying white gloves and pink persian' (L, 2): so says Austen's earliest extant letter, from January 1796. The letters go on in the same vein; this is from May 1801, and is worth quoting at length to give an impression of quite how detailed its concerns are:

Wednesday. – Mrs. Mussell has got my gown, & I will endeavour to explain what her intentions are. – It is to be a round Gown, with a Jacket, & a Frock front, like Cath: Bigg's to open at the side. – The Jacket is all in one with the body, & comes as far as the pocketholes; – about half a quarter of a yard deep I suppose all the way round, cut off straight at the corners, with a broad hem. – No fullness appears either in the Body or the flap; the back is quite plain . . . and the sides equally so. – The front is sloped round to the bosom & drawn in – & there is to be frill of the same to put on occasionally when all one's handkerchiefs are dirty – which frill *must* fall back. – She is to put two breadths & a half in the tail, & no Gores; – Gores not being so much worn as they were; – there is nothing new in the sleeves, – they are to be plain, with a fullness of the same falling down & gathered up underneath, just like some of Marthas – or perhaps a little longer. – Low in the back behind, & belt of the same. – I can think of nothing more – tho' I am afraid of not being particular enough. – My Mother has ordered a new Bonnet, & so have I; – both white chip, trimmed with white ribbon. – I find my straw bonnet looking very much like other peoples & quite as smart. Bonnets of Cambric Muslin . . . on the plan of Ly Bridges' are a good deal worn, & some of them are very pretty; but I shall defer one of that sort till your arrival. – Bath is getting so very empty that I am not afraid of doing too little. – Black gauze Cloaks are worn as much as anything. – I shall write again in a day or two. – Best Love.   (L, 83)

It was around this time that Austen was working on *Northanger Abbey*, and her surviving letters from this period sound like nothing so much as Catherine Morland's guardian in Bath, Mrs Allen, perpetually, obsessively talking and thinking about linen and clothing: 'Dress was her passion. She had a most harmless delight in being fine; and our heroine's entrée into life could not take place until after three or four days had been spent in learning what was mostly worn, and her chaperon was provided with a dress of the newest' (NA, 20). But Mrs Allen is not the only character in *Northanger Abbey* to be so preoccupied: indeed, it would be nearer the truth to say that *the novel itself* habitually turns on and returns to the subject of linen. Furthermore, I want to contend here that, as in the letters, the language of fabrics and of dress is, in *Northanger Abbey* and elsewhere in Austen, a form of encoded speech. This is obvious, of course – but as well as being a semiotic system, however complex and nuanced, as it is in most, if not all, fiction, dress specifically represents here that which escapes, elides, or otherwise survives censorship.

Firstly, and importantly, given that this is a novel of courtship which deploys, in a highly and consistently self-conscious fashion, the conventions of the marriage plot, dress operates metonymically to articulate the decorous verbal silence about sex. One should not forget that the novel's very opening sentence, 'No one who had seen Catherine Morland in her infancy, would have supposed her born to be an heroine' (NA, 13), positions Catherine precisely as the heroine of the kind of novel which must inevitably culminate in her marriage, an inevitability signalled by the address at its close to 'my readers, who will see in the tell-tale compression of the pages before them, that we are all hastening together to perfect felicity' (NA, 250) – or, to paraphrase, this is a novel of courtship and marriage; you, the reader, have read many such novels, and thus know how they end; this novel ends in precisely the same way: 'Henry and Catherine were married, the bells rang, and every body smiled' (NA, 252). (As I noted in the Introduction, this conclusion is so foregone that it is not even here given a sentence to itself, nor even a dominant clause within a sentence: rather, the wedding, which should theoretically complete the plot, is offered in a relative clause, as just another piece of information.) The opening chapter records Catherine changing across puberty, from tomboy to nascent heroine:

> the Morlands...were in general very plain, and Catherine, for many years of her life, as plain as any. She had a thin awkward figure, a sallow

skin without colour, dark lank hair, and strong features; – so much for her person; – and not less unpropitious for heroism seemed her mind. She was fond of all boys' plays, and greatly preferred cricket not merely to dolls, but to the more heroic enjoyments of infancy, nursing a dormouse, feeding a canary-bird, or watering a rose-bush. Indeed, she had no taste for a garden; and if she gathered flowers at all, it was chiefly for the pleasure of mischief – at least so it was conjectured from her always preferring those which she was forbidden to take. . . . Such was Catherine Morland at ten. At fifteen, appearances were mending; she began to curl her hair and long for balls; her complexion improved; her features were softened by plumpness and colour, her eyes gained more animation, and her figure more consequence. Her love of dirt gave way to an inclination for finery, and she grew clean as she grew smart; she had the pleasure of hearing her father and her mother remark on her personal improvement. 'Catherine grows quite a good-looking girl, – she is almost pretty to-day,' were words which caught her ears now and then; and how welcome were the sounds!' (NA, 13–15)

These changes in her body mean that she can now have children. Catherine, then, is, by the end of Chapter 1, marriageable. At the beginning of Chapter 2 she is taken to Bath by Mrs. Allen as a saleable new commodity on the marriage-market. We should not forget that she is taken there quite deliberately to find a husband, and that is precisely what she does.

That husband, Henry Tilney, is a true connoisseur of women's clothing. He knows a great deal about fabrics, and is able to engage a delighted Mrs Allen on equal terms on her sole topic:

They were interrupted by Mrs Allen: – 'My dear Catherine,' said she, 'do take this pin out of my sleeve; I am afraid it has torn a hole already; I shall be quite sorry if it has, for this is a favourite gown, though it cost but nine shillings a yard.'

'That is exactly what I should have guessed it, madam,' said Mr Tilney, looking at the muslin.

'Do you understand muslins, sir?'

'Particularly well; I always buy my own cravats, and am allowed to be an excellent judge; and my sister has often trusted me in the choice of a gown. I bought one for her the other day and it was pronounced to be a prodigious bargain by every body who saw it. I gave but five shillings a yard for it, and a true Indian muslin.'

Mrs Allen was quite struck by his genius. 'Men commonly take so little notice of these things,' said she: 'I can never get Mr Allen to know one of my gowns from another. You must be a great comfort to your sister, sir.'

'I hope I am, madam.'

'And pray, sir, what do you think of Miss Morland's gown?'

'It is very pretty, madam,' said he, gravely examining it; 'but I do not think it will wash well; I am afraid it will fray.'

'How can you,' said Catherine, laughing, 'be so –' she had almost said, strange.

'I am quite of your opinion, sir,' replied Mrs Allen; 'and so I told Miss Morland when she bought it.'

'But then, you know, madam, muslin always turns to some account or other; Miss Morland will get enough out of it for a handkerchief, or a cap, or a cloak. – Muslin can never be said to be wasted. I have heard my sister say so forty times, when she has been extravagant in buying more than she wanted, or careless in cutting it to pieces.'   (NA, 28–9)

Henry is rendered 'almost...strange' by this expertise, which amounts, I shall argue, to a kind of cross-dressing. As such, it is one of a number of instances of Austen's deployment of either cross-dressing or that which it tends to signify, a destabilised masculinity. In *Mansfield Park*, Roger Sales suggests that Tom Bertram 'is associated with some of the transgressive forms of cross-dressing and masquerade common in the Regency period', and that his behaviour in Sir Thomas's absence precipitates the novel's very own miniature Regency Crisis.[5] Furthermore, this crisis is, in *Mansfield Park*, a crisis of *masculinity*, implying the emasculation, effeminacy or gender destabilisation of virtually all of the younger generation of men in the novel. Tom, enthusiastic in his promotion of *Lovers' Vows* for the theatricals, volunteers for himself the part of the cottager's wife, or more precisely the part of the cottager's wife in drag as her husband:

We cannot have two Agathas, and we must have one Cottager's Wife; and I am sure I set her [Julia] the example of moderation myself in being satisfied with the old Butler. If the part is trifling she will have more credit in making something of it; and if she is so desperately bent against every thing humorous, let her take Cottager's speeches instead of Cottager's wife and so change the parts all through; *he* is solemn and pathetic enough I am sure. It could make no difference in the play; and as for Cottager himself, when he has got his wife's speeches, *I* would undertake them with all my heart.   (MP, 134)

Lovers' Vows also shows the imbecilic Mr Rushworth in his true colours, which are 'a blue dress, and a pink satin cloak'

(MP, 138) – the latter garment, in particular, 'whisked away' (MP, 179) by Mrs Norris as soon as Sir Thomas Bertram arrives back at Mansfield, lest he begin to entertain further doubts about his prospective son-in-law's masculinity and thus cast a shadow over the prospects of such a financially lucrative match. And Mr Rushworth's uncertain masculinity has directly political implications for *Mansfield Park*, Austen's most explicit Condition of England novel, as Mrs Grant suggests to Mary Crawford that Sir Thomas plans to establish his future son-in-law in a rotten borough: 'I dare say he *will* be in parliament soon' (MP, 161). Mary teasingly hints at Rushworth's effeminacy as she observes him watch Henry and Maria act together: 'I thought he began to look a little queer' (MP, 169). One of the reasons Mary constitutes such a danger within the novel, which closes with her expulsion, is because of her tendency verbally to emasculate or queer the men around her. Most notoriously, she has a fondness for making jokes about buggery in the navy: 'Certainly, my home at my uncles brought me acquainted with a circle of admirals. Of *Rears*, and *Vices*, I saw enough. Now, do not be suspecting me of a pun, I entreat' (MP, 60). This remark resonates with William Price's complaint that due to his lowly status in the navy, he is unable to attract women: 'One might as well be nothing as a midshipman. One *is* nothing indeed. You remember the Gregorys; they are grown up amazing fine girls, but they will hardly speak to *me*, because Lucy is courted by a lieutenant' (MP, 249). Jill Heydt-Stevenson argues that William's description of himself as 'nothing' has as its intertext *Hamlet*'s famous example of bawdry:

> *Hamlet*: Do you think I meant country matters?
> *Ophelia*: I think nothing, my lord.
> *Hamlet*: That's a fair thought to lie between a maid's legs.
> *Ophelia*: What is, my lord?
> *Hamlet*: Nothing.[6]

'The emphasis on nothing,' Heydt-Stevenson writes, 'a term with sexual connotations of women's lack, suggests that Price sees himself transformed into a portionless woman.'[7] Similarly portionless through primogeniture and through his brother's wasteful Regency dissipation, Edmund Bertram is himself the subject of Mary Crawford's emasculating rhetoric: when she hears that he is to be ordained, she tells him, 'A clergyman is nothing' (MP, 92). She later uses his name as the vehicle for a very Lawrentian penis-joke: 'Mr Edmund is no more than Mr John or Mr Thomas' (MP, 211). The motif of the emasculated clergyman recurs in *Emma* in the person of Mr Elton, who is playfully accused of impotence when Emma examines the parcel of Harriet's keepsakes from her infatuation with him: 'Emma was quite eager to see this superior treasure. It was the end of an old pencil, – the part without any lead' (E, 339).

Henry Tilney's interest in the specifics of women's clothing marks him out as willing to cross over into an overtly female sphere of knowledge, and in this it is intimately connected with his great enthusiasm for novel reading, and particularly for the works of Ann Radcliffe: 'I have read all Mrs Radcliffe's works, and most of them with great pleasure. The Mysteries of Udolpho, once I had begun it, I could not lay down again; – I remember finishing it in two days, my hair standing on end the whole time' (NA, 106). After all, as the Introduction argued, Austen's justly celebrated 'defence' of her chosen literary form, which occupies much of Chapter 5 of *Northanger Abbey*, posits the novel (quite correctly for the 1790s) as a literary form written by, about, and for women, and appeals to contemporary novelists themselves, in quasi-Wollstonecraftian terms, as an oppressed sisterhood: 'Alas! if the heroine of one novel be not patronized by the heroine of another, from whom can she expect protection and regard? I cannot approve of it. ... Let us not desert one another; we are an injured body' (NA, 37). The passage then offers three novels in particular, Frances Burney's *Cecilia* and *Camilla* and Maria Edgeworth's *Belinda*, as exemplars of the form in which 'the greatest powers of the mind are displayed, in which the most thorough knowledge of human nature, the happiest delineations of its varieties, the liveliest effusions of wit and humour are conveyed to the world in the best chosen language' (NA, 38). Henry's confession of fondness for Radcliffe's novels comes in response to Catherine's comment that 'you never read novels, I dare say? ... Because they are not clever enough for you – gentlemen read better books', and follows his own statement that 'the person, be it gentleman or lady, who has not pleasure in a good novel, must be intolerably stupid' (NA, 106). Henry concludes this conversation with yet another assertion of his ability to engage with specifically female forms of knowledge on, at the very least, an equal footing: 'Do not imagine,' he tells Catherine, 'that you can cope with me in a knowledge of Julias and Louisas' (NA, 107) – that is to say, heroines of novels of the very type to which

Northanger Abbey has, from its opening sentence, identified Catherine as belonging.

Set against Henry is the perhaps more normative version of masculinity embodied by John Thorpe, who tells Catherine that 'I never read novels; I have something else to do. ... Novels are all so full of nonsense and stuff; there has not been a tolerably decent one come out since Tom Jones, except the Monk; I read that t'other day; but as for all the others, they are the stupidest things in creation' (NA, 48). Commenting on this limited choice of reading material, Margaret Anne Doody suggests that Thorpe 'has learned nothing from *Tom Jones*, and his classing it with *The Monk* shows that he reads both only for sexual stimulus'.[8] When Henry reads *Udolpho* with 'my hair standing on end the whole time', he is reading 1790s Gothic with etymological exactitude, for the word 'horror' has its origins in the Latin *horrere*, meaning 'to bristle', describing the way in which the hair stands on end at moments of excitement or fear.[9] It is not, however, to make his *hair* stand on end that Thorpe reads *The Monk*, but rather as an example of what Tom Wolfe has evocatively termed 'one-handed literature'.

Thorpe's presence in the novel signifies a sexual threat. In the unfinished *Sanditon*, the penniless baronet Sir Edward Denham is described as a man whose 'great object in life was to be seductive. ... He felt that he was formed to be a dangerous Man – quite in the line of the Lovelaces. – The very name of Sir Edward, he thought, carried some degree of fascination with it' (MW, 405). The reference here is of course to Samuel Richardson's deadly rake, Robert Lovelace, who dominates his gargantuan novel *Clarissa*. In *Northanger Abbey*, the operative Richardson novel is not *Clarissa* but *Sir Charles Grandison*. Catherine Morland's mother, we are told, 'very often reads Sir Charles Grandison' (NA, 41), and, as R. T. Jones has pointed out, this obviously doesn't mean that she reads it from cover to cover, all 1500 or so pages, but rather that she very often *consults* it. Richardson himself, after all, considered *Grandison* to be 'a gauntlet thrown out' to the reader, structured around a series of interpretive moral challenges rather than a sequential plot.[10] It is for this reason that Richardson, disturbed by the interpretive doubleness inherent in his chosen epistolary form, which led to perceived misreadings of *Clarissa* from Lovelace's point of view, added to later editions of *Grandison* an index, which allowed readers to go straight to the required passages, and contained suggestions for the correct interpretation of that passage.

Since Richardson's technique of 'writing to the moment' forbids, on principle, his own authorial intrusion as a moral guide, it relies rather on its readers' innate ability to recognise and deplore vice when they see it. Lovelace, however, was just too well-drawn – in being rendered sufficiently seductive to pose a serious challenge to the virtuous value-system of Clarissa Harlowe, he was also rendered too seductive for many readers, who fell for him. These readers included, fictionally, Sir Edward Denham:

> With a perversity of Judgement, which must be attributed to his not having by Nature a very strong head, the Graces, the Spirit, the Sagacity, & the Perseverance of the Villain of the Story outweighed all his absurdities & all his Atrocities with Sir Edward. With him, such Conduct was Genius, Fire & Feeling. – It interested & inflamed him; & he was always more anxious for its Success & mourned over its Discomfitures with more tenderness than c[oul]d ever have been contemplated by the Authors. (MW, 404)

According to Austen's nephew James Edward Austen-Leigh's *Memoir of Jane Austen* (1870), 'Her [Austen's] knowledge of Richardson's works was such as no one is likely again to acquire, now that the multitude and the merits of our light literature have called off the attention of readers from that great master. Every circumstance narrated to Sir Charles Grandison, all that was ever said or done in the cedar parlour, was familiar to her; and the wedding-days on Lady L. and Lady G. were as well remembered as if they had been living friends.'[11] (Clearly, Austen-Leigh is proving himself right here in his assertion that no reader of his times was really familiar with Richardson's work, since Lady L. is already married when the novel begins.) Austen was to return to *Grandison*'s depiction of virtuous masculinity later in her career, in the characters of Mr Darcy and Mr Knightley, but in *Northanger Abbey* it is not Sir Charles himself who interests Austen, but rather the novel's inept would-be seducer, Sir Hargrave Pollexfen, on whom John Thorpe is, in part, modelled. Most particularly, Thorpe's driving away with Catherine Morland, against her will, in his 'well-hung' gig (NA, 46) – 'Mr Thorpe...laughed, smacked his whip, encouraged his horse, made odd noises, and drove on' (NA, 103) – directly echoes Sir Hargrave's attempted abduction of the heroine Harriet Byron, in Volume I of *Grandison*. Indeed, at around the time Austen was writing *Northanger Abbey* (certainly no later than

1800), she also composed the playlet *Sir Charles Grandison; or, The Happy Man*, which compresses the vast bulk of Richardson's novel to a mere 19 printed pages. Austen's *Grandison* is concerned, if not exclusively, then predominantly, with the episode of Harriet's abduction by Sir Hargrave, and the subsequent attempted enforced marriage ceremony: this takes up all of Act II, by far the largest space given to any single episode in Richardson's novel. For Jane Austen, at least during the 1790s, this episode was clearly the centrepiece of Richardson's novel, that to which it could be reduced. Austen's *Grandison opens*, however, with long discussion of clothing and millinery: the play's opening line is 'So, you have brought the dresses, have you?'[12]

II. CROSS-DRESSING

Henry Tilney's interest in women's clothing also has a particular contextual political significance for the 1790s, the decade in which *Northanger Abbey* is firmly set. Though its action takes place around 1798, when Austen started to write it, the novel was not published until 1818, posthumously, with *Persuasion*. Revising the novel for publication in 1816, Austen saw the need to preface it with an 'ADVERTISEMENT BY THE AUTHORESS', explaining its provenance:

> some observation is necessary upon those parts of the work which thirteen years have made comparatively obsolete. The public are entreated to bear in mind that thirteen years have passed since it was finished, many more since it was begun, and that during that period, places, manners, books, and opinions have undergone considerable changes. (NA, 10)

Importantly, then, even when it was first published, *Northanger Abbey* was always an historical novel, its setting and concerns some twenty years out of date. This is particularly significant in 1816: 22 years of war with France had concluded at Waterloo the previous year. Indeed, over the course of a 'long eighteenth century', from 1689 to 1815, Britain and France were at war on seven different occasions and for a total of some 52 years – though, as Linda Colley has noted, it is perfectly possible to view these as one extended war, 'less a series of separate and conventional wars, than one peculiarly pervasive and long-drawn out conflict which rarely had time to become a cold war in the twentieth-century sense.'[13] *Northanger Abbey*'s companion piece in 1818, *Persuasion*, is quite avowedly a post-war novel, largely set amongst newly demobbed sailors on the south coast of England who are trying to make a new life for themselves in peacetime. Unquestionably, then, *Northanger Abbey*'s return to the post-revolutionary fears and ideologies of the 1790s required some explanation in 1816, and especially perhaps its preoccupation with the specifics of dress and clothing.

The eighteenth century itself was a terrific time for cross-dressers, and consequently a difficult time for those in whom such perceived category violations raised anxieties. In part, as the theorist of cross-dressing Marjorie Garber has noted, this is because of a general relaxation in formal sumptuary legislation, the prescribing and proscribing of forms of dress as a matter of law. Queen Elizabeth I, for example, had commanded that a 'Homily Against Excess of Apparel' be preached from church pulpits: 'Yea, many men are become so effeminate, that they care not what they spend in disguising themselves, ever desiring new toys and inventing new fashions.'[14] As Garber notes, sumptuary concerns, whether formally legislative or enforced by tradition and custom, *politicise* dress, making it primarily a vehicle for control and regulation:

> The ideal scenario – from the point of view of the regulators – was one in which a person's social station, social role, gender, and other indicators of identity in the world could be *read*, without ambiguity or uncertainty.[15]

Thus, in February 1737, the periodical *Common Sense* could declare that

> Ugly women, who may more properly be called a Third Sex, than a part of the Fair one, should publickly renounce all Thoughts of their Persons, and turn their Minds another Way; they should endeavour to be honest good-humour'd Gentlemen, they may amuse themselves with Field Sports, and a cheerful Glass; and if they could get into Parliament, I should, for my own Part, have no Objection to it.

In September of that year, the same publication suggested that women who 'stray beyond' the 'Bounds allotted to their Sex' should 'declare themselves in form Hermaphrodites, and be register'd as such in their several Parishes'.[16]

In one of *Sir Charles Grandison*'s many debates on morality, Richardson's hero poses his audience this question: 'Can there be characters more odious than that of a masculine woman and an effeminate man?'[17] The 'masculine woman' to whom Sir Charles refers here is Miss Barnevelt, a manly lesbian who clearly has designs on Harriet Byron (designs which Harriet appears to have at least a subconscious desire to reciprocate). Richardson's directive index to later editions of *Grandison* glosses this as Miss Barnevelt being 'Pleasantly censured by Sir Charles Grandison' (which sounds fairly mild).[18]

In 1755, the year after the publication of the last volume of *Grandison*, Charlotte Charke published her *Narrative of the Life of Mrs. Charlotte Charke*. Charke, a noted actress and the daughter of Poet Laureate Colley Cibber, was memorably described as 'the well-known trouble-maker', and her narrative revealed how she had for many years lived as a man, and had even taken a wife, cohabiting as Mr and Mrs Charles Brown.[19] As an actress, Charke was part of a mid-eighteenth-century vogue for casting women actors in traditional male theatrical roles, which were known as 'Breeches Parts'.[20] In 1777, for example, Mrs Farrell played the part of Macheath in a bowdlerised version of *The Beggar's Opera*, 'cleaned up' on the advice of magistrate Sir John Fielding (Henry's half-brother), who suggested that 'by condoning vice [the play] was a prime cause of the increase in London crime'.[21] (This seems to imply that, for one prominent jurist, at least, theatrical cross-dressing was a public-spirited gesture, which helped to keep crime levels down.)

The most celebrated of all eighteenth-century cross-dressers was the French spy, diplomat and courtier, the Chevalier d'Eon de Beaumont. Though d'Eon lived out his/her youth as a man, he/she was sent to Russia in 1755 to act as a spy in the court of the Empress Elizabeth at St Petersburg, where he/she took the guise of a woman. D'Eon went to London in 1762 to serve for the next 15 years as Minister Plenipotentiary for the French Foreign Service, under the name of 'William Wolff', and was widely taken for a woman in drag as a man (there was vigorous betting on the subject, with the odds 7 to 4 in favour of d'Eon's being a woman). D'Eon ended his/her career in France as a woman, working as a fencing mistress, and living in a lesbian relationship with a Mrs Cole. When, after d'Eon's death in 1810, the coroner's report revealed that d'Eon was biologically male, with 'the male organs in every way perfectly formed', Mrs Cole was apparently deeply shocked, as was the surgeon who had attended d'Eon's last illness.[22] The 1790s, however, witnessed a new and specifically ideological interest in the politics of cross-dressing. As Colley notes:

> Anxiety about women wearing pseudo-masculine dress was particularly prominent at the time, and seems in retrospect absurdly overdone.... Yet, as the dozens of satirical prints devoted to this topic make clear, the changing silhouette of some women was interpreted as further demonstration that the world was shifting dangerously. As so often happens, the debate over the position of women at the time became the meeting point of much broader anxieties. Under enormous pressure from war and revolution without, and more rapid social and economic transformations at home, Britons seized upon the comparatively minor changes in women's state as a symbol of all that seemed disturbing and subversive.[23]

When in 1778 Lady Eleanor Butler and Sarah Ponsonby, a pair of Irish nobles, eloped and set up home together in Plas Newydd, Llangollen, they became, in their way, celebrated figures, much visited by cultural tourists to and from Ireland, from Dr Johnson to Wordsworth (Llangollen was on the main Holyhead to London road). It was not until the 1790s that they became figures of scandal, victims of a muckraking article in the *General Evening Post*, 24 July 1790:

> Miss Butler is tall and masculine, and she always wears a riding habit, hangs her hat with the air of a sportsman in the hall, and appears in all respects a young man, if we except the petticoats which she still retains.
> Miss Ponsonby, on the contrary, is polite and effeminate, fair and beautiful...[24]

In part, this characteristic concern of the 1790s in dress and its implications for gender and politics is because these were the terms in which so much of that decade's 'Revolution Debate' were framed and articulated. Burke famously noted that, to dispense with the monarchy, or even to apply to it the cold gaze of Enlightenment thinking, was tantamount to 'tear[ing] down all the decent drapery of life', and presents the revolutionary moment as a rapacious *unclothing* of the queen, forced to flee from her attackers 'almost naked'.[25] The vehemence and high emotionalism of Burke's rhetoric was attacked by Thomas Paine and many of Burke's other critics as unhinged ranting, a sign of mental instability: John Barrell writes that 'The alarmism of Burke is frequently described as the effect of a "wild", "distempered", "disordered", "deranged", or "diseased" imagination, with the apparent implication that he was suffering from a temporary madness or infatuation when he wrote the *Reflections*.'[26] It is a short step from accusations of hysteria to accusations of effeminacy, especially since, as Claudia L. Johnson suggests, a feminised sensibility in English political discourse was deliberately cultivated by Burkean anti-Jacobins as a necessary corrective to the cold rationalism of Enlightenment radicalism.[27] Johnson further suggests that this feminised masculinity finds its way into Austen's work through the person of Mr Woodhouse in *Emma*, associated both in the action of the novel and symbolically with a group of middle-aged and old women, particularly Miss and Mrs Bates, in whose company he seems most comfortable.[28] Noting especially the contrasting of the effeminate Mr Woodhouse with the Grandisonian masculinity embodied by Mr Knightley, I would go further, and suggest that this has serious implications for our reading of *Emma*. Uncontroversially, Mr Knightley performs the role of Emma's surrogate father within the novel. However, such is the feminisation of Mr Woodhouse that I would suggest that, within a *strictly realist* economy, there is simply no way that he can be Emma's father. The man has never had sex in his life. Conversely, Mr Knightley's very name, as well as suggesting a gentlemanly courtliness, also implies a sexual potency. I would suggest, therefore, that the logic of the novel is such that it pushes us towards seeing Mr Knightley as Emma's biological, as well as symbolic father: after all, in this rigorously endogamous novel, once we have ruled out Mr Woodhouse himself, there are simply no other candidates.

While Edmund Burke was being attacked by radicals for effeminacy, Mary Wollstonecraft found herself accused by counter-revolutionary commentators of masculinity: her desire to participate in the masculine sphere of politics and government being seen as a wish to become male. Horace Walpole, in a letter to Hannah More, famously called Wollstonecraft a 'hyena in petticoats',[29] while a wag from the *Anti-Jacobin* wrote this notorious couplet:

For Mary verily would wear the breeches
God help poor silly men from such usurping b – s.[30]

Conservative commentators could only conclude that Wollstonecraft, as a woman writer questioning issues of gender and politics, just wanted to be a man: as Miriam Brody argues, her political agenda was reduced to a case of penis envy.[31] However, Wollstonecraft herself pre-empted such accusations:

> From every quarter have I heard exclamations against masculine women, but where are they to be found? If by this appellation men mean to inveigh against their ardour in hunting, shooting and gaming, I shall most cordially join in their cry.[32]

Despite this, the accusations stuck. In his *Memoirs of the Author of 'The Rights of Woman'*, William Godwin writes of Wollstonecraft that 'those whom curiosity prompted to seek the occasion of beholding her, expected to find a sturdy, muscular, raw-boned virago'.[33]

The publication, indeed, of Godwin's *Memoirs* in 1798, with England under threat of a French invasion, led to what Margaret Kirkham has called 'the Great Wollstonecraft Scandal of 1798'.[34] Godwin's candid account of Wollstonecraft's relationship with Gilbert Imlay, her suicide attempts, and her conception of his own child before marriage, as well as his (partially inaccurate) account of her rejection of Christianity, led to vicious denunciations of her character. The index to the *Anti-Jacobin* of that year lists Wollstonecraft under 'Prostitution'.[35] 1798 also saw the publication of the Rev. Richard Polwhele's wild and undiscriminating attack on Wollstonecraft and other women writers, *The Unsex'd Females*, which accused them of being 'To Gallic freaks or Gallic faith resign'd!' In his notes to the poem Polwhele acknowledges the impetus of Godwin's *Memoirs*: 'I know nothing of Miss Wollstonecraft's character or conduct, but from the memoirs of Godwin, with whom this lady was afterwards connected.'[36] Polwhele also attacks Wollstonecraft's sister-feminist, Mary Hays, most particularly her views on sexual democracy put forward in *Letters and Essays, Moral and Miscellaneous* (1793). In her novel *Memoirs of Emma Courtney* (1796) – which fictionalises many of Wollstonecraft's arguments from the *Vindication*, and which contains, in the person of the philosophical Mr Francis, a laudatory portrait of Godwin – Hays dared to suggest that women could have an autonomy of passion in courtship. This position resembles Austen's in *Northanger Abbey*, which sets out in part to refute Richardson's contention in a letter to *The Rambler* that a woman could not love a man before he loved her: 'That a young lady should be in love, and the love of the young gentleman undeclared, is an heterodoxy which prudence, *and even policy*, must not allow.'[37] '[I]f it be true,' Austen writes, 'that no young lady can be justified in falling in love before the gentleman's love is declared, it must be very improper that a young lady should dream of a gentleman before the gentleman is known to have dreamt of her' (NA, 29–30). In 1800, Samuel Taylor Coleridge met Mary Hays, and, in a subsequent letter to Robert Southey, depicts her with a characteristic mixture of physical and intellectual scorn:

> Of Miss Hayes' intellect I do not think so highly as you, or rather, to speak sincerely, I think not *contemptuously* but certainly *despectively* thereof...for to hear a thing, ugly and petticoated, ex-syllogize a God with cold-blooded precision, and attempt to run religion through the body with an icicle, an icicle from a Scotch Hog-trough! *I* do not endure it; my eye beholds phantoms, and 'nothing is but what is not'.[38]

The implication here is obvious: by both the Scottish reference and the quotation from *Macbeth*, Coleridge is likening Hays to the archetypal demonic political woman, Lady Macbeth, assertive because 'unsexed', and threatening a potential for generalised emasculation: 'nothing is but what is not.'

Two of the novels Austen singles out for praise in *Northanger Abbey*, *Belinda* and *Camilla*, are to varying degrees participants in this debate of the 1790s. *Belinda* contains cross-dressers of both the feminised Burkean and the masculinised Wollstonecraftian varieties. Clarence Hervey, who, since it is he who marries the heroine Belinda, may be presumed to act with a degree of authorial tolerance, dresses in women's hoops at a social gathering – 'he was convinced that he could manage a hoop as well as any woman in England, except Lady Delacour' – with the aim of deceiving 'the purblind dowager Lady Boucher', to whom he is introduced as 'The countess de Pomenars', a French *émigrée*.[39] Conversely, the novel famously contains the character of Mrs Freke, a sadistic cross-dressing lesbian, who gets to articulate her philosophy in a chapter entitled 'Rights of Woman': as a grotesque version of Wollstonecraftian thinking, Mrs Freke is the pre-eminent 1790s 'unsex'd female', the demonic political woman who 'had no conscience, so she was always at ease; and never more so than in male attire, which she had been told became her particularly. She supported the character of a young rake with such spirit and *truth*, that I am sure no common conjurer could have discovered anything feminine about her.'[40] As well as Wollstonecraft, Mrs Freke is also, I think, a version of Lady Eleanor Butler: the Butler family were the earls of Ormond, and well known to the Edgeworths – Maria Edgeworth's last Irish novel, it should be remembered, is actually called *Ormond* (1817) – and certainly it is strongly implied that Mrs Freke is herself Irish (the Frekes of Castle Freke were landowners in West Cork). In 1812, Edgeworth published her penultimate Irish novel, *The Absentee*, a novel so Burkean that it even contains a character called Mr Burke, who is the very model of a benign, responsible Irish land-agent. In *Belinda*, the novel's paragon of masculinity, Mr Percival, quotes Burke with approval, and significantly does so in debate with Mrs Freke in the chapter 'Rights of Woman':

'But if you want to know,' said Mrs Freke, 'what I would do to improve the world, I'll tell you: I'd have your sex taught to say, "Horns! horns!" I defy you!'

'This would doubtless be a great improvement,' said Mr Percival; 'but you would not overturn society to attain it would you? Should we find things much improved by tearing away what has been called the decent drapery of life?'

'Drapery, if you ask me my opinion,' cried Mrs Freke, 'drapery, whether wet or dry, is the most confoundedly indecent thing in the world.'

'That depends on *public* opinion, I allow,' said Mr Percival. 'The Lacedæmonian ladies, who were veiled only by public opinion, were better covered from profane eyes, than some English ladies are in wet drapery.'

'I know nothing of the Lacedæmonian ladies, I took my leave of them when I was a schoolboy – girl – I should say.'[41]

In *Northanger Abbey*, John Thorpe dismisses Burney's *Camilla* as not worth reading:

'I was thinking of that other book, written by that woman they make such a fuss about, she who married the French emigrant?'

'I suppose you mean Camilla.' [Catherine says]

'Yes, that's the book; such unnatural stuff! – An old man playing at see-saw! I took up the first volume once and looked it over, but I soon found it would not do; indeed I guessed what sort of stuff it must be before I saw it: as soon as I heard that she had married an emigrant, I was sure I could never be able to get through it.'

'I have never read it.'

'You had no loss I assure you: it is the horridest nonsense you can imagine; there is nothing in the world in it but an old man's playing at see-saw and learning Latin; upon my soul there is not.'   (NA, 49)

What Thorpe has in mind here are the activities of Sir Hugh Tyrold – *Camilla*'s good-hearted, patrician idiot – which take up much of the action of the first volume. What Thorpe *doesn't* mention, though, is that Sir Hugh gets dressed as a woman:

> Sir Hugh...suffered his darling little girl [Camilla] to govern and direct him at her pleasure....She metamorphosed him into a female, accoutring him with her fine new cap, while she enveloped her own small head in his wig; and then, tying the maid's apron round his waist, put a rattle into his hand, and Eugenia's doll upon his lap, which she told him was a baby he must nurse and amuse.[42]

Burney's contemporaries immediately recognised Sir Hugh's political import. The Whig activist Frances Crewe, an enthusiastic subscriber to *Camilla* (1796) (as was one Miss J. Austen of Steventon), tried to enlist Burney's support for an anti-Jacobin periodical, to be entitled *The Breakfast Table*, featuring a fictitious editor, of Burney's creation, who 'should be supposed to live in the vicinity of Sir Hugh Tyrold, whose simplicity of truth, perplexity of doubts and humility, and laughable originality of dialect, might produce comic effect to enliven the serious disquisitions.'[43]

III.   'THE HIGHEST POINT OF EXTASY'

In *Northanger Abbey*, Catherine Morland's first night at the abbey, about which she has been constructing vivid Gothic fantasies, involves, centrally, an encounter with linen. In her bedchamber, she discovers 'An immense heavy chest!' with a 'mysterious cypher' on the lid, which turns out to contain 'a white cotton counterpane' (NA, 163–4), and an apparently locked cabinet containing a forbidden manuscript, indecipherable in darkness, but which, perused the following morning, turns out to be a laundry list. That both of Catherine's discoveries are concerned with clean linen is worth examination, and for a number of reasons. Clean linen, especially when accompanied by a laundry list, implies its opposite: dirty, soiled, or stained linen. *Northanger Abbey* is a novel recurringly preoccupied with dirt and the fear of dirt, at least throughout Volume I, largely set in a rain-soaked Bath. As a child, Catherine 'hated confinement and cleanliness, and loved nothing so well in the world as rolling down the green slope at the back of the house' (NA, 14). Henry Tilney fears that Catherine's prospective new gown will not 'wash well' (NA, 28). When Catherine befriends Isabella Thorpe, 'if a rainy morning deprived them of other enjoyments, they were still resolute in meeting in defiance of wet and dirt, and shut themselves up, to read novels together' (NA, 37) (Chapter 5's 'defence' of the novel follows immediately on from this passage). On the morning in which Catherine is engaged to walk with the Tilneys, it threatens to rain:

'No walk for me to-day,' sighed Catherine; – 'but perhaps it may come to nothing, or it may hold up before twelve.'

'Perhaps it may, [says Mrs Allen], but then, my dear, it will be so dirty.'

'Oh, that will not signify; I never mind dirt.'

'No,' replied her friend very placidly, 'I know you never mind dirt.' (NA, 82)

Shortly afterwards, John and Isabella Thorpe try to impress the muddiness of the day upon Catherine:

'It is very odd! [says Catherine] but I suppose they [the Tilneys] thought it would be too dirty for a walk.'

'And well they might, [says Thorpe] for I never saw so much dirt in all my life. Walk! you could no more walk than you could fly! it has not been so dirty the whole winter; it is ancle-deep every where.'

Isabella corroborated it: – 'My dearest Catherine, you cannot form an idea of the dirt'. (NA, 85–6)

The most celebrated instance of dirtiness in Austen's work must surely occur in Chapter 7 of *Pride and Prejudice*, where Elizabeth walks three miles across country to Netherfield to visit her sick sister Jane, confined to the Bingley's home with a cold. Mrs Bennet objects to this seeming impropriety: 'How can you be so silly...as to think of such a thing, in all this dirt? You will not be fit to be seen when you get there' (PP, 32). Elizabeth proceeds nevertheless:

Elizabeth continued her walk alone, crossing field after field at a quick pace, jumping over stiles and springing over puddles with impatient activity, and finding herself at last within view of the house, with weary ancles, dirty stockings, and a face glowing with the warmth of exercise. (PP, 32)

The dirty stockings and the glowing face here are correlaries (they equate to one another), both signifying Elizabeth's sexual identity and desirability: certainly, Darcy, on seeing Elizabeth, registers his 'admiration at the brilliancy which exercise had given to her complexion' (PP, 33). (In his book *Jane Austen and the Body*, John Wiltshire has commented on the psychoanalytic significance of the blush in Austen's novels.)[44] Furthermore, women in the eighteenth and early-nineteenth centuries did not wear knickers: they wore stockings which came above the knee, tied with a garter, and voluminous petticoats (the 'pink persian' silk to which Austen makes reference in her 1798 letter was too flimsy for dresses themselves, but was rather used for lining or in the manufacture of petticoats),[45] but no garment which resembled underpants (the bloomer is a Victorian invention). Thus the red cheeks and the dirty stockings operate here, I would contend, as synechdoches, representing the unspeakable, but also uncovered, female genitalia – that is, as displaced symbols for Elizabeth Bennet's vagina.

As I argued earlier, then, the clean bed-linen which Catherine Morland discovers in the chest in her room also suggests its opposite, dirty sheets, especially given the novel's preoccupation with dirt up to that point. To understand this a little more fully, I shall turn again to some of Austen's metafictional textual sources for *Northanger Abbey*. Although it is *The Mysteries of Udolpho* which Catherine reads during the course of the novel (her reading of *Udolpho* parallels ours of *Northanger Abbey* – they are both taking place at the same time), it is, as R. W. Chapman first suggested, another Radcliffe novel, *The Romance of the Forest* (1791), which provides Austen with the framework and the referent for many of the most directly 'Gothic' episodes and elements, and especially here the scene of Catherine's exploration of the chest and cabinet on her first night at the abbey.[46] At the very end of Volume I, Radcliffe's heroine Adeline, hiding out in a ruined abbey under the uneasy protection of the La Mottes, who have themselves been forced to flee their creditors in seventeenth-century Paris, has a nightmare in which she opens a coffin she finds in 'a suite of very ancient apartments, hung with black and lighted up as if for a funeral'. This is one of the passages on which Austen draws in her depiction of Catherine's first night at Northanger, but here the forbidden casket contains something rather different:

> The man she had before seen, soon after stood by the coffin, and, lifting the pall, she saw beneath it a dead person, whom she thought to be the dying Chevalier she had seen in her former dream; his features were sunk in death, but they were yet serene. While she looked at him, a stream of blood gushed from his side, and descending to the floor, the whole chamber was overflowed; at the same time some words were uttered in the voice she heard before; but the horror of the scene so entirely overcame her, that she started and awoke.[47]

It is always tempting to read Romantic Gothic, and Radcliffe's novels especially, as providing a pre-Freudian vocabulary of the unconscious, and certainly this passage is overwhelming in its Freudian implications: Adeline's adolescent sexual anxieties are projected onto the nightmare figure of the Chevalier's corpse; the gash in his side from which blood pours out unstoppably, filling the chamber, is a terrifying vaginal symbol, as, famously, in his case study of the 'Wolf Man', Freud suggested that 'women are castrated, that instead of a male organ they have a wound which serves for sexual intercourse, and that castration is the necessary condition of femininity'.[48] The bedchamber full of blood in *The Romance of the Forest* becomes in *Northanger Abbey* the blood-stained sheet, which has two distinct but related symbolic resonances, as signifying either loss of virginity with the rupturing of the hymen (hence the emblematic display of bloodstained sheets to confirm the consummation of marriages contracted for patriarchal or dynastic reasons), or, far more commonly, as signifying the presence of a menstruating woman. Though one should not too readily conflate these meanings, I would suggest that the symbolic presence of either in the novel suggests that Catherine Morland is operating within a sexual economy: she is potentially marriageable and childbearing. Unquestionably, the presence of the Gothic, and of Radcliffe in particular, suggests the irruption into the domestic order of Austen's world of a discourse of sexuality and desire:

> Northanger Abbey! – These were thrilling words, and wound up Catherine's feelings to the highest point of extasy. Her grateful and gratified heart could hardly restrain its expressions within the language of tolerable calmness.... She was to be their chosen visitor, she was to be for weeks under the same roof with the person whose society she mostly prized – and,

in addition to all the rest, this roof was to be the roof of an abbey! – Her passion for ancient edifices was next in degree to her passion for Henry Tilney – and castles and abbies made usually the charm of those reveries which his image did not fill. To see and explore either the ramparts and keep of the one, or the cloisters of the other, had been for many weeks a darling wish, though to be more than the visitor of an hour had seemed too nearly impossible for desire. (NA, 140–1)

The rhetoric of Catherine's exploration of the cabinet in her bed-chamber is also the rhetoric of desire and uncontainable sexual excitement, which I would want to call masturbatory. In *The Poetics of Space*, Gaston Bachelard, who dedicates a chapter to 'Drawers, Chests and Wardrobes', suggests that:

> Chests, especially small caskets, over which we have more complete mastery, are objects *that may be opened*. When a casket is closed, it is returned to the general community of objects; it takes its place in exterior space.... But from the moment a casket is opened, dialectics no longer exist. The outside is effaced with one stroke, an atmosphere of novelty and surprise reigns. The outside has no more meaning. And quite paradoxically, even cubic dimensions have no more meaning, for the reason that a new dimension – the dimension of intimacy – has just opened up.[49]

Finally alone in her room at the abbey, Catherine undresses for bed, and sets about exploring the cabinet:

> in the centre, a small door, closed also with a lock and key, secured in all probability a cavity of importance.
> Catherine's heart beat quick, but her courage did not fail her. With a cheek flushed by hope and an eye straining with curiosity, her fingers grasped the handle of a drawer and drew it forth. It was entirely empty.... The place in the middle alone remained now unexplored ... It was some time however before she could unfasten the door,... but at length it did open; and not in vain, as hitherto, was her search; her quick eyes directly fell on a roll of paper pushed back into the farther part of the cavity, apparently for concealment, and her feelings at that moment were indescribable. Her heart fluttered, her knees trembled, and her cheeks grew pale. She seized, with an unsteady hand, the precious manuscript. (NA, 169)

What Catherine discovers in the 'cavity of importance', while exploring 'the place in the middle' with 'unsteady' hands and 'trembling' knees, is of course, the laundry list. The first thing to say about this is that it is an inventory of *gentleman's* laundry; the second, that it belongs not to Henry, but to Eleanor Tilney's absent, nameless fiancé, about whom we learn at the close of the novel, and whose marriage to Eleanor in the last chapter precipitates Henry and Catherine's own wedding. The laundry list is, in fact, that which represents the fiancé, and thus by extension marriage, in the novel, since he does not himself appear: he is reduced to an inventory of clothing. Indeed, the attentive reader will have noticed that Eleanor is herself identified as bridal throughout the novel: Mrs Allen, who does notice these things, informs Catherine that 'Miss Tilney always wears white' (NA, 91). These are the contents of the laundry list:

> [Catherine's] greedy eye glanced rapidly over a page. She started at its import. Could it be possible, or did not her senses play her false? – An inventory of linen, in coarse and modern characters, seemed all that was before her! If the evidence of sight might be trusted, she held a washing-bill in her hand. She seized another sheet, and saw the same articles with little variation: a third, a fourth, and a fifth presented nothing new. Shirts, stockings, cravats and waistcoats faced her in each. Two others, penned by the same hand, marked an expenditure scarcely more interesting, in letters, hair-powder, shoe-string, and breeches-ball. (NA, 172)

What is a 'breeches-ball'?[50] It is, simply, a ball, usually of a chalky composition, used for cleaning breeches – that is, men's trousers. As *Northanger Abbey*'s recurring interest in dirty clothes and how to clean them suggests, laundry was at this time a relatively complex and time-consuming business. The breeches-ball, of the same colour as the material of the breeches themselves (often an off-white), was rubbed on stains, thus covering them over, precluding the need for washing every time the breeches got some dirt on them. At the very beginning of the novel, remember, we are told that, at age fifteen, Catherine 'began to curl her hair and long for balls'. Though obviously this carries the primary, though emphatically sexual, meaning of longing to dance, to be 'out' in society, there is also the related truth that the longed-for ball which Catherine gets at the end of the novel is this, the breeches-ball: that is to say, the balls which remove dirt from men's breeches. Certainly, Catherine ends her first night at Northanger with an awareness of the significance both of dirt and of men's trousers.

2

Sense and Sensibility

I. THE PROBLEM TEXT

Is Marianne Dashwood pregnant? Is the 'putrid fever' (SS, 330) which threatens her life and robs her of her looks in Volume 3 of *Sense and Sensibility*, and which is itself a consequence of her disastrous romantic encounter with the rakish Willoughby, a decorous euphemism? At the heart of the novel there lies not, as Tony Tanner once suggested, 'a muffled scream from Marianne', but a hidden narrative, barely touched upon but of enormous resonance (Marianne Dashwood's scream, 'muffled' by biting her handkerchief, is, it is true, a part of this resonating effect, but it is a symptom, not the thing itself).[1] This is the story of Eliza Williams, Colonel Brandon's niece, and her mother Eliza Brandon, his sister-in-law. Brandon's tale is, in Barbara K. Seeber's words, one of Austen's 'narrative cameos', which

> all speak of sexual and financial exploitation that the main narrative tries to elide. Yet this subversive content cannot be contained. The stories spill over into the main narrative, disturbing the peace of the narrative that has been privileged by traditional criticism. They talk back to the central plot and reveal its inability to accommodate their stories; in this way, Austen reveals ideology as a constructed 'truth'.... The narrative cameos challenge some common assumptions about Austen. The novels are narrow in their social milieu; yet the cameos deal with illegitimate children, fallen women, and abject poverty. Austen is conservative, for she reconciles the desire of the individual with the structure of society; the cameos show just the opposite: individuals for whom the social order has failed. The cameos provide a countercurrent to the main narrative.[2]

This buried story, which threatens to surface throughout the first half of the novel, distorted by rumour and gossip (in which Austen, by withholding information, makes her readers collusive – we, too, are gossips) and, when finally told, done so stumblingly, is central to the novel, the key to its many seeming mysteries. For one thing, it provides a real explanation for Tanner's invented subtitle for the novel, 'Secrecy and Sickness';[3] but more than this, it provides the novel's *internal* rationale for what has traditionally been viewed as its most vexing feature. Much critical unease has tended to focus on the novel's close, and particularly on the way in which Marianne Dashwood is, it seems, summarily married off to Colonel Brandon in order to satisfy the novel's formal requirement: the novel's device of twin heroines, Elinor and Marianne Dashwood, presupposes a double marriage-plot, and therefore *must* end with the marriages of both sisters. Colonel Brandon, as the only eligible man left standing at the end of the novel, *must* therefore marry Marianne, however psychologically implausible such a resolution might seem.[4] Brandon, after all, is initially presented, mediated through Marianne's consciousness, as a middle-aged dullard, who seems much older than his 35 years: he wears the Regency equivalent of thermal underwear, a flannel waistcoat, which means that he must be 'old and ... feeble' (SS, 38):

'[Colonel Brandon] is old enough to be *my* father; and if he ever were animated long enough to be in love, must have long outlived any sensation of the kind. It is too ridiculous! When is a man to be safe from such wit if age and infirmity do not protect him.' (SS, 37)

This raises further troubling questions: what *is* this respectable man approaching middle age doing lusting silently after 17-year-old girls? After all, Elinor does suggest to Marianne that 'Perhaps thirty-five and seventeen had better not have anything to do with matrimony together' (SS, 37–8). Alternative possibilities suggest themselves perhaps too readily for this novel. Might it have been more emotionally satisfying had *Elinor* married Brandon? He and Marianne, after all, hardly speak throughout the whole novel, whereas it is Elinor to whom Brandon relates his life-story. On a purely formal level, the imperative of the double-heroine trope seems to cut across that of the marriage plot – formally, at least, the novel might make more sense had Elinor and Marianne married *each other*. That is to say, marriage would effect the dialectical resolution of their initially antithetical subject-positions, in keeping with the quasi-Hegelian structures which Austen deployed success-fully elsewhere, in *Emma* and, archetypally, in *Pride and Prejudice.*

Sense and Sensibility was Jane Austen's first published novel (1811), and it has traditionally been one which has afforded readers and commentators problems, and that because of its perceived schematic nature. Writing in 1965, A. Walton Litz, for example, was sure that *Sense and Sensibility* is 'the least interesting of Jane Austen's major works'.[5] Many of the most powerful voices in Austen criticism up to and including the 1960s were deeply troubled by the novel, unable to assimilate it or its implications. D. W. Harding suggested that 'we should in any case feel [difficulty] in accepting the transformation of Marianne herself, and entering wholeheartedly into her new fortunes with Colonel Brandon'.[6] This was expressing things far too temperately for some: Marvin Mudrick, ever hyperbolic, suggested that 'Marianne, the life and center of the novel, has been betrayed, and not by Willoughby', and it is an ending for which, Andrew H. Wright suggested, 'we can hardly forgive Jane Austen'.[7] Modern feminist criticism has tended to agree: Patricia Meyer Spacks somewhat wearily notes that the moral to be drawn from the novel is 'a woman must satisfy her needs with little', while Eve Kosofsky Sedgwick sees the novel as a prime example of the 'spectacle of a girl being taught a lesson'.[8]

Tony Tanner, one of the most influential of all Austen's critics (not least in his role as editor of a number of the Penguin Classics editions of Austen's novels, in print from the 1960s to the 1990s), summed up this response well. Marianne, he suggested, 'is tamed and ready for "citizenship"':

> This points to what is certainly the weakest part of the book – the way Marianne is disposed of at the end. She is married to Brandon to complete a pattern, to satisfy that instinct for harmonious arranging which is part of the structure both of that society and of the book itself. Her energy is sacrificed to the overriding geometry.[9]

The novel itself, in fact, seems acutely aware of this problem, and recounts the marriage in extraordinarily problematic terms:

> Precious as was the company of her daughter to her, [Mrs Dashwood] desired nothing so much as to give up its constant enjoyment to her valued friend [Brandon]; and to see Marianne settled at the mansion house was

equally the wish of Edward and Elinor. They each felt his sorrows, and their own obligations, and Marianne, by general consent, was to be the reward of all.

With such a confederacy against her – with a knowledge so intimate of his goodness – with a conviction of his fond attachment to herself, which at last, though long after it was observable to everybody else – burst on her – what could she do?   (SS, 378)

What indeed? Marianne is the subject, or victim, of a conspiracy; she is offered as a reward or trophy to Brandon. Louis Menand, further extending the novel's problematics to cover the Elinor–Edward relationship, suggests that Austen's novel is burdened by the characterisation of 'the diffident sad sack Edward Ferrars...and the stolid sad sack Colonel Brandon'; it is these flaws which subsequent re-readings, re-writings and re-visions of the novel must serve, Menand implies, to correct.[10] Furthermore, Tanner seems to suggest above that in a novel whose concerns are overridingly formal, what happens to Marianne takes on a ritualistic aspect: she is 'sacrificed' – but also murdered, 'disposed of'. Seeber, more explicitly and self-consciously, writes that 'Marianne dies and is reborn, and this birth is the birth into another ideology.'[11] Here, Tanner hints at a resolution and Seeber posits one – Marianne's death – which, I shall argue, Austen entertained as a real narrative possibility, but also one which she must quite consciously have rejected.

So apparently problematic is the Marianne–Brandon marriage that it was, as it were, subject to correction from the very beginning. Lady Bessborough, sister of the late Duchess of Devonshire and friend of the Prince Regent, thought the novel ended 'stupidly'.[12] By as early as 1815, *Sense and Sensibility* had been translated into French by the Swiss romantic novelist, Isabelle de Montolieu, as *Raison et Sensibilité ou les deux manières d'aimer*.[13] Jeanne-Isabelle-Pauline Polier de Bottens, dame de Montolieu, baronne de Croussaz, to give her resplendent full name, was a successful writer of sentimental fictions, probably now best remembered as the author of *Caroline de Lichtfield* (1786), which was itself translated into English (also in 1786) by the radical novelist Thomas Holcroft to considerable critical acclaim: Samuel Badcock in the *Monthly Review* called it a 'beautiful and interesting novel'.[14] As Edgeworth's *Belinda* was one of those novels singled out for praise by Austen in *Northanger Abbey*, so, in a neat historical touch, does Edgeworth herself in *Belinda* single out Montolieu's work as an example of the novel at its finest: 'Were all novels like those of madame de Croussaz...[I] would adopt the name of novel with delight.'[15] Montolieu's 'free translation' of *Sense and Sensibility* radically de-ironised Austen's original in its concentration on the predicament of Marianne (here recast as the more conventionally romantic-sounding 'Maria') as a straightforward sentimental heroine, effectively unmediated by Elinor's controlling ironic gaze and discourse. De Montolieu's translation also rewrote the ending, heightening Austen's partial vindication of Willoughby by having him marry Eliza Williams, Colonel Brandon's ward; Brandon himself is also rewritten in more conventionally romantic-heroic terms. A similar 'solution' was arrived at in the 1990s when Emma Thompson adapted the novel for the 1997 film directed by Ang Lee, in which she co-starred as Elinor alongside Kate Winslet's Marianne. Here, casting was to prove the key, as Colonel Brandon was played, black-clad and brooding, by Alan Rickman, who came with a screen pedigree, as a dashing, dangerous, sexy older man. Furthermore, as Cheryl L. Nixon points out, the film's re-presentation of Brandon is contingent upon a partial effacing of Willoughby, largely achieved through displacing some of Willoughby's romantic-heroic characteristics onto Brandon himself, an effect achieved in large part through the drawing of explicit parallels between Brandon and Willoughby across a number of scenes. Thus, both men love Marianne's music, both bring her flowers, both read her poetry, both rescue her in the rain:

> In having Brandon mimic the physical shorthand for emotional depth that we see Willoughby enacting, the film slowly erases the emotional distinctions between the two....Brandon has performed the ultimate metonymic substitution: he has substituted himself for the courtship hero. The elderly, staid, emotionally repressed Brandon is accepted as a believable substitute for the youthful, vigorous, and emotionally expressive Willoughby.[16]

Valérie Cossy, indeed, explicitly (and rather disapprovingly) connects De Montolieu's 'free translation' of *Sense and Sensibility* with that of Lee, Thompson and Rickman: 'the press coverage of Emma Thompson's adaptation of *Sense and Sensibility* suggests the "popular", sentimental and moralistic Austen invented by Montolieu is very much alive, many commentators finding it still beneath their dignity to treat her work as serious literature.'[17]

II. DOUBLE HEROINES

In part, these problems arise from the novel's complex composition history. Though published in 1811, *Sense and Sensibility*, like *Northanger Abbey* and *Pride and Prejudice*, was initially a product of Austen's formative writing years in the 1790s. Specifically, the novel began life perhaps as early as 1795, as *Elinor and Marianne*, an epistolary fragment whose twin heroines were juxtaposed as the quasi-allegorical embodiments of polarised worldviews.[18] As Marilyn Butler notes, there was a brief vogue for twin-heroined novels in the mid-1790s.[19] Jane West's *A Gossip's Story* (1795), clearly somewhere near the front of Austen's mind when writing *Sense and Sensibility*, balances the narratives of its twin heroines, the sensible Louisa Dudley and her romantic sister, here also called Marianne. *A Gossip's Story* is ideologically very different from *Sense and Sensibility*: it is animated and everywhere coloured by West's conservative political and didactic agenda, which naturally skews the novel's ideological balance toward Louisa/Sense. This is most directly articulated through a number of speeches and letters instructing and endorsing female piety and subservience, the necessity of submission at all times to forms of patriarchal authority, represented by husbands and especially, it seems, fathers (the didactic homily is Mr Dudley's preferred discursive mode). Eliza Fenwick's extraordinarily melodramatic Jacobin Gothic, *Secresy; or, The Ruin on the Rock*, which plays off the rational Caroline Ashburn against the romantic Sibella Valmont, also dates from 1795. In a grotesque version of the Rousseauan theories of upbringing (a reflection of Fenwick's association with Mary Wollstonecraft, Rousseau's most trenchant critic in the 1790s), Sibella is brought up in isolation under the governance of her uncle, 'the most absurd ridiculous misanthrope of his age', while Caroline acknowledges that 'I have heard myself called pedantic, inflexible, opinionated; I have been told, by some gentler people, that I am severe'.[20] Another direct model for Austen here is the 'Letters of Julia and Caroline' from Maria Edgeworth's *Letters for Literary Ladies*, again from 1795. Here, the impulsive Julia articulates her position in a manner which should be familiar:

> If the genius said to me, 'Choose' – the lot of one is great pleasure, and great pain – great virtues, and great defects – ardent hope, and severe disappointment – ecstasy, and despair: – the lot of the other is calm

happiness unmixed with violent grief – virtue without heroism – respect without admiration – and a length of life, in which to every moment is allotted its proper portion of felicity: – Gracious genius! I should exclaim, if half my existence must be the sacrifice, take it; *enthusiasm is my choice.*... Such, I had almost said, is my *system*, but I mean my *sentiments*. I am not accurate enough to compose a *system*. After all, how vain are systems, and theories, and reasonings![21]

As an educational theorist of the Enlightenment, Edgeworth obviously sets up Julia's position in order to reject it, privileging the rational Caroline at every point. Robert Bage's Jacobinical *Hermsprong* (1796) attempts a rigorous ideological balance between its two heroines, the conventionally virtuous Caroline Campinet and the Wollstonecraftian Maria Fluart, whose role is diminished here to that of the heroine's foil or sidekick – as, much later and with a concomitant moral diminishment, is Elinor Joddrell, confidante and rival to the heroine Juliet Granville in Frances Burney's *The Wanderer* (1814), a novel which revisits, from the historical perspective of the Napoleonic Wars, the climate and ideas of the 1790s, their effect on Franco-British cultural and political relations, and thus on domestic ideologies.

But when Austen resumes writing *Sense and Sensibility*, after the mysterious rejection of *Northanger Abbey* and the years of silence in Bath, she is no longer writing in this mode. That is to say, a newer narrative form – we might, crudely, want to call it a 'nineteenth-century' form: psychological realism articulated through the heavy use of Austen's characteristic narrative technique of free indirect speech – is placed on top of an older, eighteenth-century narrative – epistolary, schematic and didactic, or even architectural, in which characters are not autonomous self-authorising agents but embodiments of an overarching ideological purpose. This is a complex theoretical issue, however, since the dominant modern conception of realism has things the other way around: for structuralist and poststructuralist theory, realism is a great epistemological bugbear, purporting as it does to represent an external reality independent of its own linguistic patterning, the greatest of heresies in post-Saussurean linguistic and literary theory. Thus Roland Barthes can write, seemingly counter-intuitively but with absolute accuracy, that 'The writing of realism is far from being neutral, it is on the contrary loaded with the most spectacular signs of fabrication'.[22] Following the theories of Bakhtin on the one hand, and of much

Modernist and New Critical narrative thinking on the other, contemporary theorising tends to valorise the dialogic over the monologic, mimesis over diegesis, showing over telling, though as Wayne Booth famously demonstrated, all of these ostensibly differing narrative techniques deploy rhetorical strategies which are recognisably similar.[23] Thus, theories of realism have focused on its subsuming of competing voices into an overarching or imperialising monology – one voice, one vision – and its consequent silencing of dissidence in its imposition of a dominant, centralising consensus; its ideological function, in Noam Chomsky's famous phrase, as a manufacturer of consent.[24] Conversely, the epistolary novel has been quite properly understood as a potentially radical form, allowing in its very polyphony for the free play of competing discourses.[25] *Sense and Sensibility* seems trapped between the imperatives of these apparently contradictory narrative theories: to put it simply, the trouble is, it seems, that the newer narrative does not fit perfectly on top of the old one. We can see the joins. As the philosopher Gilbert Ryle suggested, for all its realist trappings, the novel still labours under 'the tyranny of antithesis'.[26]

Certainly the novel *is* antithetical, or more properly dialectical, and that on a number of levels. The novel's doubleness is displayed symbolically through the image of the scissors which Edward Ferrars destroys in frustration shortly before he proposes to Elinor:

> He rose from the seat and walked to the window, apparently not knowing what to do; took up a pair of scissors that lay there, and while spoiling both them and their sheath by cutting the latter to pieces as he spoke, said, in an hurried voice,
> 'Perhaps you do not know – you may not have heard that my brother is married to – to the youngest – to Miss Lucy Steele.' (SS, 360)

The breaking of the sheath here seems hymenal, symbolically foreshadowing Edward and Elinor's marriage. This marriage will also sunder the doubleness of Elinor and Marianne – thus, in breaking the sheath, Edward also spoils the scissors.

The twin heroines espouse and at least partially embody the title's two abstract nouns, 'sense' and 'sensibility', whose historically fortuitous semantic combination of homonymy (deriving, of course, from a shared etymology) and antonymy govern its meaning – like Elinor and Marianne, they are the same but opposite. The *OED* dates 'sense' in Austen's meaning here of 'Natural understanding, intelligence, esp. as bearing on action or behaviour; practical soundness of judgement' from 1684, and 'sensibility' as 'Capacity for refined emotion; delicate sensitiveness of taste; also readiness to feel compassion for suffering, and to be moved by the pathetic in literature or art' from 1756. That is to say, the 'sensibility' of the novel would have been a relatively modern coinage, but already, by the time of *Sense and Sensibility*, a dated one: the two great novels of sensibility in English, Henry Mackenzie's *The Man of Feeling* and Laurence Sterne's *A Sentimental Journey*, date from the 1760s and 1770s. Indeed, Austen's own frames of literary, cultural and aesthetic reference in the novel seem to belong more to the 1780s than to the 1810s when it was published. In Chapter 10, following Willoughby's first visit to Barton Cottage after rescuing Marianne from her fall, Elinor remarks:

> 'Well, Marianne... for one morning I think you have done pretty well. You have already ascertained Mr Willoughby's opinion in almost every matter of importance. You know what he thinks of Cowper and Scott; you are certain of his estimating their beauties as he ought, and you have received every assurance of his admiring Pope no more than is proper.' (SS, 47)

Later in the novel, Edward Ferrars remarks of Marianne: 'And books! – Thomson, Cowper, Scott – she would buy them all over and over again' (SS, 92). Although Scott's *Lay of the Last Minstrel* does date from 1805, and his three-volume *Border Minstrelsy* from 1802–3, this is an interpolation which attempts to bring the published 1811 edition up to date culturally, but which instead only serves to put the slight anachronism of the other references into sharper relief. William Cowper was perhaps the defining poet of the 1780s: his popular ballad, 'The Journey of John Gilpin', dates from 1783 and his great work *The Task* (which Fanny Price also quotes in *Mansfield Park*), written 'to recommend rural ease and leisure', was the great poetic success of 1785. James Thomson, of course, was even earlier: his classic rural epic *The Seasons*, an obvious favourite for Marianne, dates from 1726–30. Thomson may be best (or most frequently) remembered now as the author of 'Rule Britannia' (itself only the most celebrated work of a consistently patriotic *oeuvre* which also included the poems 'Liberty' and 'Britannia'), significant as a reminder of the way in which Austen was and remains, as the Introduction argues, embedded in British polity (see Chapter 5 for more on 'Rule Britannia'). It is notable, then, that – Scott notwithstanding – Marianne's aesthetics should be backward-looking, her tastes for Thomson and Cowper rather than, as might be expected from a twenty-first-century perspective, Wordsworth and Coleridge, or even, say, Southey, Burns, Crabbe or Thomas Moore, all variously too formally or politically radical, too disreputable or (in the cases of Crabbe or Southey) perhaps too serious and heavy for the gentry drawing-room c.1810. This curious potential anachronism partially explains the presence of two of the novel's rather more puzzling cultural references, Mrs Dashwood's remark to Edward that 'your sons will be brought up to as many pursuits, professions, and trades as Columella's' (SS, 103), an allusion to Richard Graves's 1776 novel *Columella, the Distressed Anchoret*, and Robert Ferrars's boast that 'My friend Lord Courtland came to me the other day on purpose to ask my advice, and laid before me three different plans of Bonomi's' (SS, 255) – that is, Joseph Bonomi (1739–1808), the architect and garden-designer, dead by the time the novel saw print. More significantly, it also explains the novel's total silence on the subject of the Napoleonic Wars – an understated but pervasive presence in *all* of Austen's other published novels, except for the claustrophobically centripetal *Emma*, though visible even there. Rather, Colonel Brandon's career as a successful soldier, colonist and trader in the East Indies, a world, in Willoughby's dismissive words, of 'nabobs, gold mohrs, and palanquins' (SS, 51), returns readers not to the 1810s nor even the 1790s, but to the 1770s and 80s, the time of Warren Hastings, famously, and perhaps notoriously, godfather to Austen's cousin Eliza Hancock. Notoriously because, as David Nokes suggests, Hastings may in fact have been Eliza's father, having had an affair with her mother Philadelphia. As evidence of this, Nokes cites a letter from Lord to Lady Clive: 'In no circumstances whatever keep company with Mrs Hancock, for it is beyond a doubt that she abandoned herself to Mr Hastings.'[27] This, we shall see, offers tempting parallels with *Sense and Sensibility*.

By the 1790s, sensibility had, as we saw in Chapter 1, an ambivalent status: ideologically, its connection with Edmund Burke meant that it carried overtones both of effeminacy and patriotism, making it often confusing and contradictory. However, as Janet Todd has noted, sensibility 'was always on the defensive', always an easy target for ridicule.[28] Certainly it was easy to ridicule, not least because of its association with fashion, with empty stances and meaningless jargon. In one of the great novels of the 1780s, Burney's *Cecilia* (1783), the social sage Mr Gosport provides a neat sociological taxonomy of the *personae* of the *ton*, early 1780s fashionable London society, which includes an account of the 'JARGONIST' Captain Aresby, who has emptied his discourse of all meaning, and in doing so has lost the ability to speak English, relying instead on the small pool of French phrases which constitutes his entire vocabulary:

> '[Captain Aresby] has not an ambition beyond paying a passing compliment, nor a word to make use of that he has not picked up at public places. Yet this dearth of language, however you may despise it, is not merely owing to a narrow capacity: foppery and conceit have their share in the limitation, for though his phrases are almost always ridiculous or misapplied, they are selected with much study, and introduced with infinite pain.'

However, Aresby, Burney's narrative informs us, 'wanted not courage, however deeply in vanity and affectation he had buried common sense',[29] and D. Grant Campbell notes:

> The fashionable adjectives surrounding Aresby, both in his own speech and that of the narrator, repeatedly express tyranny, despair and ruin. Aresby displays 'half-dying fatigue' and 'horror': in the course of [his] conversation he is progressively *accablé, obsedé, au desespoir, assomé*, and finally *âbimé*. Aresby's final verdict on Vauxhall is . . . : '*assez de monde*, but nobody here! a blank partout!'[30]

Captain Aresby ends up '*âbimé*', swallowed up or destroyed, by the society of the novel, suggesting a degree of awareness of the absurdity, or even the *horror* of his condition; a horror which, however, he has lost the linguistic ability genuinely to express or escape.

Aresby, consumed by fashionable rhetoric as he is by his novel's economy of credit and consumption, is antithetical to Marianne, yet subject to the same critique of sensibility. Much like the term 'political correctness' today, the word 'sensibility' denoted in broad terms a set of highly desirable social and political attitudes (sensitivity, openness, tolerance) which, because threatening to a conservative order, was treated with disdain, as if it were *inherently* ridiculous. It is not, though, and while there is much affectation and self-conscious posturing in Marianne's adoption of the persona of sensibility (and she *is* only seventeen, after all!), she nevertheless embodies a set of values – openness, honesty – which most twenty-first-century readers consider preferable to Elinor's code of 'sense', which means repression, denial, and silence, and which proves extraordinarily damaging, both to herself (because of her refusal to divulge or act upon what she knows about Edward's engagement to Lucy Steele) and to Marianne (because her refusal to ask Marianne – *her own sister!* – whether she is or is not actually engaged to Willoughby means that she proceeds as though Marianne *were*, thus both compounding Marianne's misery and making the assumption that Marianne is as habitually duplicitous as Elinor is herself). The historian of sensibility G. J. Barker-Benfield has given a detailed account of sensibility's associations with humanitarian reform which provides – certainly from a modern perspective but also, I would suggest, from Austen's own – a powerful vindication of Marianne's position, arguing that while sensibility eventually 'became convention', it was rooted in a 'criticism of selfishness and materialism', and thus 'signified revolution, promised freedom, threatened subversiveness'.[31] Amongst the causes with which sensibility was associated were:

> The cruel treatment of animals, the mistreatment of children, of the sick, and the insane; the corporal punishments of public flogging and executions; imprisonment for debt; dueling, war, and imperialism; the abuse of the poor, their economic exploitation, unrelieved by charity; the press-gang and injustice generally; political corruption; and the slave trade and slavery.[32]

Importantly for our purposes here, Barker-Benfield argues that 'sentimental literature was part and parcel of the campaign for the reformation of manners and...a primary target of that campaign was men's brutalization of women'.[33]

Elinor, in fact, is an habitual liar. This is revealed most glaringly in her relationship, played out across a number of scenes and dialogues, with Lucy Steele, a relationship of mutual loathing in which both parties behave in a very similar fashion. In Chapter 23, for example, Elinor, visiting Lady Middleton, bows out of a game of Casino, ostensibly to help Lucy in her basket-work for Annamaria ('I should like the work exceedingly', she says) (SS, 145), but really to ply Lucy for more information about her engagement to Edward. The discursive dynamic of Elinor and Lucy's dialogue here and elsewhere is predicated on a wholly conscious mutual dislike, with the fiction that is their friendship deployed on both sides for information-gathering and point-scoring:

> In a firm though cautious tone, Elinor thus began.
> 'I should be undeserving of the confidence you have honoured me with, if I felt no desire for its continuance, or no farther curiosity on its subject. I will not apologize therefore for bringing it forward again.'
> 'Thank you,' cried Lucy warmly, 'for breaking the ice; you have set my heart at ease by it; for I was somehow or other afraid I had offended you by what I told you that Monday.'
> 'Offended me!' How could you suppose so? Believe me,' and Elinor spoke with truest sincerity, 'nothing could be farther from my intention, than to give you such an idea. Could you have a motive for trust, that was not honourable and flattering to me?' (SS, 146)

'Elinor spoke with truest sincerity'? If, as Marvin Mudrick once suggested, Austen never deploys irony against Elinor, then how are we to read this statement?[34] After all, a few pages earlier, immediately following the events of 'that Monday' (when Lucy divulges her secret engagement to Elinor), Elinor has decried Lucy as 'illiterate, artful and selfish' (SS, 140). 'How, we ask ourselves, have we been persuaded to endorse a system of values with which we have no real sympathy at all?' David Lodge famously asked of *Mansfield Park*.[35] Since the novel's controlling narrative point of view is almost invariably that of Elinor, this is a question we might also fruitfully ask of *Sense and Sensibility* if we are to understand the novel's structure, as many critics seem to, as fundamentally antithetical, since reading the novel in this way must interpret it as an endorsement of Elinor's values, in keeping with the ideological schemas of West's and Edgeworth's works, and a recognition that it is *Marianne* who is in need of education, development and maturity. Even Lee and Thompson, who, as we have seen, go to great lengths to recast the Marianne–Brandon romance as sympathetically as possible, can never bring themselves to criticise or even to question Elinor (no doubt in part because Elinor is played by Thompson herself, who clearly empathises with her character).

III. INHERITANCE

The novel opens in overwhelming complexity. Its opening chapter, as Jan Fergus rightly suggests, 'sets up all the contrasts which will be refined and worked out through the novel'.[36] These are effected through a series of narrative doublings which themselves further redouble the Elinor/Marianne, Sense/Sensibility pairings which control the novel (it is tempting, in passing, to wonder whether *Sense and Sensibility* has the same exploratory/critical relationship to the double-heroine novel that *Northanger Abbey*, which Austen began slightly later, has to the Gothic). Thus, *Sense and Sensibility* begins not with the Dashwood girls but with two patriarchs, the unmarried 'old gentleman' and 'his nephew Mr Henry Dashwood' (SS, 3), who himself married *twice*, which gives us two branches of the Dashwood family (Elinor, Marianne and Margaret are the children of his second marriage). The legally sanctioned dead hands of these two patriarchs, who feature only in the opening paragraph, are to govern Elinor and Marianne's lives from beyond the grave, establishing a theme of female disempowerment through patrimony ('the old gentleman' keeps his sister as a presumably unpaid 'housekeeper', that is, a de facto servant) (SS, 3) and beginning a process of disinheritance brilliantly worked out in the succeeding chapter, where the John Dashwoods exploit the fact that Mrs Dashwood and her daughters have no legal claim on inheritance or property systematically to deny them any claim on status, material comfort, or social identity. They are cast adrift in the West Country, dependent on men, be it in the form of the good-hearted patrician beneficence of Sir John, or, in the case of Elinor and Marianne, forming romantic attachments with two young men who are effectively killing time until they come into their own inheritances.

Inheritance may well be the real theme of *Sense and Sensibility*, and it is an issue which materially affects not only the Dashwoods' domestic existence at Norland and then at Barton, but is central to the working and resolution of both the novel's marriage plots. Inheritance, one might say, drives the novel. As Claudia L. Johnson argues, *Sense and Sensibility*

> methodically examines the sexual relations gentlemen pursue, either to strengthen patriarchal interests or to relieve the tedium of their existences, which are doomed to dependency and ennui until the death of a near relation will supply the money and liberty they crave.[37]

Clearly, this is Willoughby's situation, dependent ultimately upon the good will of his elderly relative Mrs Smith, and it is this which governs his entire behaviour towards Marianne, as he later explains to Elinor:

> 'My fortune was never large, and I had always been expensive, always in the habit of associating with people of better income than myself. Every year since my coming of age, or even before, I believe, I had added to my debts; and though the death of my old cousin, Mrs Smith, was to set me free; yet that event being uncertain, and possibly far distant, it had been for some time my intention to re-establish my circumstances by marrying a woman of fortune. To attach myself to your sister, therefore, was not a thing to be thought of.'   (SS, 320)

Waiting for Mrs Smith to die, Willoughby has nothing to do but fritter away what allowance he has, and more – he is heavily in debt, and disinherited by Mrs Smith for his treatment of Eliza Williams, which is why he has to marry the wealthy Miss Grey, whose name, even, signals her undesirability. What he also does with his time is seduce women: this is the focus of his otherwise unfocused, undisciplined energy. These conditions obtain equally for Edward Ferrars (though presented in less graphic terms), who contracts his youthful engagement to Lucy out of boredom, to pass the time: 'It was a foolish, idle inclination on my side,' Edward finally admits, 'the consequence of ignorance of the world – and want of employment...I had...nothing in the world to do, but fancy myself in love' (SS, 362). Like Willoughby, Edward is himself disinherited for sexual conduct deemed improper.

IV.   FALLEN WOMEN

Marianne, Brandon and Willoughby are narratively and symbolically interconnected throughout the novel. When the Dashwoods ask Sir John Middleton for information about Willoughby, the conversation flips to Brandon, uniting them in terms of hunting, sex and sexual entrapment, and injury:

> '[Willoughby] is as good a sort of fellow, I believe, as ever lived,' repeated Sir John. 'I remember last Christmas at a little hop in the park, he danced from eight o'clock till four, without once sitting down.'
> 'Did he indeed?' cried Marianne with sparkling eyes, 'and with elegance, with spirit?'

'Yes, and he was up again at eight to ride to covert.'

'That is what I like; that is what a young man ought to be. Whatever his pursuits, his eagerness in them should know no moderation, and leave him no sense of fatigue.'

'Aye, aye, I see how it will be,' said Sir John, 'I see now how it will be. You will be setting your cap at him now, and never think of poor Brandon. . . . Poor Brandon! he is quite smitten already, and he is very well worth setting your cap at, I can tell you, in spite of all this tumbling about and spraining of ancles.' (SS, 45)

But it is not until the proposed excursion to Whitwell, slightly later, that this connection begins to make sense. Brandon, whose presence is necessary to gain entrance, gets a mysterious letter at breakfast – 'he took it, looked at the direction, changed colour, and immediately left the room' (SS, 63) – which causes him to depart in a rush and without explanation. A flurry of gossip follows, which readers, currently clueless as to Brandon's real motives, must provisionally take at face value:

'I can guess what [Colonel Brandon's] real business is, however,' said Mrs. Jennings, exultingly.'

'Can you, ma'am?' said almost everybody.

'Yes, it is about Miss Williams, I am sure.'

'And who is Miss Williams?' asked Marianne.

'What? You do not know who Miss Williams is? I am sure you must have heard of her before. She is a relation of the Colonel's, my dear: a very near relation. We will not say how near, for fear of shocking the young ladies.' Then, lowering her voice a little, she said to Elinor, 'She is his natural daughter.'

'Indeed!'

'Oh! yes; and as like him as she can stare. I dare say the Colonel will leave her all his fortune.' (SS, 66)

This passage, apart from implicating the reader in a general climate of gossip, does two important things: it refutes, provisionally, the received notion (Marianne's) of Colonel Brandon as a somewhat decrepit old man (there was life in the old dog once, there may be still), and it places this chapter of the novel (Chapter 13), firmly in a context of sexual impropriety. This, particularly, is important for what happens next: Willoughby and Marianne, who 'never looked happier than when she got into it' (SS, 67), drive off together in his carriage without waiting for the others:

He drove through the park very fast, and they were soon out of sight; and nothing more of them was seen till their return, which did not happen till after the return of all the rest. They both seemed delighted with their drive, but said only in general terms that they had kept to the lanes, while the others went on the downs.   (SS, 67)

This is one of the novel's many narrative *lacunae*, invariably filled by gossip and rumour – this indeed is largely Mrs Jennings's function in the first half of the novel, and here she is able to answer the first question with confidence: she has information from Willoughby's groom that they have been to Allenham, Mrs Smith's house, 'and spent a considerable time in there walking about the garden and going all over the house' (SS, 67). But what did they do there? Readerly responses to this event are mediated initially through Elinor's reactions. She suspects some nameless but terrible impropriety:

Elinor could hardly believe this to be true, as it seemed very unlikely that Willoughby should propose, or Marianne consent to enter the house while Mrs Smith was in it, with whom Marianne had not the smallest acquaintance. . . .

'Yes, Marianne, but I would not go in there while Mrs Smith was there, and with no other companion than Mr Willoughby. . . I am afraid . . . that the pleasantness of an employment does not always evince its propriety. . . . But, my dear Marianne, as it has already exposed you to some very impertinent remarks, do you not now begin to doubt the discretion of your own conduct? . . . If [Allenham] were one day to be your own, Marianne, you would not be justified in what you have done.'

[Marianne] blushed at this hint.   (SS, 68)

The 'very impertinent remarks' were made by Mrs Jennings, who has just a page or two previously been making some similarly 'impertinent remarks' to Elinor regarding *Colonel Brandon's* 'conduct' – that is, pre-marital sex leading to pregnancy and childbirth out of wedlock. Given that this is the context in which the events of this chapter unfold, and given the novel's technique of deliberately withholding information in order to implicate readers in its climate of gossip, then one has to ask whether *Marianne* is herself seduced and 'ruined' by Willoughby? After all, Marianne's first meeting with Willoughby might be seen as providing a prefiguring metaphor of their subsequent relations: in a display of emotional and physical abandon, Marianne runs down the steep hill to Barton Cottage in the rain, loses her footing, and falls. She is rescued by Willoughby, and though Marilyn Butler notes that 'His entrance [is] like that of the "preserver" of the heroine in a romantic novel', this first appearance itself encodes a warning.[38] He is figured in terms of sexual symbolism from the start. The first description of him is as 'a gentleman carrying a gun' (SS, 42), and as well as carrying the predatory associations of hunting, the image of the gentleman with a gun is a familiar one from eighteenth-century portraiture, particularly the public or 'Swagger' portraiture designed to display both physical prowess and material status:

> 'Swagger' implies a degree of self-consciousness on the part of the artist, if not the sitter (though the two will often collide), which causes the portrait to transcend the private statement (in which the sitter communes with a single viewer), and address itself to the public at large. There is an element of rhetoric in it, even of challenge – the 'insolence' that was always inherent in the meaning of the word. That challenge can often be erotic: swagger nearly always demands sex appeal. It is in its element in the theatre, and the interrelationship between theatrical and other kinds of ostentatious portraiture is an important facet of the subject.... A common device for this purpose is billowing drapery: the wind often blows in swagger portraits; it rarely does in others.[39]

The gun in these portraits was unambiguously phallic, symbolising both physical or material power and sexual potency, and often in these portraits laid at rest, *couchant* (uncocked, as it were) across the sitter's lap. Thomas Gainsborough's celebrated 'Mr and Mrs Andrews' (1750), though not formally a Swagger portrait (it is a Conversation Piece, a depiction of a group of figures), positions Robert Andrews and his wife slightly off-centre, allowing the viewer's gaze to trail off into the farmland, woods and mountains beyond, all of which comprise the Andrews estate (considerably enlarged by his recent marriage). Andrews stands protectively at the shoulder of his sitting wife: she too forms a part of his property. A large gun rests under Andrews's right arm; a gun-dog at his heels – like Willoughby, he is symbolically associated with that most phallic-sounding of hunting dogs, the pointer: the full opening decription of Willoughby is of 'a gentleman carrying a gun with two pointers playing round him' (SS, 42), reinforced slightly later by Sir John's account of his having 'the nicest little black bitch of a pointer I ever saw' (SS, 44). That Willoughby should be introduced both as a hunter and a phallus provides a forewarning of what we discover about him as the novel progresses. Willoughby and Marianne's first meeting, then, encodes a metaphorical tableau representing one interpretive possibility, at least, of their entire relationship: the fallen woman and the predatory libertine. Marianne's climactic sickness and Colonel Brandon's own history of seduced, ruined, sick, and dying maidens serves subsequently to provide further suggestions of the novel's concern with the *potential* of Marianne's passionate relationship with Willoughby.

'You will find me an awkward narrator, Miss Dashwood,' Colonel Brandon says to Elinor, signalling the commencement of his authoritative version of what has hitherto been a genuinely 'awkward', troubling narrative presence in the novel, a narrative unfolding in hints and guesses, silence and absence, gossip and rumour, 'I hardly know where to begin' (SS, 204–5). Brandon tells Elinor the story of his wealthy, orphaned cousin Eliza, brought up under the guardianship of his father. For reasons of patrimony (*the* theme of *Sense and Sensibility*), although she and Brandon are in love, Eliza is forced by her guardian, at age 17 (the same age as Marianne), to marry Brandon's older brother: 'Her fortune was large, and our family much encumbered.... My brother did not deserve her, he did not even love her' (SS, 205). In accordance with the novel's structuring principle of symmetry and parallelism (everything happens *twice*), Brandon is initially attracted to Marianne because she strongly reminds him of Eliza: 'there is a very strong resemblance between them, in mind as well as in person. The same warmth of heart, the same eagerness of spirits'(SS, 205).

This resemblance would seem to be *Sense and Sensibility*'s version of the paternal recognition scene familiar from a number of the period's novels. In Burney's *Evelina* (1778), Sir John Belmont finally recognises Evelina Anville as his legitimate daughter when, on meeting her, he sees in her the double of his beloved dead wife, Caroline Evelyn, whom he has also refused to own, having contracted a secret marriage and then burned the certificate. This is a scene which carries strong incestuous overtones entirely in keeping with that novel's troubled politics of familial identity, and it is worth dwelling on this novel here for the light it casts on *Sense and Sensibility*'s preoccupations (and it *is* an explicit intertext – Austen names her own rake, John Willoughby, in honour of *Evelina*'s rake Sir Clement Willoughby). Affirmation of identity tends finally, in the novels of Austen and her contemporaries, to be achieved through marriage, but that marriage is only made possible, as *Northanger Abbey* suggested, by a process of reification, in which a young woman is objectified into the market commodity known as 'an heroine'. The case of *Evelina* offers something of a slant on this norm, as the novel's heroine is simultaneously seeking both parental legitimisation and the legitimising marriage certificate which will end her narrative as her father's burning of *his* marriage certificate both ended Caroline's story and began Evelina's. Indeed, the novel conflates these two forms of legitimisation, parental and marital, by having Sir John Belmont, as Amy J. Pawl notes, view Evelina, when he finally sees her, as both daughter *and* wife:[40]

> The moment I reached the landing-place, the drawing-room door was opened, and my father, with a voice of kindness, called out, 'My child, is it you?'
>
> 'Yes, Sir,' cried I, springing forward and kneeling at his feet, 'it is your child, if you will own her!'
>
> He knelt at my side, and folding me in his arms, 'Own thee!' repeated he, 'yes, my poor girl, and heaven knows with what bitter contrition!' Then, raising both himself and me, he brought me into the drawing room and shut the door, and took me to the window, where, looking at me with great earnestness, 'Poor unhappy Caroline,' cried he, and to my inexpressible concern, he burst into tears.[41]

Belmont recognises Evelina as his daughter because he sees before him the image of her mother – 'never was likeness so striking'[42] – and therefore because he is able to view her simultaneously as daughter and wife: 'Oh then, thou representative of my departed wife, speak to me *in her name*'[43] – that is, in the name of Caroline Evelyn. In doing so, he confers simultaneous legitimacy on both his daughter and his wife: 'Acknowledge thee, Caroline! – yes, with my heart's best blood would I acknowledge thee!'[44]

Until this moment, Evelina has no fixed identity. Hers is an epistolary novel, but this is the first letter she is able to sign 'Evelina Belmont'. Her previous pseudonymous surname, 'Anville', is merely an image of her unstable self: it is an anagram of 'Evelina', which is itself only a reiteration, with the obligatory heroine's suffix –a, of a commodifying label, of her mother's redundant surname – Caroline Evelyn, who was, but was never allowed to call herself, Caroline Belmont. Her name is a solipsism, its self-referentiality redoubling the novel's incestuous sexual economy (we shall see this significant doubling of names again in *Sense and Sensibility*). Indeed, not only is

Anville an anagram of Evelina, but *both* these names, 'Evelina Anville' are themselves near-anagrams of the names of the novel's other patriarchal figures, her guardian Mr Villars and her eventual husband Lord Orville (curiously, a practice Burney continues with *Cecilia*'s Mortimer Delvile and *The Wanderer*'s Juliet Granville). This can be no accident. Evelina is a composite name, a collage made up of fragments of other names. Without the stabilising, legitimising 'Belmont', Evelina is the sum of a disparate collection of influences; not a 'character' but the projection of the desires and dictates of men.

A near-identical scene, not exactly of identification, but of parental recognition and generational conflation, occurs in Mary Shelley's *Mathilda* (1819–20), here with an overtly incestuous agenda – though for historicising purposes *Mathilda* is bound to remain a liminal case as the manuscript remained unpublished until 1959, though this was for reasons which present commentators with fertile interpretive possibilities, largely because of the many explicit parallels it offers to Mary Shelley's own troubled family life. At the beginning of Shelley's novel, Diana, Mathilda's mother, dies giving birth to her. Stricken by grief, her father, a radical freethinker, 'a Patriot; and an enlightened lover of truth and virtue', leaves his baby daughter in the care of her aunt, who brings her up in Rousseauan isolation on a remote Scottish estate.[45] Shortly after Mathilda's sixteenth birthday, her father returns from his wanderings and commences life with his daughter. In London, Mathilda gains a suitor; her father is consumed by jealousy, and removes her to his estate in Yorkshire, where, on a wild and stormy night, he confesses his unnatural, incestuous love for his daughter before taking his own life by throwing himself off a cliff. Before this, however, he writes a letter to his daughter, explaining that his desire comes from a conflation of mother and daughter: Mathilda *now* resembles and for him becomes Diana *then*: 'If I grieved, it was for your mother, if I loved it was your image...I dared say to myself – Diana gave her birth; her mother's spirit was transferred into her frame, and she ought to be as Diana to me.'[46] The novel closes with a grotesque version of the marriage-plot resolution, as Mathilda gives herself over to death:

> In truth I am in love with death; no maiden ever took more pleasure in her bridal attire than I in fancying my limbs enwrapt in their shroud: is it not my marriage dress? Alone it will unite me to my father when in an eternal mental union we shall never part.[47]

In 1820, Mary Shelley sent the manuscript to her *own* father William Godwin. Perhaps unsurprisingly, he never returned it, and it remained undiscovered amongst his papers for almost a century and a half.

Brandon's narrative, his confession to Elinor, corroborates Marianne's first impression of him as a dull old bachelor, but explains, as Mrs Jennings implied, that he has a romantic past: 'my affection for [Eliza] as we grew up was such, as perhaps, judging from my present forlorn and cheerless gravity, you might think me incapable of having felt' (SS, 205). Brandon's 'forlorn and cheerless gravity' comes as a result of Eliza's history, and his confession attempts narratively to position him as a doomed lover with a tragic past, though as Mary Poovey argues, such a positioning has deeper implications for the patriarchal positioning of women, as the narrative demonstrates 'intense anxiety... produced by his fear of female sexuality'. Austen, Poovey suggests, 'at least intuits the twin imperatives that anchor patriarchal society: men want women to be passionate, but, because they fear the consequences of this appetite, they want to retain control over its expression.'[48] Prevented at the last moment from eloping together to Scotland, Brandon went off to the East Indies with his regiment, and Eliza was forced to marry. This marriage is vicious as well as loveless: Brandon's brother 'had no regard for her: his pleasures were not what they ought to have been, and from the first he treated her unkindly' (SS, 206). 'His pleasures were not what they ought to have been' – this temptingly open phrase raises any number of narrative possibilities, as the activities of wayward husbands in the novels of the period range from drunken dissolution (Lord Delacour in *Belinda*) to incarcerating their wives in lunatic asylums (Mr Venables in Wollstonecraft's *The Wrongs of Woman*), and this without mentioning the various and ingenious male depravities offered by the Romantic Gothic novel. Whatever these 'pleasures' are, they are serious – serious enough for Eliza to commit herself to the social doom of deserting her husband for another man. Troublingly, Brandon offers this break as an excess of carnality: 'I could not trace her beyond her first seducer, and there was every reason to believe she had removed from him only to sink deeper in a life of sin' (SS, 207). Colonel Brandon's beloved Eliza is a *bona fide* fallen woman, divorced for adultery by her husband (she may even, it is implied, have taken to prostitution). It is her adultery and divorce, rather than her husband's evidently horrific brutality, which Brandon considers the most distasteful aspect of his story: 'The shock which her marriage had given me ... was of trifling weight – was nothing, to what I felt when I heard, about two years afterwards, of her divorce. It was *that* which threw this gloom – Even now the recollection of what I suffered –' (SS, 206). Brandon spends six months searching for her before he finds her in a 'spunging-house', a form of debtor's prison, where she lies dying – and, as she is 'ruined' goods, no longer a marketable commodity, this comes as a relief to him: 'That she was, to all appearances, in the last stages of consumption, was – yes, in such a situation it was my greatest comfort' (SS, 207).

It is this pervasive view of women which *Sense and Sensibility* ultimately rejects. For a sense of the cultural depth of the issues with which Austen is dealing here, it is necessary to examine their theoretical, philosophical and theological underpinnings. The philosopher Susan Griffin, writing on pornography, says this:

> In the pornographic mind, a great fissure exists between spiritual and carnal love, for the pornographer can never love one woman in both body and soul. The Marquis de Sade has told us, for instance, that he liked to be friends with 'ugly' women. He could not befriend a woman whom he desired. After an act of coitus with a woman, he found her repulsive and hated her company.... Here we find an old and familiar duality. Now the body and the soul, which we are used to thinking of as divided, are represented by the virgin and the whore. The virgin is 'pure', her soul can be loved precisely because her body has not been touched. She is without sexual knowledge. But the whore, who knows sexual experience, is defiled.... We know this thinking from the church fathers.[49]

Julia Kristeva theorises that the 'symbolic order' of patriarchy necessarily represents women as the boundaries of that order, that which, in Toril Moi's gloss, 'shields the symbolic order from the imaginary chaos' outside.[50] Such a construct necessarily predicates the dualist vision of female sexuality. Kristeva writes:

> no other civilization [than the Judaeo-Christian] seems to have made the principle of sexual difference so crystal clear: between the two sexes a cleavage opens up. This gap is marked by their different relationship to the law (both religious and political), a difference which is in turn the very condition of their alliance. Monotheistic unity is sustained by the radical separation of the sexes: indeed, it is this very separation which is its prerequisite. For without the gap between the sexes, without this

localization of the polymorphic, orgasmic body, desiring and laughing, in the *other* sex, it would have been impossible, in the *symbolic realm*, to isolate the principle of One Law.... Universalist as it is, Christianity does associate women with the symbolic community, but only providing they keep their *virginity*. Failing that, they can atone for their carnal *jouissance* with their martyrdom.[51]

Failing in turn to atone by martyrdom, sexualised women are represented as *partaking* of the external chaos and consequently symbolically demonised as Lilith or the Whore of Babylon. Lilith, we remember, was Adam's first wife (or variously his second wife, mother of his demonic offspring after his separation from Eve – and since Chapters 1 and 2 of Genesis present two discrete and completely different accounts of the creation of woman, there is some scriptural evidence for Lilith), according to some sources dismissed for wantonness (she wanted to have sex on top, presumably seen by the primal patriarchs, God and Adam, as a dangerously revolutionary or powerful position), and thereafter demonised as an embodiment of evil. In his study *On the Nightmare*, the psychoanalyst Ernest Jones traces the etymology of Lilith's name back to sexual and vampiric origins:

> The Hebrew Lilith...the princess who presided over the Succubi, came from the Babylonian Lilitu, who was definitely a vampire; incidentally, the name is now thought to be derived from *lulti*, 'lasciviousness', and not, as the Rabbis used to maintain, from the Hebrew Lailah, 'night'.[52]

Clearly, this kind of thinking has its most profound contextual resonances for our subject in the Gothic novel of the 1790s. It provides, in fact, a most accurate description of the gender politics of Matthew Lewis's *The Monk* – John Thorpe's favoured reading, we remember, in *Northanger Abbey*. Lewis's mad monk Ambrosio is consumed with desire for the lovely Antonia, the more desirable for her 'purity', 'virtue', 'innocence', those imperatives which, as the Introduction noted, were transformed into moral categories signifying femininity. Ambrosio makes a Satanic pact to gratify his desire for Antonia, who is drugged, kidnapped and imprisoned in a tomb, where Ambrosio rapes her. Immediately thereafter, he lashes out at her:

> 'Wretched Girl, you must stay here with me! Here amidst these lonely Tombs, these images of Death, these rotting loathsome corrupted bodies!

Here you shall stay, and witness my sufferings, witness, what it is to die in the horrors of despondency, and breathe the last groan in blasphemy and curses! And who am I to thank for this? What seduced me into crimes, whose bare remembrance makes me shudder? Fatal Witch! was it not thy beauty? Have you not plunged my soul into infamy? Have you not made me a perjured Hypocrite, a Ravisher, an Assassin!... You will tell my Judge, that you were happy, till *I* saw you; that you were innocent, till *I* polluted you!... And 'tis you, who will accuse me! 'Tis you, who will cause my eternal anguish! You, wretched Girl! You! You!'[53]

Having crossed the boundary of the symbolic order into the external chaos, Antonia is represented here as both demonic – she is a 'Fatal Witch' – and as metonymically associated with the decaying corpses which surround her – she is rotten flesh, dead meat. Shortly thereafter, Antonia atones for her carnality (Ambrosio's carnality, of course, projected onto her) through her martyr's death. Lest readers be at all unclear about this, her place in the text is taken by another beautiful young woman, whose name is Virginia.

V. SEDUCED MAIDENS

As Susan Staves suggests, such narratives as Colonel Brandon's offer a somewhat more complex version of the traditional Christian sexual dialectics of virgin and whore: 'the very idea of the seduced maiden seems paradoxical. Seduced maidens are certainly not lascivious whores; indeed, their intrinsic delicacy is so great that once violated they are apt to die.'[54] Brandon offers a qualified example of a woman forced to 'atone for [her] carnal jouissance with...martyrdom', figuring Eliza as a fallen woman for whom death is redemptive. From the perspective of Enlightenment feminism with which Austen is frequently associated, such a figuring was anathema, and associated with all that was worst about the feminine ideologies of domestic fiction. In her unfinished novel *The Wrongs of Woman*, Wollstonecraft's incarcerated heroine is given an unanswerable condemnation of the prevailing sexual double standard:

'But the misfortune is, that many women only submit in appearance, and forfeit their own respect to secure their reputation in the world. The situation of a woman separated from her husband is undoubtedly very different from that of a man who has left his wife. He, with lordly dignity, has shaken off a clog; and the allowing her food and raiment, is thought sufficient to secure his reputation from taint. And, should she have been inconsiderate, he will be celebrated for his generosity and forbearance. Such is the respect paid to the master-key of property! A woman, on the contrary, resigning what is termed her natural protector (though he never was so, but in name) is despised and shunned, for asserting the independence of mind distinctive of a rational being, and spurning at slavery.'[55]

The *locus classicus* of the eighteenth-century 'seduced maiden' is Samuel Richardson's Clarissa Harlowe, and both Wollstonecraft and her feminist contemporary Mary Hays attacked Richardson's decision to have Clarissa wane away to a redemptive death as, in Johnson's phrase, 'a twisted testimonial to *male* power'.[56] Indeed, as far back as 1709, Mary Delariviere Manley had attacked the injustice of this state of affairs in her feminist Utopia *The New Atalantis*:

> Men may regain their Reputations, tho' after a complication of Vices, *Cowardice, Robbery, Adultery, Bribery*, and *Murder*, but a Woman, once departed from the Road of Virtue, is made incapable of return; sorrow and scorn overtake her, and … the World suffers her to perish loath'd and unlamented.[57]

A radical fiction such as Bage's *Barham Downs* (1784) not only overturned the convention of the death of the seduced maiden, but made sure that the woman received a financial reward as compensation for her seduction.[58]

In her letters, Austen herself wrote disparagingly of the idea of a young woman dying for, or because of, love: 'it is no creed of mine … that such sort of Disappointments kill anybody' (L, 281). When Austen revisits the trope of the seduced maiden with the narrative of Lydia Bennet's elopement with Wickham in *Pride and Prejudice*, the conservative response is rejected on principle and out of hand by being given to Mary Bennet and Mr Collins, the novel's absurd and (in the latter case) objectionable conduct-book moralists. Mary speechifies, while 'Elizabeth lifted up her eyes in amazement':

> 'Unhappy as the event may be for Lydia, we may draw from it this useful lesson; that the loss of virtue in a female is irretrievable – that one false step involves her in endless ruin – that her reputation is no less brittle

than it is beautiful, – and that she cannot be too much guarded in her behaviour towards the undeserving of the other sex.' (PP, 289)

Mr Collins helpfully informs Mr Bennet that 'The loss of your daughter would have been a blessing in comparison of this' (PP, 296–7) – which, as a matter of fact, comes close to Brandon's sentiments about Eliza.

Marianne, then, though she wanes in sickness, does *not* die like Eliza, though Johnson argues that her death is figured as desirable, and even willed, by both Willoughby and Brandon.[59] Seeing Marianne after her sickness, Mr John Dashwood, for one, believes her now to be unmarriageable, effectively 'ruined':

'Poor Marianne, 'said [Mr. John Dashwood] to Colonel Brandon in a low voice, as soon as he could secure his attention, – 'She has not such good health as her sister, – she is very nervous, – she has not Elinor's constitution; – and one must allow that there is something very trying to a young woman who *has been* a beauty, in the loss of her personal attractions. You would not think it, perhaps, but Marianne was remarkably handsome a few months ago, quite as handsome as Elinor. – Now you see it is all gone.' (SS, 236–7)

John Dashwood, of course, has a vested interest in denigrating Marianne here, comparing her unfavourably to Elinor, since he is hatching a scheme to encourage Brandon, whom he admires for his wealth, to marry Elinor, thus helping to relieve him for good of the already non-existent burden of supporting his step-family. However, even Edward Ferrars, a more disinterested commentator, immediately notices, when visiting the sisters at Mrs Jennings's London home, 'Marianne's altered looks' (SS, 242).

Brandon decribes the dying Eliza's appearance in a way which anticipates these accounts of Marianne after her sickness:

'So altered – so faded – worn down by acute suffering of every kind! hardly could I believe the melancholy and sickly figure before me, to be the remains of the lovely, blooming, healthful girl on whom I had once doated.' (SS, 207)

Eliza has a daughter by her first lover, and she too is called Eliza (it is only fitting that there should be *two* Elizas in this outrageously doubled text), and becomes Colonel Brandon's ward, the Miss Williams of Mrs Jennings's speculations. She is not, then, his 'natural daughter', though symbolically that *is* the position she occupies in the text. At the age of 17 – Marianne's age, Eliza 1's age – she goes to Bath, where she meets and falls in love with Willoughby, who afterward deserts her. Brandon tells Elinor that

> '[Willoughby] left the girl whose youth and innocence he had seduced, in a situation of the utmost distress, with no creditable home, no help, no friends, ignorant of his address! He had left her promising to return; he neither returned nor wrote, nor relieved her.'   (SS, 209)

This contains far too many parallels with Willoughby's treatment of Marianne. That *Marianne* is 'a girl whose youth and innocence [Willoughby] had seduced', is, I suggest, offered at least initially by the novel as an ambiguity. Certainly by connecting Marianne both narratively and symbolically with both ruined Elizas, both of whom bear illegitimate children, and by giving her a romance with Willoughby which parallels his own with Eliza 2 (including most importantly, the connection with Brandon, who seems to be a professional rescuer of 17-year-old girls), the novel offers a ruined Marianne as a narrative possibility – if not indeed, as Butler suggests, a seeming inevitability: 'Another contemporary novelist – Mrs. West, Mrs. Hamilton, or the young Maria Edgeworth – would almost certainly have had Marianne seduced and killed off, after the errors of which she has been guilty.'[60]

Butler's verdict bespeaks truth, but may be a little hard on Jane West, at least as far as *A Gossip's Story*, Austen's readiest model here, is concerned. Nevertheless, to demonstrate and highlight the extent of Austen's conscious, and radical, disavowal of accepted ideological models, it is worth concentrating on West for a moment. The relationship between Marianne Dudley and her suitor and eventual husband, Mr (later Lord) Clermont, clearly foreshadows that of Marianne Dashwood and Willoughby in Austen. Their first meeting is staged as a romantic rescue, when Marianne's horse takes fright and gallops away, but is heroically and athletically brought to a halt by a handsome stranger. The young couple soon discover shared tastes for the Romantic sublime:

> Never was such a wonderful coincidence of opinion! Both were passionate admirers of the country; both loved moonlit walks, and the noise of distant waterfalls; both were enchanted by the sound of the sweet-toned harp, and the almost equally soft cadence of the pastoral and elegiack muse;

in short whatever was passionate, elegant, and sentimental in art; or beautiful, pensive, and enchanting in nature.[61]

Marianne and Clermont marry, though since their marriage is based on passion and romance, rather than the rational companionship which Marianne's father Mr Dudley continually advocates, its foundations are shown to be weak. Marianne and Clermont grow apart, largely through the agency of a loose confederacy of scheming, malicious or interfering women (the titular gossips' circle, a group of frustrated middle-aged women; Clermont's jealous and gorgonish mother; Marianne's confidante Eliza and her maid Patty). At the end of the novel, news of Mr Dudley's death causes the pregnant Marianne to miscarry, 'by which not only Lord Clermont's anxious expectations of an heir were frustrated, but her own life was endangered, and the affections of her husband further alienated'. Marianne loses her bloom, 'faded by sickness and distress' – so much so that on visiting her, her former suitor, the virtuous Mr Pelham, 'beheld the beauty of Mrs. Clermont withering under the worm of discontent, her features contracted by peevish melancholy, and her temper rendered irritable by disappointment'.[62] With Mr Dudley's deathbed blessing, Mr Pelham marries Louisa: it is an ideal marriage, which, in contrast to the thwarted dynastic ambitions of Clermont, soon produces a young son (Mr Pelham also has built on the grounds of his estate 'a fine Dorick temple...dedicated to Integrity and Fortitude', whose centrepiece is a white marble bust of the late Mr Pelham, complete with laudatory verses!).[63] Clermont enters public life and becomes effectively estranged from Marianne, who closes the novel as an unloved recluse:

> Her time passes very uncomfortably. She has in a great degree secluded herself from society, some of her neighbours say she is deranged, others think her intolerably proud; all blame her for living unhappily with a handsome, generous, well-behaved husband. Few can understand her sorrows, and fewer have courage to stem the torrent of publick opinion by pitying them.[64]

A Gossip's Story at least provided for its Marianne a *relatively* liberal conclusion: unhappy and possibly insane, but alive. Narratives of the dead maiden abounded. This, raving in sickness on the decline to death, is, after all, the destiny of Clarissa Harlowe (and Jocelyn Harris has drawn many parallels between Sense and Sensibility and

Clarissa),[65] as well as of Sibella Valmont, Marianne's counterpart in Eliza Fenwick's *Secresy*. *Secresy*, whose outlandish plot verges on incoherence, multiplies its images of the seduced and dying maiden in ways which, again, resemble *Sense and Sensibility*. Like Brandon, Mr Davenport is forced overseas by his tyrannical father who refuses to countenance his son's love for the fair but impecunious Arabella: 'my father gave her the character of an abandoned strumpet, and vowed I should die in prison if I did not renounce her for ever.'[66] Returning from France after his father's death, he discovers that Arabella has borne him a child in his absence. Wearied by poverty and sickness, she is discovered close to death but antici- pating redemption: 'she calmly looks forward to that abode where *the wicked cease from troubling and the weary are at rest.*'[67] Arthur Murden, meanwhile, warns Clement Montgomery against an affair with the beautiful but wicked Janetta Landy, which he likens with hilarious symbolism to the eruption of Vesuvius:

> Rememberest thou, Montgomery, the terrific and awful minutes we past on Vesuvius! Was that not a scene which, while it gratified curiosity and exhausted wonder, made nature shrink with repugnance from the situ- ation? – Yet, in all the horrors of a night worse than that hour, lighted only by the flame of destruction, with showers of thundering dangers obstructing my footsteps, yet, had I been *thee*, Clement! would I have climbed that summit – aye and precipitated myself into the gulph of ruin, rather than forever blacken the sheet of love, by sinking to the embraces of a prostitute!
> Oh'tis a stain indelible![68]

The close of the novel sees Murden falling dead in the arms of his beloved Sibella, whom he has rescued from the clutches of the wicked Lord Filmar. Filmar abducts Sibella, 'seiz[ing] her unattired in bed', whose hand he has been promised in marriage by her misanthropic uncle, and, in a familiar story, imprisons and impreg- nates her. Her uncle responds to the news thus: 'she, poor child, suffers sufficiently, and I am willing to forgive her though I can never be reconciled to her. Her pregnancy will now be known to the world; and, were I again to receive her, I should co-operate in disgracing my family.'[69] He needn't have worried, as Sibella herself drops dead immediately after Murden does.

Closest of all here is Edgeworth's 'Letters of Julia and Caroline'. For *Sense and Sensibility*, Austen splits Julia in two: her excess of sensibility is given to Marianne, but her tragic demise belongs to Eliza Brandon. Julia has two suitors, the wealthy but vain and proud Lord V —, and Caroline's sensible and suitable brother, Mr Percy. In spite of Caroline's warning that 'The belief in that sympathy of souls, which the poets suppose declares itself between two people at first sight, is perhaps as absurd as the late fashionable belief in animal magnetism', Julia chooses unwisely, contracting a marriage to Lord V — which soon turns sour and results in their separation, affording Caroline the opportunity for some Wollstonecraft-type musings on the lot of the separated wife. A fallen woman, Julia flees to France, only to be reunited with Caroline at the close, when she is discovered at an inn, mad and close to death:

> Upon a low matted seat beside the fire sat Lady V —; she was in black; her knees were crossed, and her white but emaciated arms flung on one side over her lap; her hands were clasped together, and her eyes fixed upon the fire; she seemed neither to hear nor see any thing round her, but, totally absorbed in her own reflections, to have sunk into insensibility. I dreaded to rouse her from this state of torpor; and I believe I stood for some moments motionless: at last I moved softly towards her – she turned her head – started up – a scarlet blush overspread her face – she grew livid again instantly, gave a faint shriek, and sunk senseless into my arms.

She expires shortly thereafter, exhorting her daughter to '*be good and happy*'.[70] This is of course Marianne Dashwood's fate, which Austen narratively displaces onto Eliza Brandon. It is, I think, a gesture of formal and ideological radicalism on Austen's part that she chooses to reject this destiny for Marianne.

3

Pride and Prejudice

I. FAIRYTALES

The first thing to say about *Pride and Prejudice* is that it is a fairytale. The fact that it is set in the village of Meryton, or 'Merry Town', provides the first clue to this. Setting the novel here is akin to setting it in Happy Valley or Pleasantville, an untroubled community reflective of a larger, idealised polity: all is well with the world.[1] We are, ostensibly at least, in Little (conceivably even in 'Merrie') England, where the famous aphorism with which the novel opens, however ironically presented it may be, is nevertheless vindicated by its close: 'It is a truth universally acknowledged, that a single man in possession of a good fortune, must be in want of a wife' (PP, 3). Its fairytale narrative economy, in which Opposites Attract, and in which a feisty, intelligent heroine in financially straitened circumstances overcomes the opposition of a backward-looking tradition and authority, as well as the preconceptions about class and money to which her own sceptical intelligence has initially predisposed her, to win the hand of a man who is effectively the richest man in England, provides the template for innumerable subsequent redactions upon the same theme. It is, I would suggest, *the* major source for most subsequent romantic comedies, particularly movies in the Hollywood tradition.

It is also this fairytale element which has led to *Pride and Prejudice*'s being the most enduringly popular of all Jane Austen's novels. 'The Republic of Pemberley', the astonishing fan-based Austen website named, of course, for Darcy's Derbyshire residence, provides a good example of this. On the Internet, websites such as the

Republic of Pemberley have potentially democratised the literary canon by opening Austen up to a fan-base going public for the first time with theories and interpretations of beloved novels, and also offering a forum for fan-fiction in the form of new versions, sequels, continuations, homages, available for all to read. However, rather than opening up interpretation, the traditional 'Janeism' of many of these responses – hostile as it often is to academic discourse – might paradoxically be said to shore up and confine interpretations.

The power of the stranglehold *Pride and Prejudice* has on the popular imagination is very graphically demonstrated by a search of the Republic of Pemberley's 'Bits of Ivory', its extensive and ongoing collection of submitted Austen sequels and spin-offs. At the time of writing (September 2003), all five of the ongoing stories take their lead from *Pride and Prejudice*. Thus, for example, Louise Barada's *An Encounter at Netherfield* juxtaposes two conversations, one between Darcy and Bingley, the other between Elizabeth and Jane, both reporting Darcy's successful proposal of marriage: the first ends, fancifully but rather touchingly, with Bingley planning 'a double wedding. We are to be brothers the same day' – a conclusion which is, frankly, at least as satisfying and plausible as the authentic doubled resolution of *Sense and Sensibility*. Each sequel in its turn is the subject of vigorous discussion, which tends to be naïve and uncritical, though again touchingly supportive. Thus, for example, 'HopeElyse' responds 'Lovely! Simply lovely. There is not much more too [*sic*] say', 'Else' comments 'I've loved every word of it! Thank you so much!' while 'Judith O' says, 'you've done an excellent job with this story. Very like the original, and I can picture each scene in my imagination. Please do continue!' More strikingly still, the Bits of Ivory archives contain more stories based on *Pride and Prejudice* than on all the other Austen novels combined – a whopping 316 completed stories, compared with 27 for *Persuasion*, 26 for *Sense and Sensibility*, 23 for *Emma*, 14 for *Mansfield Park*, and a meagre 8 for *Northanger Abbey*. A search of the Republic of Pembeley's archives did not merely confirm my suspicions about *Pride and Prejudice*'s cultural dominance, it spectacularly outdid them.

Part of *Pride and Prejudice*'s appealing fairytale quality also lies in the ways in which the novel touches upon many of the issues which recur in other Austen novels as thorny, difficult, oppressive or ideologically contradictory, but does so smoothly, in ways which render them untroubling, easily resolved. Here, certainly, the realist novel's tendency towards consensus, identified by Ermarth, Watson and Seeber and discussed in detail in the previous chapter, seems uncomplicated and absolute. While the appeal of this tactic is obvious, and makes *Pride and Prejudice* Austen's most harmonious novel, it also makes it her most glib, a condition which might be said to apply *a fortiori* in the case of academic critics trained to sniff out difficulties and ambiguities: 'We will certainly,' writes Claudia Johnson, 'misrepresent [Austen's] accomplishment if we posit this singular novel as the one against which the others are to be judged.'[2] There is, however, and self-evidently, a considerable readerly pleasure to be gained from having one's generic expectations *precisely* confirmed, and this is the kind of pleasure which *Pride and Prejudice* seems to afford.

The novel begins from the same premise as *Sense and Sensibility*, the unfair treatment afforded women under primogeniture. The celebrated opening sentence is one of the subtlest instances of Austen's use of free indirect speech, as it is really only to Mrs Bennet that this 'truth universally acknowledged' obtains this early. The most materially pressing truth is this:

> Mr Bennet's property consisted almost entirely in an estate of two thousand a year, which, unfortunately for his daughters, was entailed in default of heirs male, on a distant relation; and their mother's fortune, though ample for her situation in life, could but ill supply the deficiency of his. Her father had been an attorney in Meryton, and had left her four thousand pounds. (PP, 28)

Mr Bennet, then, has no male heir, and therefore in accordance with its entail, his Longbourn estate devolves to 'my cousin, Mr Collins, who, when I am dead, may turn you out of this house as soon as he pleases' (PP, 61). Recognising that this form of disinheritance is likely to cast her daughters adrift effectively penniless, like the Dashwood girls, Mrs Bennet 'continued to rail bitterly against the cruelty of settling an estate away from a family of five daughters, in favour of a man whom nobody cared anything about' (PP, 62). She is quite correct, of course, and even Lady Catherine de Bourgh says that she sees 'no occasion for entailing estates from the female line' (PP, 164). The fact that Mr Collins is an objectionable buffoon, 'a conceited, pompous, narrow-minded, silly man' (PP, 135), serves only to underline this. It is precisely these iniquitous laws of inheritance whose consequences are so devastating to the

Dashwoods, and which have here, no less seriously, conspired to drive Mrs Bennet insane (which she undoubtedly is): 'I am sure I do not know who is to maintain you when your father is dead. – *I* shall not be able to keep you' (PP, 113), she says to Elizabeth after her rejection of Mr Collins's proposal of marriage. The famous exchange between the Bennets on the subject of Mrs Bennet's nerves is certainly clever and amusing, but it is also indicative of a rather callous disregard for women on Mr Bennet's part, a refusal of imaginative sympathy with his wife and a refusal to acknowledge his own dereliction of paternal duty towards his daughters:

> 'Mr Bennet, how can you abuse your children in such a way? You take delight in vexing me. You have no compassion for my poor nerves.'
>
> 'You mistake me, my dear. I have a high respect for your nerves. They are my old friends. I have heard you mention them with consideration these twenty years at least.'　(PP, 5)

This discussion draws on an Enlightenment tradition of medical speculations about the function of the nervous system, particularly in women, its relation to sensibility and therefore its presence in theories of the novel.[3] This is a rich and complex subject, and one which elsewhere, even in another Austen novel, would have been treated with the seriousness it merits. Thus, in a manner characteristic of the novel's tendency to smooth over differences and difficulties, the conditions which were to predicate *Sense and Sensibility*, making it Austen's gloomiest novel, are here deflected, rendered ideologically safe by being made the vehicle for an admittedly funny joke. But Mrs Bennet's obsession with marrying off her daughters at all costs stems from real practical parental concern – if they do not marry, they may starve, especially given that Mr Bennet himself has made no provision for his daughters' futures but seems instead to be in a form of denial – he retreats to his library. This amounts to a condition every bit as pathological, and considerably more culpable, than his wife's, as even Elizabeth eventually comes to recognise:

> Elizabeth, however, had never been blind to the impropriety of her father's behaviour as a husband...that continual breach of conjugal obligation and decorum which, in exposing his wife to the contempt of her own children, was so highly reprehensible. But she had never felt so strongly as now, the disadvantages which must attend the children of so

unsuitable a marriage, nor ever been so fully aware of the evils arising from so ill-judged a direction of talents; talents which rightly used, might at least have preserved the respectability of his daughters, even if incapable of enlarging the mind of his wife. (PP, 236–7)

This is potentially grim stuff, and in *Sense and Sensibility* it makes for actually grim stuff. *Pride and Prejudice*, however, elides the implications of these issues by making for the two oldest Bennet girls, at least, marriages which are, by any standards, spectacularly lucrative, but which serve yet again to demonstrate the novel's tendency towards compromise.

II. PROPERTIES

Bingley is 'a young man of large fortune from the north of England' with 'four or five thousand a year' (PP, 4): he is, that is to say, new money, the cash-rich heir of an industrial family from the north of England. Bingley was and is a mill-town just to the north of Bradford, which was a major centre for the manufacture of textiles during the industrial revolution, when the invention of the flying shuttle (1733), the spinning jenny (1770) and 'Crompton's Mule' (1779), revolutionised the industry. Bradford in particular became a boom-town after the introduction of the first steam-powered mill in 1798 made large-scale factory-systems possible here as elsewhere across the north. Bingley, then, is a textile magnate whose family, at least, wish to launder their fortune through marriage into the gentry: thus Caroline Bingley has designs on Darcy, 'a gentleman' (as Elizabeth reminds Lady Catherine de Bourgh), while Bingley himself marries Jane, 'a gentleman's daughter' (PP, 356). Bingley's social mobility is symbolically represented, as it was later to be in *Persuasion*, through the fact that he lives in rented accommodation:

> Mr Bingley inherited property to the amount of nearly an hundred thousand pounds from his father, who had intended to purchase an estate but did not live to do it. – Mr Bingley intended it likewise, and sometimes made choice of his county; but as he was now provided with a good house and the liberty of a manor, it was doubtful to many of those who best knew the easiness of his temper, whether he might not spend the remainder of his days at Netherfield, and leave the next generation to purchase. (PP, 15)

The 'property' which he inherits, a vast fortune, is presumably in factories, and he initially thinks of buying his way into the gentry through purchase of property: 'I will buy Pemberley itself if Darcy will sell it.... I should think it more possible to get Pemberley by purchase than imitation' (PP, 38).

Pemberley itself is the most straightforwardly symbolic of Austen's great houses, the nearest she comes to the tradition of great Country House literature, of Ben Jonson's Penshurst and Andrew Marvell's Appleton House, whose significance in mythologising a national polity (the management of the estate represents the management of the state) Raymond Williams has analysed in *The Country and the City*.[4] In the England of the 1790s, and through to the end of the Napoleonic Wars, this image of the estate as a microcosm for the nation and an expression of the ideal of English polity gained further topical currency because of its use by Edmund Burke as a recurring image in *Reflections on the Revolution in France*, that powerful formulation of English conservatism, as that which needs shoring up as a protection against revolutionary Jacobinism:

> You will observe, that from the Magna Charta to the Declaration of Right, it has been the uniform policy of our constitution to claim and assert our liberties, as an *entailed inheritance* derived to us from our forefathers, and to be transmitted to our posterity; as an estate specially belonging to the people of this kingdom without any reference whatsoever to any other more general or prior right. By this means our constitution preserves an unity in so great a diversity of its parts. We have an inheritable crown, an inheritable peerage; and an house of commons and a people inheriting privileges, franchises, and liberties, from a long line of ancestors.[5]

Almost immediately, the landed estate became a discursively contested site to a degree even greater than it had been across the eighteenth century: in 1793, Charlotte Smith's *The Old Manor House*, in a conscious Jacobin counterblast to Burke, presented *its* landed estate, Rayland Hall, as a crumbling pile peopled by antiques and relics, badly in need of ideological renovation. The complexities and ambiguities of estate management and improvement which, as the next chapter will demonstrate, bedevil *Mansfield Park* are nowhere in evidence, however, in *Pride and Prejudice*. While it is the case that the Bennets' entailed estate devolves out of their hands to Mr Collins, and that there is in this an implied critique of Mr Bennet's familial mismanagement, the outrageously successful marriages of Elizabeth and Jane magically overcompensate the family for this loss, embedding them further still within Burke's model Tory constitution.

The great eighteenth-century exemplar of virtuous masculinity, Samuel Richardson's Sir Charles Grandison, is in part Austen's model for Darcy, not least in his management of his estate, Grandison Hall, which, as Edward Malins has suggested, bears all the hallmarks of Capability Brown's handiwork:[6]

> This large and convenient house is situated in a spacious park; which has several fine avenues leading to it.
>
> On the north side of the park, flows a winding stream, that may well be called a river, abounding with trout and other fish; the current quickened by a noble cascade, which tumbled down its foaming waters from a rock, which is continued, to some extent, in a kind of ledge of rock-work rudely disposed.
>
> The park itself is remarkable, for its prospects, lawns, and rich-appearing clumps of trees of large growth; which must therefore have been planted by the ancestors of the excellent owner; who, contenting himself to open and enlarge many fine prospects, delights to preserve, as much as possible, the plantations of his ancestors; and particularly thinks it a kind of impiety to fell a tree, that was planted by his father.
>
> On the south side of the river, on a natural and easy ascent, is a neat, but plain villa, in the rustic taste, erected by Sir Thomas; the flat roof of which presents a noble prospect. The villa contains convenient lodging-rooms; and one large room in which he used sometimes to entertain his friends.
>
> The gardener's house is a pretty little building. The man is a sober diligent man, he is in years: Has a housewifely good creature of a wife. Content is in the countenance of both: How happy they must be![7]

Pride and Prejudice's version of Sir Charles's happy gardener is Mrs Reynolds, Darcy's happy housekeeper, who swears that:

> 'He is the best landlord and the best master...that ever lived. Not like the wild young men now-a-days who think of nothing but themselves. There is not one of his tenants or servants but will give him a good name. Some people call him proud, but I am sure I never saw anything of it. To my fancy, it is only because he does not rattle away like the other young men.' (PP, 249)

Elizabeth's visit, with the Gardiners, to Pemberley, provides, after Darcy's letter to Elizabeth, the novel's second narrative *peripeteia*.

The description of the grounds, influenced according to John Dixon Hunt and Peter Willis by Humphry Repton, provides a veritable pornography of estate management, designed to display its owner not only, as Elizabeth notes, in 'an amiable light' (PP, 249), but in the most sensational of lights:[8]

> The park was very large, and contained great variety of ground. They entered it in one of the lowest points, and drove for some time through a beautiful wood, stretching over a wide extent.
>
> Elizabeth's mind was too full for conversation, but she saw and admired every remarkable spot and point of view. They gradually ascended for half a mile, and then found themselves at the top of a considerable eminence, where the wood ceased, and the eye was instantly caught by Pemberley House, situated on the opposite side of a valley, into which the road with some abruptness wound. It was a large, handsome, stone building, standing well on rising ground, and backed by a ridge of high woody hills; – and in front a stream of some natural importance was swelled into greater, but without any artificial appearance. Its banks were neither formal, nor falsely adorned. Elizabeth was delighted. She had never seen a place for which nature had done more, or where natural beauty had been so little counteracted by an awkward taste. They were all of them warm in their admiration; and at that moment she felt, that to be mistress of Pemberley might be something! (PP, 245)

Indeed. And the end of the novel has Elizabeth confessing to Jane that it is precisely this visit to Pemberley which has made all the difference:

> 'Will you tell me how long you have loved him?'
>
> 'It has been coming on so gradually, that I hardly know when it began. But I believe it must date from my seeing his beautiful grounds at Pemberley.' (PP, 373)

Pemberley, landscaped and improved 'but without any artificial appearance' enacts in bricks and mortar, wood and water, the novel's synthesising, ameliorating middle way: 'There is,' Alistair Duckworth writes, 'a kind of scenic *mediocritas* about the estate, a mean between the extremes of the improver's art and uncultivated nature.'[9] So too with the events at Pemberley, and the social inclusiveness which they symbolise. When Darcy initially proposes to Elizabeth, he deplores 'the inferiority of [her] connections'

(PP, 192) – the Gardiners, who 'lived by trade, and within view of [their] own warehouses' in Cheapside (PP, 139) (that is, they have not begun to gentrify themselves through the renting of a country estate, as Bingley has). However, in Pemberley, Darcy encounters Elizabeth and the Gardiners on a symbolically unifying 'simple bridge' (PP, 253), and a class rapprochement begins, a rapprochement which closes with the novel itself, whose last words are not specifically of Elizabeth and Darcy, but of the importance of the Gardiners to their lives:

> With the Gardiners, they were always on the most intimate terms. Darcy, as well as Elizabeth, really loved them; and they were both sensible of the warmest gratitude towards the persons who, by bringing her into Derbyshire, had been the means of uniting them.   (PP, 388)

III. LETTERS

If *Pride and Prejudice* is a novel about a house, then it is also a novel about a letter: Darcy's letter to Elizabeth, which takes up most of Volume 2 Chapter 12 (Chapter 35 in some modern editions), and on which the entire text hinges. In an archaeological account of Austen's novels, B. C. Southam suggests a possible explanation for the prominence of this letter. Remarking that, in the novel, 'a very credible system of letters [carries] much of the story in an epistolary version', Southam suggests that '*Pride and Prejudice* was originally a novel-in-letters'.[10] Certainly, the novel's crucial narrative event is a piece of writing, and Darcy's letter has the status of an autonomous and co-existent parallel text which effects a rewriting of much which has proceeded it. As readers, in effect, Darcy's letter causes us to read the first half of the novel *twice*. Darcy's letter operates as a synoptic device within the text, a kind of narrative split-screen effect. The purpose of this is to allow for Elizabeth's negotiation between two simultaneous stories, which now occupy the same narrative space, and its outcome is that Elizabeth effects a renegotiation of the terms of her own story, and concludes that 'actions were capable of a very different construction' (PP, 258). 'Can there be any other opinion on the subject?' Jane asks when she and Elizabeth offer each other very different interpretations of another letter, Caroline Bingley's to Jane. 'Yes there can,' Elizabeth replies, mine is totally different' (PP, 118).

The whole novel offers Elizabeth an exercise in interpretation; Darcy's letter sets about dismantling her confidence in the fixity of the meaning of these interpretations: 'How differently did everything now appear' (PP, 207), she thinks after reading it, 'Till this moment I never knew myself' (PP, 208). *Pride and Prejudice*'s initial working title, 'First Impressions', itself suggests the significance of the 'second impression': the letter, then, allows the text formally to enact its own ideological 'double vision', to have it both ways. At Pemberley, a major symbolic component in the novel's double vision, Elizabeth 'admired...every point of view' (PP, 245), thus enacting in spatial terms Elizabeth's new-found capacity for a generous understanding of its owner.

A number of critics have in fact made reference to Austen's, and specifically to *Pride and Prejudice*'s 'double vision',[11] this in the sense of the novel's 'balancing act',[12] its tendency to accommodate or smooth over ideological differences which can amount to a refusal or inability to subscribe to a single narrative or political position (Johnson suggests that the novel's every argument is undercut by 'a built-in countervailing argument').[13] Elizabeth herself has frequently been read as a female fantasy figure, but she embodies a contradictory double fantasy. She is, on the one hand, as several critics have pointed out, 'a fantasy of female autonomy', a heroine willing and able to articulate effective resistance to the power-structures of class, money and gender: a radical, therefore, or even potentially a revolutionary heroine.[14] Conversely, as Marilyn Butler, ever eager to read a Tory Austen, has noted, *Pride and Prejudice* contains the archetypal plot of the conservative novel: 'An impulsive or mistaken protagonist, frequently someone whose first choice in love was rash, now uses sober judgement and external evidence to select a partner in marriage.'[15] Marriage, furthermore, the novel's 'double vision' shows, to a man who, though proud abroad, dispenses from his Pemberley estate a Grandisonian largesse. Darcy, then, is a genuine conservative model of the benign aristocracy, an embodiment of a social organisation straight out of Edmund Burke. But it is he and not Elizabeth who articulates the nearest that the novel comes to open Jacobinism, an Enlightenment feminist programme for women's education which echoes Wollstonecraft's call for a redefinition of women's education in the *Vindication of the Rights of Woman*, and one which sets him explicitly against the conservative conduct-book moralising of Mr Collins and of Mary Bennet. Darcy suggests a programme so radical in its implications that Elizabeth refuses to believe it possible. In the *Vindication*, Wollstonecraft writes witheringly of the limitations inherent in the series of 'alluring' accomplishments which comprised the standard female education, and which have served effectively to cretinise generations of women, denying them a stake in the Enlightenment:

> The conduct and manners of women, in fact, evidently prove that their minds are not in a healthy state; for, like the flowers which are planted in too rich a soil, strength and usefulness are sacrificed to beauty; and the flaunting leaves, after having pleased a fastidious eye, fade, disregarded on the stalk, long before the season when they ought to have arrived at maturity. One cause of this barren blooming I attribute to a false system of education, gathered from the books written on this subject by men who, considering females rather as women than human creatures, have been more anxious to make them alluring mistresses than affectionate wives and rational mothers; and the understanding of the sex has been so bubbled by this specious homage, that the civilized women of the present century, with a few exceptions, are only anxious to inspire love, where they ought to cherish a nobler ambition, and by their virtues exact respect.... It is acknowledged that [women] spend many of the first years of their lives acquiring a smattering of accomplishments; meanwhile, strength of body and mind are sacrificed in libertine notions of beauty, to the desire of establishing themselves – the only way women can rise in the world – by marriage.[16]

Miss Bingley, who certainly wishes to establish herself and rise in the world by marriage to Darcy, offers a conventional account of women's accomplishments, to which Darcy adds a crucial Wollstonecraftean condition:

> 'I cannot boast of knowing more than half a dozen [women], in the whole range of my acquaintance, that are really accomplished.'
> 'Nor I, I am sure,' said Miss Bingley.
> 'Then,' observed Elizabeth, 'you must comprehend a great deal in your idea of an accomplished woman.'
> 'Yes; I do comprehend a great deal in it.'
> 'Oh! certainly,' cried his faithful assistant [Miss Bingley], 'no one can be really esteemed accomplished, who does not greatly surpass what is usually met with. A woman must have a thorough knowledge of music, singing, drawing, dancing, and the modern languages, to deserve the word; and besides all this, she must possess a certain something in her air and manner of walking, the tone of her voice, her address and expressions, or the word will be but half deserved.'

'All this she must possess,' added Darcy, 'and to all this she must yet add something more substantial, in the improvement of her mind by extensive reading.'

'I am no longer surprised at your knowing *only* six accomplished women. I rather wonder now at your knowing *any*.'

'Are you so severe upon your own sex, as to doubt the possibility of all this?'

'*I* never saw such a woman. *I* never saw such capacity, and taste, and application, and elegance, as you describe, united.' (PP, 39–40)

The irony here, of course, is that it is precisely Elizabeth herself who does unite all of these qualities, as a version of the Wollstonecraftean heroine.

In a novel which, from its very opening sentence, makes marriage for the Bennet sisters an imperative of overpowering (in Mrs Bennet's case, crushing) financial importance, the ultimate fantasy may not be Elizabeth's acts of verbal rebellion but the fact that she manages to make herself such an astonishingly good match. More precisely, of course, these apparently contradictory impulses, of rebellion and conservatism, are brought together as the novel offers a synthesis of ideological opposites, a proto-Hegelian social dialectic which succeeds in uniting desirable qualities from both sides, having the best of both worlds, having it both ways through the elision or harmonising of discord. Little wonder, then, that the novel has proven so popular: it is calculatedly Austen's most inoffensive work. Critics, predictably, have divided along party lines when faced with this tendency, with Butler and Johnson as ever, it seems, articulating interpretive poles: either *Pride and Prejudice* is 'a categorically happy novel' (Johnson, for once voicing an opinion which the good folks of the Republic of Pemberley would only too happily endorse), or it closes at an impasse with its own intentions, in 'moral limbo' (Butler).[17]

The novel closes by resolving, as it were magically, what is initially a conflict of imperatives, the sexual and the economic. In purely financial terms, even marrying Mr Collins would, given the entail which hangs over the Bennet family, be a prudent move for Elizabeth. In a conversation significantly placed immediately after the ball in which Elizabeth confirms her unfavourable 'First Impression' of Darcy, she and Charlotte Lucas, discussing Jane and Bingley's burgeoning relationship, and through that the pragmatics of the marriage market in general, reveal very different outlooks:

'Jane [says Charlotte] should make the most of every half an hour in which she can command his attention. When she is secure of him, there will be leisure for falling in love as much as she chuses.'

'Your plan is a good one,' replied Elizabeth, 'where nothing is in question but the desire of being well married; and if I were determined to get a rich husband, or any husband, I dare say I should adopt it. But these are not Jane's feelings; she is not acting by design.'...

'Well,' said Charlotte, 'I wish Jane success with all my heart; and if she were married to him tomorrow, I should think she had as good a chance of happiness, as if she were studying his character for a twelve-month. Happiness in marriage is entirely a matter of chance. If the dispositions of the parties are ever so well known to each other before-hand, it does not advance their felicity in the least. They always grow sufficiently alike afterwards to have their share of vexation; and it is better to know as little as possible of the defects of the person with whom you are to share your life.' (PP, 22–3)

Elizabeth, despite her denial of the primacy (even, perhaps, the necessity) of financial security in marriage, is forced to negotiate between a desire which includes the sexual (mutual attractiveness, compatibility, knowledge) and 'the desire of being well married', that is, of getting 'a rich husband'. The two other marriages which take place during the course of the novel illustrate the danger of veering too close to either pole of desire, and if they do so somewhat schematically it is because they are narrative devices, there to point up Elizabeth and Darcy's own centralising course.

'I certainly *have* had my share of beauty' (PP, 4), says Mrs Bennet, and the Bennets' marriage is entirely down to her youthful sexiness, wherein lies the problem:

[Mr Bennet] captivated by youth and beauty, and that appearance of good humour, which youth and beauty generally give, had very early in their marriage put an end to all real affection for her. Respect, esteem, and confidence, had vanished for ever; and all his views of domestic happiness were overthrown. (PP, 236)

Mrs Bennet admits, with a kind of touching honesty which belies her husband's, and the novel's, antipathy towards her as 'a woman of mean understanding, little information, and uncertain temper' (PP, 5), that 'When a woman has five grown up daughters, she ought to give over thinking of her own beauty' (PP, 4). Amongst these 'five grown up daughters' it is Lydia who has inherited her mother's status as a teenage sex-bomb:

> Lydia was a stout, well-grown girl of fifteen, with a fine complexion and good-humoured countenance.... She had high animal spirits, and a sort of natural self-consequence, which the attentions of the officers, to whom... her easy manners recommended her, had increased into assurance. (PP, 45)

The handsomest of these officers is Wickham, 'the happy man towards whom every female eye was turned' (PP, 76). Elizabeth is certainly susceptible to his magnetism: 'Whatever he said, was said well; and whatever he did, done gracefully. Elizabeth went away with her head full of him. She could think of nothing but Mr Wickham' (PP, 84). Elizabeth is shocked at Lydia's shameless lack of remorse when she returns from her elopement married to Wickham, a marriage whose strong mercenary element Lydia is aware of and perhaps even collusive in. As Susan Staves notes in her study of 'seduced maidens', seduction *could* be a collusive act: a correspondent to the *Gentleman's Magazine* wrote in 1773, 'Oh, ye powers, did you not give the lovely Sophia less love, or more resolution to resist.'[18] In the same way, in *Sense and Sensibility*, Willoughby attempts to justify his treatment of Eliza Brandon to Elinor:

> 'I do not mean to justify myself, but at the same time cannot leave you to suppose that I have nothing to urge – that because she was injured she was irreproachable, and because *I* was a libertine, *she* must be a saint. If the violence of her passions, the weakness of her understanding – I do not mean, however, to defend myself.' (SS, 322)

Like the lovely Sophia, Lydia has little or no 'resolution to resist'.

'Happiness in marriage,' Charlotte, we remember, tells Elizabeth, 'is entirely a matter of chance' (PP, 23). Despite Elizabeth's confidence in telling Charlotte 'that you would never act in this way yourself' (PP, 23), Charlotte marries Mr Collins. It is of course a marriage for security's sake, a settlement based on not so much 'the desire... to get a rich husband' and the desire to get 'any husband': 'marriage was the only honourable provision for well-educated young women of small fortune, and however uncertain of giving happiness, must be their pleasantest preservative from want'

(PP, 122–3). Charlotte is 'twenty-seven, without ever having been handsome' (PP,123), and when Mrs Bennet says to Bingley, 'Not that I think Charlotte so *very* plain – but then she is our particular friend' (PP, 44), we know that it is in her interest to downplay Charlotte's desirability in order to boost her own daughters', but nevertheless all honest readers will acknowledge that 'plain' is here and remains a euphemism for ugly. Charlotte is an ugly woman approaching thirty, and the novel registers her family's 'apprehension of Charlotte's dying an old maid' (PP, 122). While, two novels later, *Emma* will show its heroine adamant that a wealthy young woman should have no particular need for marriage, here Charlotte quite unambiguously accepts Mr Collins's proposal 'solely from the pure and disinterested desire of an establishment' (PP, 122), as aware as Elizabeth is that her husband-to-be is, in the words of Lilian S. Robinson, 'a schmuck'.[19] Here, Charlotte is again under no illusions: 'I am not romantic, you know,' (PP, 125) she tells Elizabeth, indicating a willingness to efface her own sexuality – indeed, of the positive desirability under these circumstances, which obtained for many women, of as low a sex-drive as possible. Elizabeth considers it 'humiliating' and 'disgracing' that Charlotte has 'sacrificed every better feeling to worldly advantage' (PP, 125) – including, unquestionably or even perhaps primarily, the 'better feelings' of sex. Nevertheless, the patrilineal imperative which drives Mr Collins to marry means that the marriage must be consummated, an heir produced. But to minimise her contact with her husband, Charlotte's marriage becomes a kind of game of 'musical rooms': as often as possible Charlotte ensures that, wherever Mr Collins is, she is somewhere else, deliberately spending much of her time in an uninviting room or suggesting that he tend his garden: 'To work his garden was one of his most respectable pleasures; and Elizabeth admired the command of countenance with which Charlotte talked of the healthfulness of the exercise, and owned she encouraged it as much as possible' (PP, 156). Interestingly, then, the Gardiners aren't the novel's only gardeners: the future, this passage implies, belongs to Mr Collins too.

Mr Collins's status as a potential lover has led to some fascinating critical speculations. Robinson draws our attention to the fact that 'whether Jane Austen wishes to remember it or not, the repulsive Mr Collins cannot be avoided in bed'.[20] Dorothy Van Ghent went further, offering a memorably grotesque fantasy of Mr Collins's 'grampus-like erotic wallowings'![21] In Robert Z. Leonard's MGM production of *Pride and Prejudice* (1940), Mr Collins is played with terrific sliminess by Melville Cooper. Perfect casting, but Cooper was not the only actor up for the role. In what could have been an inspired choice, the young Phil Silvers – Sergeant Bilko himself! – was also up for the part. In his autobiography, *The Man Who Was Bilko*, Silvers recalls how, dressed in a wig last worn by Edward G. Robinson in Howard Hawks's *Tiger Shark* and affecting an accent he'd picked up from conversations with Robert Morley, he tested for the English casting director:

> ME: My dear Dame Elizabeth, your modesty does you no dissoivice –
> BASIL: Cut. It's dis-service, Mr Silvers.
> ME: Okay . . . dis-service in my eyes. You can hardly doubt the poipuss –
> BASIL: Cut. Purr-pose, Mr Silvers.
> ME: . . . purr-pose of my discourse. My attentions have been too marked to be avoided. (On my knees.) Oh! forgive this passion.

He didn't get the part, but, Silvers recalls, 'These three minutes were perhaps the funniest I've done.'[22]

Elizabeth's dominant mode, in the first half of the novel at least, is a verbal irony which Darcy characterises as 'easy playfulness' (PP, 23). The purpose and function of this irony is to deflect meaning (in this she is her father's daughter, as both acknowledge), and the meaning deflected is predominantly sexual, the advances of Mr Collins and (at first) Darcy. One of Elizabeth's commonest discursive strategies to deflect Darcy's signification in the first half of the novel is to 'speak for' him, anticipating his discourse and mimicking it, turning the gaze of his 'satirical eye' (PP, 24) back upon himself: 'You expect me,' he says, 'to account for opinions which you chuse to call mine, but which I have never acknowledged' (PP, 50). For example, at the Netherfield ball, Darcy asks her to dance:

> She smiled, but made no answer. He repeated the question, with some surprise at her silence.
> 'Oh!' said she, 'I heard you before, but I could not immediately determine what to say in reply. You wanted me, I know, to say "Yes", that you might have the pleasure of despising my taste, but I always delight in overthrowing those kind of schemes, and cheating a person out of their premeditated contempt. I have therefore made up my mind to tell you, that I do not want to dance a reel at all – and now despise me if you dare.' (PP, 52)

(Alice Chandler reads a sexual innuendo here: 'The word *reel* did have a sexual connotation in Jane Austen's time. The phrases "the reels o'Bogie", "the reels of Stumpie" [!] and "dance the miller's reel" are all slang terms for sexual intercourse.' This being the case, one might want to render Elizabeth's put-down in the modern vernacular as something like 'I wouldn't have sex with you if you were the last man on earth'.[23]) This verbal agility, Elizabeth's second-guessing of Darcy's speech, allows her consistently to evade his meaning, to reinterpret his motives, and to misinterpret them, to turn the first half of the novel into a series of misreadings. Thus, when Elizabeth tells Darcy that his 'defect' is 'a propensity to hate every body', Darcy replies ('with a smile') that hers 'is wilfully to misunderstand them' (PP, 58). In effect, Elizabeth will not allow Darcy to speak to her. 'I beg your pardon,' she tells him, 'one knows exactly what to think' (PP, 86), and when dancing in conspicuous silence, Darcy, ostensibly talking about books, suggests to Elizabeth that 'We may compare our different opinions', she simply turns him down: 'No – I cannot talk about books in a ball-room; my head is always full of something else'(PP, 93).

Darcy's letter does not put a total stop to Elizabeth's self-authorising ironic discourse, thank heavens, but it *does* effect a diminishing or tempering of it. By the end of the novel, Elizabeth countenances restraint in her repartee with Darcy: 'she checked herself. She remembered that he had yet to learn to be laught at, and it was rather too early to begin' (PP, 371). Early in the novel, she famously states that 'follies and nonsense, whims and inconsistencies do divert me, I own, and I laugh at them whenever I can' (PP, 57). But Elizabeth comes to an awareness of her own 'inconsistencies', and realises, as Emma Woodhouse never does, that 'nonsense' can contain meaning. When eventually, towards the novel's close, Elizabeth and Darcy engage in a dialogue which *does* signify, they discuss his letter:

> Darcy mentioned his letter. 'Did it,' said he, 'did it *soon* make you think better of me? Did you go on reading it, give any credit to its contents?'
> She explained what its effect on her had been, and how gradually all her former prejudices had been removed. (PP, 368)

One thing the letter does not contain is a better phrased reiteration of Darcy's botched proposal: Elizabeth's witheringly accurate elucidation of her reasons for not wanting to marry him have put paid to that. The purpose of the letter is rather to clear Darcy of the 'two offences of a different nature, and by no means equal magnitude... laid at my charge' (PP, 196) – his separation of Bingley from Jane on account of the unsuitability of the Bennet family, and his having 'blasted the prospects of Mr Wickham... Wilfully and wantonly' (PP, 196).

It's no surprise, perhaps, that Darcy should find Mrs Bennet's 'total want of propriety' to be 'objectionable' (PP, 198). It *is* objectionable. The novel itself, through its narrative voice (largely speaking from Elizabeth's point of view), has asserted this from the opening chapter, we have seen, with its seemingly dispassionate account of her 'mean understanding, little information, and uncertain temper'. Elizabeth certainly feels this way, and the narrative records her feelings on one of the occasions which led to the formation of Darcy's opinion about Mrs Bennet: 'Her mother would talk of her views in the same intelligible tone. Elizabeth blushed and blushed again with shame and vexation' (PP, 100). At the same gathering, Elizabeth's views of other members of her family foreshadow Darcy's denunciation: Mary's singing has her 'in agonies' (PP, 100). Like most families, perhaps, the Bennets can be excruciatingly embarrassing. Darcy's real 'offence' may have been his refusal to accommodate, to suppress this awareness in his actions, to keep his opinions to himself. Elizabeth's family pride, her sense of being 'a gentleman's daughter' (PP, 356), is offended by Darcy's actions – but then again the Bennets are not, as things stand, his family. The novel's equalising 'balancing act' sees to it that Darcy, too, is provided with an embarrassing relative, Lady Catherine de Bourgh, every bit as cringe-making as Mrs Bennet, and considerably more malicious. Here, a familial imperative analogous to Elizabeth's obliges him to stifle his overt reaction to her equally 'objectionable' behaviour, which Elizabeth is quite properly willing to challenge with all her verbal resources: 'Mr Darcy looked a little ashamed of his aunt's ill breeding, and made no answer' (PP, 173).

The more serious offence with which Elizabeth charges Darcy is his effective disinheritance of Wickham. Given that Darcy's and Wickham's account of the same events radically contradict each other, this is simply a case of whose evidence is the more believable: 'on both sides it was only assertion' (PP, 205). Reuben A. Brower, in what for me remains the finest single piece ever written on *Pride and Prejudice*, suggests that 'The passages in which Elizabeth reviews the letter present an odd, rather legalistic process...

[in which] the evidence on both sides is weighed and a reasonable conclusion is reached.'[24] This seems perfectly true: 'She put down the letter, weighted every circumstance with what she meant to be impartiality, deliberated on the probability of each statement' (PP, 205). But there is nothing necessarily 'odd' about this legalistic process: rather, Elizabeth responds in kind to the terms of Darcy's letter, whose vocabulary ('justice', 'offences', 'charge') quite clearly places the affair in terms of a criminal trial, with Elizabeth as judge: 'I demand of [this letter] your justice,' he writes (PP, 196). This response in kind presupposes on Elizabeth's part a nascent willingness to do what had previously been unthinkable, accept Darcy's point of view. Wickham also appeals to Elizabeth to accept the veracity of his own version of events through the adoption of legal discourse: 'I have known [Darcy] too long and too well to be a fair judge. It is impossible for *me* to be impartial' (PP, 77); 'I cannot do justice to [Darcy's father's] kindness' (PP, 79). 'Why did you not seek legal redress?' Elizabeth asks him (PP, 79).

Elizabeth initially considers Wickham 'A young man...whose very countenance may vouch for [his] being amiable' (PP, 80–1). The letter provides an awareness of 'inconsistencies' of which Elizabeth was not aware, and which she could not 'laugh at':

> Again, she read on. But every line proved more clearly that the affair, which she had believed impossible that any contrivance could so represent, as to render Darcy's conduct in it less than infamous, was capable of a turn which must make him entirely blameless throughout the whole. (PP, 205)

Elizabeth re-reads Wickham: 'She could see him instantly before her, in every charm of address, but could remember no more sub-stantial good than the general approbation of the neighbourhood, and the regard which his social powers had gained him in the mess' (PP, 206). She comes to realise that Darcy's 'character was by no means so faulty, nor Wickham's so amiable, as they had been considered in Hertfordshire' (PP, 258). Darcy's letter, and Elizabeth's subsequent visit to Pemberley, allow her to place *him*, conversely, 'in an amiable light' (PP, 249). Stuart M. Tave has discussed the significance for Austen of the amiable (as opposed to the merely 'agreeable'):[25] in *Emma*, Mr Knightley, as Chapter 5 will discuss more fully, sets great store by Frank Churchill's being only ' "aimable" ', 'very agreeable', rather than genuinely 'amiable'

(E, 149). Darcy's letter enables Elizabeth to distinguish the sincerely 'amiable' from that which is, like Wickham, whose countenance vouches for it, only amiable-looking.

Pride and Prejudice, then, might be described as a bipartite novel, pivoting on Darcy's letter. Austen can only move into the second half of her novel, in which a synthesis is achieved, desire consummated, a marriage contracted, by effectively handing control of her narrative over to Darcy. Darcy's letter is pure meaning, signification unmediated by the narrative's tendency towards ironic deflection or deferral. Without rupturing the narrative to interpose the story which it has not been allowing Darcy to tell, this 'categorically happy novel' might never have ended so evidently to the satisfaction of (almost!) all.

4

Mansfield Park

I. THE DIVIDED TEXT

Mansfield Park is Jane Austen's great 'Condition of England' novel, and as such stands as one of a great trilogy of novels of 1814 – the others are Sir Walter Scott's *Waverley* and Frances Burney's *The Wanderer* – analysing the State of the Nation in what was to be the last full year of the Napoleonic Wars. This much we can say with certainty, though not much else, as what precisely it is that the novel has to say about the state of the nation is, to say the least, unclear. This is because *Mansfield Park* is an extraordinarily complex aesthetic and ideological text which does not and will not fit preconceived ideas, particularly if readers demand a didactic ideological stance which is consistent, univocal or internally coherent.

On 24 January 1813, while she was writing *Mansfield Park*, Austen wrote to Cassandra describing her most recent course of reading:

> I am reading a Society-Octavo, an Essay on the Military Police and Institutions of the British Empire, by Capt. Pasley of the Engineers, a book which I protested against at first, but which upon trial I find delightfully written & highly entertaining. I am as much in love with the Author as I ever was with Clarkson or Buchanan, or even the two Mr. Smiths of the city. (L, 198)

The bipolar model of Austen criticism (which figures her as either radical or conservative) finds it difficult to accommodate what are to modern sensibilities the seeming contradictions implicit in this passage. A number of commentators wishing to offer a radical *Mansfield Park* – wishing, that is, for entirely understandable reasons to view Austen as a Regency mirror of their own political liberalism – have focused on the fact that Austen appears to have been reading Thomas Clarkson's monumental *History of the Rise, Progress and Accomplishment of the Abolition of the African Slave Trade* (1808) while writing *Mansfield Park*. However, the fact that it is *Pasley*, the military analyst, not Clarkson, the abolitionist, who is the real subject of this passage has gone largely unnoticed.[1]

An analysis of Pasley's treatise offers many ready parallels with *Mansfield Park*. Pasley attempts a corrective to bullish assumptions about inherent British superiority, assumptions which, he suggests, have potentially fatal consequences for national survival. Pasley began writing in 1808, with the outcome of the Napoleonic Wars in serious doubt, and his work reads as a kind of wake-up call to the British military mindset, pointing out that the British are out-numbered five-to-one by France and its allies and subject-nations, who are able to command a revenue at least double that of Britain. Indeed, drawing on the work of Adam Smith, Pasley suggests that British commercial power is not sufficiently strong to fund and withstand an endless war with France such as the long eighteenth century had promised. Furthermore, although British naval superiority had held off a French invasion hitherto, Pasley fears that if France were properly to direct her resources to the navy (which seemed to him inevitable), this superiority would not last for long: 'the hope of our being able to rule the waves for more than a limited time against this gigantic empire appears to me so contrary to reason as scarcely to deserve a serious confutation.'[2] Pasley predicts the survival of Britain and its empire for no longer than thirty more years.

The rationale for this grim scenario is that Britain's military policy is governed by complacent, outmoded and corrupt institutions, incapable of understanding the nature of modern global power: 'The failures that have happened in our wars by land have arisen principally out of the nature of our military policy and institutions in themselves.'[3] Generals, Pasley suggests, are not in a position dispassionately to analyse the weaknesses of a military policy in which they are deeply implicated, yet this is precisely what is required. This critique of misgovernment chimes resonantly with 'radical' readings of *Mansfield Park* as displaying the consequences of the dereliction of familial and by extension national duty.

Raymond Williams has provided a rich context for understanding the way in which the Park itself partakes of a long tradition of national narratives centred on the image of the country house.[4] Here, it seems, Austen offers a picture of a landed family collapsing in on itself through incest, financially held up by slavery, and whose patriarch is further forced to sell off his daughters in disastrous mercantile marriages in order to keep afloat.

All of this would seem to suggest that, for Austen, Clarkson and Pasley were the same *kind* of author, providing fuel for *her* sustained critique of the State of the Nation. If this is indeed so, then Austen read Pasley selectively. Writing from patriotism, Pasley's home truths preface his call for a more vigorously hawkish military policy towards France in order to pre-empt inevitable long-term defeat: to act decisively and ruthlessly *now* was Britain's only hope. This was to be coupled with a more aggressive exploitation of Britain's imperial resources. These are hardly the kinds of conclusions which accounts of a 'radical' *Mansfield Park* see the novel as endorsing.

As an analysis of this valuable source and intertext demonstrates, *Mansfield Park* can confound our critical praxis, being unable to accommodate any one consistent *reading*. Critical accounts of the novel have consequently differed wildly, to a far greater extent than is the case with any other Austen novel. It has been read as Jane Austen's 'most profound novel (indeed...one of the most profound novels of the nineteenth century)'[5] and as an ideological and aesthetic mess.[6] It has been read as a text propounding a highly conservative political agenda[7] and as 'a bitter parody of conservative fiction'[8] or a novel whose heroine offers 'a radical critique of bourgeois patriarchy, its norms, and values of behaviour'.[9] While Lionel Trilling saw *Mansfield Park* as a novel which 'undertakes to discredit irony and affirm literalness',[10] the novel's use of irony has occupied other critics.[11] Fanny Price herself has been read as 'something of a prig',[12] or even as 'a monster of complacency and pride...under a cloak of shrinking self-abasement',[13] but also as a heroine who 'after Hypatia...should be the patron saint of the women's movement'.[14] Her adherence to a doctrine of stasis and silence[15] refers us back to the dictates of the eighteenth-century conduct-book, and to the silent, suffering, victimised heroines of Frances Burney's novels, yet *Mansfield Park* has been read as ahead of its time, the first Victorian novel.[16] Fanny has been read as a pious Christian heroine,[17] or as a character intended to expose the hypocrisy and salaciousness underpinning traditional representations of Christian heroineism.[18] The novel itself, indeed, seems inconsistent. Brean S. Hammond is surely correct when he refers to its 'ideological contradictions',[19] and though Michael Williams attempts to resolve these contradictions into 'compromises' (this, he suggests, is the novel's watchword),[20] it seems that *any* attempt at a coherent, internally consistent reading of the novel necessarily entails an elision of some of *Mansfield Park*'s characteristics and implications. What, then, are the novel's contradictions and inconsistencies?

At the centre of the novel lies its heroine and controlling narrative consciousness, Fanny Price. To understand the novel, or at least to recognise why it can never fully be comprehended, we must learn to read Fanny, and this is a problem. As I have suggested elsewhere in the study, perhaps Austen's greatest contribution to feminist aesthetics lies in her placing at the very centre of her novels *unapologetically* self-authorising, articulate women. However, far from displaying the 'light & bright & sparkling' (L, 203) expertise in social discourse which characterises her direct predecessor, Elizabeth Bennet, or her direct successor, Emma Woodhouse, Fanny's character seems predicated on those 'dynamics of fear' which Patricia Meyer Spacks identifies as the forces governing Burney's conception of heroineism.[21] Like Evelina and her successors, stasis, silence and repression seem to be Fanny's modes. As such, she is an archetypal example of what Mary Poovey has famously called 'The Proper Lady': her very unwillingness or inability to engage socially – her 'shyness' – as well as her physical frailty are ideals of womanhood straight out of eighteenth-century conduct-books for young women.[22] Taken at face value, this portrait of an absolutely conventional conservative heroine does seem, for Austen, both a retrograde step and an unlikely one. In *Pride and Prejudice*, as we saw, such conventional moralising is put in the mouths of characters who are variously foolish and/or reprehensible, Mary Bennet and Mr Collins, and when it came to 'Novels & Heroines', Austen wrote, 'pictures of perfection...make me sick & wicked' (L, 335).

II. RELIGION

Lionel Trilling maintained that a modern readerly difficulty in understanding or sympathising with Fanny and her values stems from a more general modern inability to understand or sympathise with the ideals, and therefore the presentation, of Christian heroism: that issues which we now find complex or even undesirable would have been straightforward and easily recognisable to Austen's contemporary readership.[23] A more recent commentator, the historian Oliver MacDonagh, even goes so far as to state, apparently without irony, that Fanny is not merely 'on the side of the angels' but 'at the extremity of the host'.[24] The novel itself seems quite clear about this: Fanny is 'the lowest and last' (MP, 221), the meek who inherits, if not the earth, then, figuratively speaking (for it is Tom Bertram who actually does so, while, perhaps significantly, by finishing the novel as the wife of the parson of Mansfield, Fanny takes *Mrs Norris's* place), that small corner of it that is Mansfield Park. The novel's ultimate lesson is of 'the necessity of self-denial and humility' (MP, 463), virtues which Fanny seems to possess in abundance.

The exact meaning of Austen's remark in a letter to Cassandra shortly prior to starting work on *Mansfield Park*, 'Now I will try to write of something else; – it shall be a complete change of subject – Ordination. I am glad to find your enquiries have ended so well' (L, 202) is highly disputed.[25] However, one need not conceive of *Mansfield Park* as being *about* 'ordination' to agree with MacDonagh that many of its major scenes 'are "calibrated" on the measures of seriousness and ordination'.[26] Thus, Mary Crawford ostensibly, from what seems to be the novel's guiding perspective (that is, Fanny's point of view), gives early hints of the moral slipperiness she is later to manifest, when she comments on ordination, the clergy, and religious practices – although in fact she is the most consistent and withering critic of the secularising tendencies of Anglicanism, and thus the novel's most powerful proponent of Evangelical reform. Considering Sir Thomas's return to the Park as a prelude both to Maria's marriage and Edmund's ordination, she uses the language of pagan idolatry: 'it does put me in mind of some of the old heathen heroes, who after performing great exploits in a foreign land, offered sacrifices to the gods on their safe return' (MP, 108). On first hearing that Edmund is to be ordained, she tells him that 'A clergyman is nothing' (MP, 92). On Sotherton's lapsed religious observances, Mary remarks:

'Cannot you imagine with what unwilling feelings the former belles of the house of Rushworth did many a time repair to this chapel? The young Mrs Eleanors and Mrs Bridgets – starched up into seeming piety, but with their heads full of something different – especially if the poor chaplain were not worth looking at – and, in those days, I fancy parsons were very inferior even to what they are now.' (MP, 87)

Her audience's response is condemnatory: 'For a few moments she was unanswered. Fanny coloured and looked at Edmund, but felt too angry for speech; and *he* needed a little recollection before he could say, "Your lively mind can hardly be serious even on serious subjects" ' (MP, 87). There is a sense in which the novel's entire discursive dynamic is encapsulated in this exchange: Mary's 'lively' discourse continually subverts the novel's tendency towards propriety, offering remarks which the narrative, always written from Fanny's point of view, figures as scandalous and counters by condemning Mary as immoral.

Ordination, then, is a 'serious subject', one which Mary should treat 'with more respect' (MP, 89). Tony Tanner points out that the word ordination 'carries connotations of authority and "order" (from Latin *ordo*)', and goes on to remark:

> Given Jane Austen's concern with the problem of how a true social order could be maintained, particularly in that troubled period, she clearly considered the role of the clergyman as being of special importance – less for the saving of souls (though there is little reason to doubt her genuine orthodox belief) and more for the saving of society.[27]

Tanner quotes Edmund's defence of the clergy – specifically the provincial rather than the metropolitan clergy – to vindicate this belief:

> 'The *manners* I speak of might rather be called *conduct*, perhaps, the result of good principles; the effect, in short, of those doctrines which it is their duty to teach and recommend; and it will, I believe, be every where found, that as the clergy are, or are not what they ought to be, so are the rest of the nation.' (MP, 93)

Mary uses the example of her brother-in-law Dr Grant to make the point that clergymen are not 'every where … what they ought to be':

> 'It is indolence, Mr Bertram, indeed. Indolence and love of ease – a want of all laudable ambition, of taste for good company, or of inclination to take the trouble of being agreeable, which make men clergymen.

A clergyman has nothing to do but be slovenly and selfish – read the newspaper, watch the weather, and quarrel with his wife. His curate does all the work, and the business of his own life is to dine.'   (MP, 110)

The number of Anglican clergymen, static thoughout the eighteenth century, rose steadily from the beginning of the nineteenth.[28] The institutional reform of the Church of England, particularly with regard to clerical practice, became an important, publicly debated issue during the years of *Mansfield Park*'s composition and publication, 1812–14. The Evangelical movement within the Church reached its peak in the years 1805–15, and was dedicated in part to just the kinds of social and moral clerical overhaul that Mary suggests is needed.[29] As seen in Chapter 1, Henry Austen's posthumous 'Biographical Notice' appended to the 1818 edition of *Persuasion* and *Northanger Abbey*, was understandably keen to promote Jane Austen's Anglican orthodoxy. By the time of his *Memoir of Miss Austen* in 1831, Henry's account of his late sister's piety had become positively Evangelical, in keeping with his own 'stern and fiery' Evangelicalism:[30] 'Jane Austen's hopes of immortality were built upon the Rock of ages. That she deeply felt, and devoutly acknowledged, the insignificance of all worldly attainments, and the worthlessness of all human services, in the eyes of her heavenly Father. That she had no other hope of mercy, pardon, and peace, but through the merits and sufferings of her Redeemer.'[31] Characteristically, however, Austen's own letters register a seeming ambivalence toward the Evangelical movement. She mentions Evangelicalism twice, in ways which apparently contradict each other: thus, in 1809, she wrote to Cassandra 'I do not like the Evangelicals' (L, 170), while in 1814, with *Mansfield Park* surely on her mind, she wrote 'I am by no means convinced that we ought not all to be Evangelicals' (L, 280). However, it may well be that Austen's dislike of the Evangelicals in the 1809 letter is an aesthetic rather than a social or theological judgement, coming as it does in a brief account of Hannah More's Evangelical novel *Coelebs in Search of a Wife* (1808), to which Austen took a strong dislike (not least because of what she saw as the pretentiousness of its title – she insisted on referring to the protagonist as 'Caleb, which has an honest, unpretending sound; but in Coelebs there is pedantry and affectation') (L, 172). Furthermore, Peter Garside and Elizabeth McDonald detect in Edmund a portrait of 'an Evangelical-type clergyman', a view apparently given credence by one of Mary

Crawford's parting shots: 'when I hear of you next, it may be as a celebrated preacher in some great society of Methodists' (MP, 458).[32] During the years of the novel's composition, the British government was headed by the Evangelical Spencer Perceval, and witnessed parliamentary campaigns to reduce the clerical practice of 'pluralities' – the holding of multiple incumbencies: that is, more than one parish – and in 1812–13 a bill was passed through parliament ensuring better pay for just the kind of overworked curates to whom Mary Crawford refers.[33]

Indeed, this was an issue which was to resonate through much of the nineteenth century. Though dating from 1871–2, George Eliot's *Middlemarch* is set in that period of post-Waterloo reform leading up to the Reform Act of 1832. It was in these years that the British political establishment realised that it was, in practice, obliged to cede at least a measure of its power to at least some of the great mass of politicised patriots who had comprised the front line of the long Franco-British wars – national liberty owed these men a great moral debt, combat veterans with a grievance could be a force to be reckoned with, and the horrified response to Peterloo in 1819 had demonstrated that the government could no longer automatically and with impunity use strongarm tactics to get its way.[34] Clerical reforms of the kind discussed in *Mansfield Park* were a part of this broad socio-political tendency. However, when he is given the living of Lowick, Mr Farebrother, *Middlemarch*'s virtuous (he is decidedly *un*-Evangelical, which is why he does not get the hospital chaplaincy for which he is a candidate) and penurious (he plays cards and billiards for money) Anglican clergyman, makes his position on the subject clear: 'I don't feel bound to give up St. Botolph's. It is protest enough against the pluralism they want to reform if I give somebody else most of the money. The stronger thing is not to give up power, but to use it well.'[35]

Bearing in mind, then, what would have been the public and highly controversial nature of this subject for contemporary readers, I wish now to turn to *Mansfield Park*'s own ordinand, Edmund Bertram. Clarence L. Branton points out that Edmund, like all of Austen's clergyman for whom this is knowable, becomes a priest without first serving as a deacon. This was in contravention of canonical law, which stated that a year's deaconship was necessary before formal ordination as a priest.[36] Edmund's formal training for the priesthood is, in fact, risibly brief: 'On the 23rd [of December] he was going to a friend near Peterborough in the same situation as himself, and they were to receive ordination in the course of the Christmas week' (MP, 255). That's it. Edmund returns to Mansfield Park a fortnight later, having 'already gone through the service once since his ordination' (MP, 340). Furthermore, Branton writes:

> The ancient (and also modern) canons of the Church require that ordinations be held on the Sundays following Ember weeks, and if for some reason it was necessary for a bishop to ordain at some other time, that he obtain special permission from the Archbishop of Canterbury.[37]

It is highly unlikely that Edmund is ordained on such a day (it is *just* possible that the Sunday following Ember Week could be December 24, but only if the Winter Ember Days, the Wednesday, Friday and Saturday following December 13, fall as late as December 20, 22, and 23), and the novel makes no reference to a dispensation from the Archbishop of Canterbury. It does not, indeed, suggest that there is *anything* unusual in the circumstances surrounding Edmund's ordination. This is not a matter that can simply be put down to Austen's ignorance of ecclesiastical arcana. She was, after all, from a family of Anglican clerics, and in this instance she had done her homework: the controversial letter of 29 January 1813 may not show that *Mansfield Park* was intended to be 'about' ordination, but it *does* reveal that Austen had asked Cassandra for information about ordination practices from their clergyman brother James.

The issue of pluralities addressed by the Evangelicals is also of concern to *Mansfield Park*. Henry Crawford, wishing to rent Thornton Lacey, Edmund's vicarage, is told by Edmund, 'I have no idea but of residence' (MP, 247). Sir Thomas Bertram's views on this subject are expressed most forcefully:

> '[Edmund's] going, though only eight miles, will be an unwelcome contraction of our family circle; but I should have been deeply mortified if any son of mine could reconcile himself to doing less. . . . [A] parish has wants and claims which can be known only to a clergyman constantly resident, and which no proxy can be capable of satisfying to the same extent. Edmund might, in the common phrase, do the duty of Thornton, that is, he might read prayers and preach, without ever giving up Mansfield Park; he might ride over, every Sunday, to a house nominally inhabited, and go through divine service; he might be the clergyman of Thornton Lacey every seventh day, for three or four hours, if that would content him. But it will not. He knows that human nature needs more lessons than a weekly sermon can convey, and that if he does not live

among his parishioners, and prove himself by constant attention their well-wisher and friend, he does very little either for their good or his own.' (MP, 247–8)

Edmund concurs: 'Sir Thomas...undoubtedly understands the duty of a parish priest. – We must hope that his son may prove that *he* knows it too' (MP, 248). Both father and son are in agreement that pluralism constitutes a neglect, at the very least, of a clergyman's pastoral duties.

Why, then, following the 'apoplexy and death' of Dr Grant 'by three great institutionary dinners in one week' (MP, 469) – that is, as a consequence of the dereliction of his real clerical duties, which only Mary really condemns him for – does Edmund seemingly close the novel as just such a pluralist?

[T]o complete the picture of good [in Fanny and Edmund's marriage], the acquisition of the Mansfield living by the death of Dr Grant, occurred just after they had been married long enough to begin to want an increase of income, and feel their distance from the paternal abode an inconvenience. (MP, 473)

Care needs to be taken here, as the narrative maintains a conspicuous silence on whether Edmund also retains the living of Thornton Lacey, though critics have tended to assume that he does.[38] This, of course, is because of the obvious assumption that having established at some length the novel's background in and beliefs about ordination and the clergy, surely Austen would have taken care to establish that Edmund *had* left Thornton Lacey before taking up the Mansfield living.

However, such an assumption rests upon the novel's internal coherence, which cannot be established. In fact, like many of the great ideological novels of the period, from *Hermsprong* or *Caleb Williams* in the 1790s, through *Belinda* or *Castle Rackrent* in the 1800s, to *Waverley* and *The Wanderer* in 1814, and forward beyond *Frankenstein* in 1818, *Mansfield Park* habitually raises issues which it finds unable to resolve. This is because, even within avowedly radical novels of the 1790s, issues of class, gender, race, religion, or nationalism admitted no firm conclusion, other than the conservative confinement, silencing, or denial – or hegemonic acceptance – offered by some of Austen's less ideologically sceptical contemporaries. Lennard J. Davis suggests that this, finally, must be the narrative condition of *all* novels – irresolution, undecidability, ambivalence, ambiguity:

> The novel must always be thought of as inherently ambivalent. It was so in its origins and it continues to be so. One might say that the quality of ambivalence is one which has permitted the novel to survive by refusing to be assigned one particular meaning or function....In its sense of ambivalence, the novel is beyond the control of even its best practitioners.[39]

Austen's avowed political affiliations may, after all, have been Tory, and her ostensible *conscious* agenda, alas, at variance with Enlightenment feminism or English Jacobinism, in spite of the best efforts of a generation of feminist-historicist critics to prove otherwise. What remains incontrovertible, however, is that her narrative skill and her ideological antennae were simply too acute for unquestioning orthodoxy. This is why *Mansfield Park*, her most directly political novel, is in danger of collapsing under the weight of its own contradictions.

Nevertheless, the readiest interpretation here, accepted by most commentators, directly implies that Austen has taken great care to establish a set of ethical discourses within *Mansfield Park* regarding ordination, only to have those characters who espouse those values in theory ignore them in practice. The question of 'duty' is measured against questions of 'inconvenience' and 'increase of income' (and Edmund is, after all, severely financially embarrassed as a result of Tom Bertram's profligacy), and counts for little. The Marxist historian R. S. Neale has famously written of the connections between 'property' and 'propriety', suggesting that the 'feminine' dictates of the latter are invariably conditioned by the 'masculine' dictates of the former: 'in [the] larger world of property the value stance expected of women may be encapsulated in the word, "propriety". One might say that among the landed classes, propriety was to women as property to men.'[40] Here, it seems, property *is* propriety; the novel's ethical discourses are elided in the name of 'increase of income', and Edmund's ideals of 'duty' are reduced to 'in the common phrase, do[ing] the duty of Thornton'.

III. 'SICK AND WICKED'

There remains, however, one sense in which *Mansfield Park* can unambiguously be termed a religious novel. It is charged with the rhetoric of dissenting Protestantism, a lexicon of judgement, damnation, sin and evil. The novel's dramatisation of Fanny's internal emotional life is well documented, commented upon by virtually every serious critic of the novel, of whatever theoretical position. There is nothing radical, therefore, in ascribing to her the novel's Jamesian controlling 'central intelligence', and so in arguing that the use of religious rhetoric is in a real sense *Fanny's* internal discourse. The novel's use of the term 'my Fanny' (MP, 461), a possessive pronoun Austen never uses for any of her other heroines, might further suggest that novel and heroine are unusually closely aligned.

David Lodge argues that in *Mansfield Park* Austen sets about 'schooling her readers in a vocabulary of discrimination which embraces the finest shades of social and moral value', suggesting that this vocabulary is divisible into two lexicons, 'an order of social or secular value' ('agreeable', 'appropriate', etc.), and 'a more moral or spiritual value ... suggested by words like conscience, duty, evil, good, principle, right, wrong, vice'[41] (such words, Garside and McDonald note, 'the Evangelicals claimed as their own'[42]). Fleishman argues that Fanny compensates for her 'submissiveness' by deploying 'conventional moral attitudes' as 'offensive weapons', making her 'the sanctimonious critic of everyone – literally everyone – in her world but her brother William'.[43] The word 'judgement', with its simultaneous connotations of discrimination and damnation, appears 37 times in the novel, expanded to 116 times when one includes its cognates ('judge', 'justice', etc.).[44] The most significant single word in the novel's religious lexicon is 'evil', occurring at least 25 times in the novel, mostly in the context of the Crawfords and their activities. Mary 'does not *think* evil, but she speaks it' (MP, 269), Edmund tells Fanny; Fanny in turn believes that 'Miss Crawford's style of writing, lively and affectionate, was itself an evil' (MP, 376); by the end of the novel, Edmund concludes that 'her's is not a cruel nature ... The evil lies yet deeper' (MP, 456). Henry Crawford 'could do nothing without a mixture of evil' (MP, 302); his 'attentions' to Fanny 'she ... felt, or fancied an evil' (MP, 366). The Crawfords are figured throughout as Satanic tempters: in Sotherton's wilderness, Mary's 'feminine lawlessness' means that she and Edmund 'have taken a very serpentine course'; the wilderness is indeed here an outward manifestation of Mary's moral lack, a mind 'led astray and bewildered', says Edmund (MP, 367). Critics have tended to respond in kind, it seems, to this rhetoric. C. S. Lewis, who, believing in its literal physical existence presumably would not have used the term lightly, describes Mrs Norris as 'genuinely evil'; David Monaghan suggests that Henry's interest in Fanny means that she is 'at last able to grapple actively with the forces of evil'; MacDonagh calls Mary 'the devil's disciple'.[45]

As the novel approaches its close, with the news of Maria and Julia's elopements, the intensity of the narrative's religious discourse spills over into a characteristically Evangelical (or even dissenting) apocalypticism. The closing chapter, wrapping up the novel's Last Things, gives us the complete eschatology – death (Dr Grant), judgement (everybody), heaven (Fanny and Edmund), and hell (Mrs Norris and Maria). To convey the intensity of this rhetoric, it is easiest to provide a list:

Mr Price cared too little about the report [of Maria's elopement] to make [Fanny] much answer. 'It might be all a lie,' he acknowledges; 'but so many fine ladies were *going to the devil* now-a-days that way, that there was no answering for any body.'   (MP, 440)

The *horror* of a mind like Fanny's, as it received *the conviction of such guilt*, and began to take in part of the *misery* that might ensue, can hardly be described. At first, it was a sort of stupefaction; but every moment was quickening her perception of the *horrible evil*...[Mary's] eager defence of her brother, her hopes of its being *hushed up* [Austen's emphasis], her evident agitation, were all of a piece with *something very bad*; and if there were a woman of character in existence, who could treat as a trifle this *sin of the first magnitude*, who could try to gloss it over, and desire to leave it *unpunished*, she could believe Miss Crawford to be the woman!   (MP, 440-1)

Fanny passed only from feelings of sickness to shudderings of horror...*it was too horrible a confusion of guilt, too gross a complication of evil, for human nature, not in a state of utter barbarism, to be capable of!* – yet her *judgement* told her it was so.   (MP, 441)

it appeared to [Fanny] that *as far as this world alone was concerned, the greatest blessing* to everyone of kindred with Mrs. Rushworth, would be *instant annihilation.*   (MP, 442)

there was no intelligence from Mansfield...This was *an evil omen.* (MP, 442)

[a letter from Edmund to Fanny:] You know our present *wretchedness. May God support you under yours....There is no end to the evil let loose upon us.*   (MP, 442-3)

The *evil* which brought such good to [Fanny]!   (MP, 443)

The happiness [Fanny] was imparting...[was] very little alloyed by the *black communication* that preceded it.   (MP, 444)

Susan...[knew] nothing personally of *those who had sinned*. (MP, 444)

Edmund was particularly struck by the alteration in [Fanny's] looks, and from his ignorance of *the daily evils of her father's house*... (MP, 446)

Mrs Norris...could have charged [Fanny] as *the daemon of the piece*. (MP, 448)

[Susan] was so provided with happiness, so strong in *that best of blessings, an escape from many certain evils.*   (MP, 449)

Lady Bertram...saw therefore in all its *enormity* what had happened, and neither endeavoured herself, nor required Fanny to advise her, to think little of *guilt and infamy*.   (MP, 449)

Sir Thomas...remained yet a little longer in town, in the hope of...snatching [Maria] from *further vice*.   (MP, 451)

'*Thank God!*' said [Edmund]. 'We were all disposed to wonder, but it seems to have been *the merciful appointment of Providence that the heart which knew no guile should not suffer*. [Mary] spoke of you [Fanny] with high praise and warm affection; yet even here, there was alloy, *a dash of evil*.'   (MP, 455)

'*The evil lies yet deeper* [says Edmund]; in Mary's total ignorance, unsuspiciousness of there being such feelings, in *a perversion of the mind which made it natural for her to treat the subject as she did*....*Her's are faults of principle, Fanny, of blunted delicacy and a corrupted, vitiated mind*. Perhaps it is *blest* for me, since it leaves me so little to regret.'   (MP, 456)

'the manner in which [Mary] treated the *dreadful crime* committed by her brother and sister [says Edmund]...recommending to us a compliance, a compromise, an acquiescence in *the continuance of the sin*.'   (MP, 457–8)

[all emphases mine except where stated]

'There is no end to the evil let loose upon us.' Satan himself, it seems, stalks the closing pages of *Mansfield Park*. Having built up to this apocalyptic crescendo, Austen opens the final chapter with a celebrated statement of denial: 'Let other pens dwell on guilt and misery. I quit such odious subjects as soon as I can' (MP, 461). It is on this page that Austen refers to her heroine, uniquely, as 'My Fanny', and the truth is that her pen has been dwelling on very little other than 'guilt and misery' for the past few chapters (perhaps for the entire novel), subjecting the Crawfords (and especially Mary – who is, after all, Fanny's rival for Edmund) to a sustained righteous verbal lashing at the behest of 'her Fanny'. Characteristically, despite authorial disclaimers, the use of this rhetoric of damnation continues unabated throughout the final chapter, which gives us 'evil', 'self-denial and humility' (MP, 463), 'punishment', 'guilt', 'mortified' (MP, 464), 'penitent', 'vice', 'judgement', 'punishment', 'evil' (MP, 465) 'guilt', 'sacrifice to right' (MP, 467). This, the narrative clearly establishes, is Fanny's distinctive, dominant rhetorical mode, habitually turning on 'odious subjects'.

IV. INCEST

Coinciding and overlapping with *Mansfield Park*'s religious rhetoric is another discursive field, that of illness and disease. The novel is shot through with the language of sickness, generally used in conjunction with, or as a symbolic articulation of, Fanny's troubled sexual identity. The first thing to say about this, of course, is that the novel's sexual economy is incestuous, and doubly so – Fanny's love for her brother William is displaced and developed onto her desire, consummated at the close, for her cousin Edmund.[46]

The incest motif, as the Introduction argued, was a common one in fiction across the long eighteenth century, in part as a reflection of the developments in the culture and ideology of marriage (consequently, of desire) which, according to sexual historians such as Lawrence Stone, typified the age.[47] Novelists from Defoe to Richardson to Fielding to Burney deployed it with such frequency that, in Glenda A. Hudson's words, 'incest becomes almost a *sine qua non* in eighteenth-century fiction, adding a frisson of shock to titillate the reading public.'[48] As previous chapters have noted, Gothic novelists (and Austen in her role as Gothic commentator) called upon it as a general means of exploring and representing issues of sexuality, power, and politics, particularly in and around the 1790s – with, as we saw in Chapter 2, Mary Shelley's *Mathilda* providing a particularly striking late instance of this. The radical potential of taboo and transgression was further explored by Romantic poets, most particularly of the second generation, for whom incest provided the readiest of symbolism for their ideological aims – witness P. B. Shelley's *Laon and Cythna*, where the brother-and-sister leaders of a doomed rebellion turn to incest in its aftermath.

The marriage of first cousins, Austen's primary concern in the sexual economy of *Mansfield Park*, was not technically incestuous at the time – that is to say, it was not proscribed by the canons of the Anglican Church, who legalised it almost immediately, in 1540 (though it was, and is, banned by the Catholic and Orthodox Churches – Anglicanism, after all, owes its existence to the desire to contract marriages banned by other churches) – though, as Hudson points out, there was considerable 'contemporary criticism of marriage between close consanguineal relations'.[49] By no means can the incestuous desire at the heart of *Mansfield Park* be written off as accidental, or as a subject with which Austen was not much concerned: 'I like first Cousins to be first cousins, & interested about each other,' she wrote to Anna Lefroy. 'They are but one remove from Br[other] & Sr [sister]' (L, 283). Certainly, it is an issue which Sir Thomas considers and discusses with Mrs Norris before inviting Fanny to live at Mansfield:

> He thought of his own four children, of his two sons, of cousins in love ... 'You are thinking of your sons – but do you not know that of all things upon earth *that* is least likely to happen; brought up, as they would be, always together like brothers and sisters? It is morally impossible. I never knew an instance of it. It is, in fact, the only sure way of providing against the connection.' (MP, 6)

But Mrs Norris has not bargained on Fanny's notions of what it means to be 'like brothers and sisters'. This is an account of William's visit to Mansfield Park:

> An advantage this, a strengthener of love, in which even the conjugal tie is beneath the fraternal. Children of the same family, the same blood, with the same first associations and habits, have some means of enjoyment in their power, which no subsequent connections can supply; and it must be a long and unnatural estrangement, by a divorce which no subsequent connection can justify, if such precious remains of the earliest attachments are ever entirely outlived. Too often alas! it is so. – Fraternal love, sometimes almost everything, is at others worse than nothing. But

with William and Fanny Price, it was still a sentiment in its prime and freshness, wounded by no opposition of interest, cooled by no separate attachment, and feeling the influence of time and absence only in its increase. (MP, 234–5)

This passage privileges 'fraternal' over 'conjugal' love at every point, and even uses the language of marital break-up ('estrangement', 'divorce') to describe how this fraternal love is threatened by marriage. Seeing Fanny and William together, Henry Crawford, who has open sexual designs on Fanny, 'wished he had been a William Price...instead of what he was!' (MP, 236). But fraternal love is, at best, only *'almost* everything': what it cannot contain, within propriety, is sex.

Edmund begins the novel as an explicit surrogate for William. He is first distinguished by Fanny when he provides writing-material for her letters to William, and it is not long before Fanny 'loved [Edmund] better than anybody in the world except William; her heart was divided between the two' (MP, 22). Hudson's theory that Austen contructs her social mechanics around the notion of 'sibships' – endogamous marital structures which hover on the margins of, but never technically become, incest – seems to me suggestive and highly persuasive. Such endogamy, Hudson suggests, makes *Mansfield Park*'s narrative dynamic rigorously *centripetal*, excluding all outside influences.

Fanny's desire for both Edmund and, by implication, William, must be understood as a projection of her own narcissism. This is a seemingly bizarre or contradictory assertion for one so rigorously self-effacing, yet this very self-effacement signifies a refusal of socialisation. Fanny is a solipsist – all signification is *her* signification, all events have existence in the novel only insofar as they cast light on Fanny herself, dramatising her own denial. As Otto Kernberg suggests, the narcissistic consciousness is characterised by a dialectic of rage and fear: 'It is the image of a hungry, enraged, empty self, full of impotent anger at being frustrated, and fearful of a world which seems as hateful and revengeful as the [narcissist] himself.'[50] Johanna M. Smith is surely right to liken Fanny's sexual identity to a mirror: when she looks at William and Edmund, she sees both her physical and her intellectual and moral doubles. Furthermore, writes Smith, the novel figures Fanny herself as a mirror, in which others (Henry, Edmund, Sir Thomas) see themselves, 'the reflection of their own consequence'.[51]

Mansfield Park tells us early that 'Having formed [Fanny's] mind and gained her affections, [Edmund] had a good chance of her thinking like him' (MP, 64), and concludes:

> With such regard for [Fanny] as [Edmund's] had long been, a regard founded on the most endearing claims of innocence and helplessness, and completed by every recommendation of growing worth...Loving, guiding, protecting her, as he had been doing ever since her being ten years old, her mind in so great a degree formed by his care, and her comfort depending on his kindness, an object to him of such close and peculiar interest, dearer by all his importance with her than anyone at Mansfield, what was there now to add, but that he should learn to prefer soft light eyes to sparkling dark ones.   (MP, 470)

The novel does not hide the fact that the marriage is based on consanguinity and similarity of character. *Mansfield Park* begins as Austen's most populous novel. The narrative's centripetal, endogamous economy, predicated on Fanny's narcissistic solipsism, distils this to two halves of the same character, Fanny and Edmund. It is with this, clearly, that the significance of Fanny's cross and chain, symbolically uniting Fanny, William and Edmund in holy union (Fanny wears William's cross on Edmund's chain), while denying Henry Crawford (whose chain she rejects) becomes clear.

Fanny, then, her desire incestuous and therefore taboo, represses eroticism, vilifying it and projecting it outward onto Mary Crawford, who inspires desire and consequently waywardness in Edmund, countering *Mansfield Park*'s narrative by acting upon him *centrifugally*, pushing him outward, away from himself and Fanny. Freudian thinking tells us that eros so repressed is compelled to return in a darker form: Gothic novels enact the return of the repressed in the form of violent incestuous desire – the desire simultaneously, that is, for violence and for incest. To Fanny, for whom any form of sexuality other than the incestuous already constitutes a form of violence (a violence, that is, to the dynamic of her own narrative), eros returns in the form of censorious hostility. She figures sex as disease.

When the Crawfords first arrive, Mrs Grant tells them 'we will cure you both. Mansfield shall cure you both – and without any taking in. Stay with us and we will cure you' (MP, 79). For Fanny, the Crawfords, like all outside influences, are contagious to Mansfield, and therefore need rejecting by the narrative body. When Sir Thomas returns from Antigua to find his house in disarray as a result of the theatricals, Tom attempts to explain the situation: 'My friend Yates brought the infection from Ecclesford, and it spread as these things always spread, you know' (MP, 184). The 'infection' which the Crawfords carry to Mansfield has its origins in their upbringing: 'that uncle and aunt!' Edmund says, 'They have injured the finest mind! – for sometimes, Fanny, I own to you, it does appear more than manner; it appears as if the mind itself was tainted' (MP, 269). Edmund closes the novel believing Mary to have 'a corrupted, vitiated mind' (MP, 456), an echo of Fanny's earlier recognition of Mary's 'corrupted mind' (MP, 225). Henry Crawford describes his burgeoning desire for Fanny as 'the pleasing plague' (MP, 292); Mary tells Henry of 'the advantage of getting away from the Admiral before your manners are hurt by the *contagion* of his, before you have *contracted* any of his foolish opinions' (MP, 295).

V. THE LANDSCAPE, THE GARDEN AND THE NATION

The visit to Sotherton provides the most symbolic section of Jane Austen's most symbolic novel, and this because it partakes and contributes to a characteristically eighteenth-century complex of aesthetic, cultural and national discourses all of which cohere around one area of symbolic investigation and display, the garden. This was the great century of landscape gardening and the development and formation of *le jardin anglais*, considered (by many English commentators, at least) not only the definitively English contribution to garden design, but indeed its crowning pinnacle of perfection, under first William Kent, then 'Capability' Brown and Humphry Repton. Alexander Pope, himself an influential landscape theorist in the eighteenth century, suggested that 'all gardening is landscape-painting',[52] and the landscape garden strove not to order and formalise nature, but to recreate it according to aesthetic theories of the picturesque, to emphasise nature's undulating 'line of beauty' through harmonising the inherent qualities of the landscape. In the celebrated words of Pope's 'Epistle to Burlington':

Consult the Genius of the Place in all;
That tells the Waters to rise, or fall,
Or helps th'ambitious Hill the heav'n to scale,
Or scoops in circling theatres the Vale,

Calls in the Country, catches opening glades,
Joins willing woods, and varies shades from shades,
Now breaks or now directs, th'intending Lines;
Paints as you plant, and as you work, designs.

'The chief proof of [Good Sense],' the poem's Argument states, 'is to follow Nature, even in works of mere Luxury and Elegance. Instanced in Architecture and Gardening, where all must be adapted to the Genius and Use of the Place, and the Beauties not forced into it, but resulting from it.'[53]

This was in overt contrast to the stylised, emblematic ostentation of the Renaissance gardens, which were, Roy Strong notes, completely eradicated from the English landscape: 'Bridgeman, Capability Brown and their imitators from 1720 onwards were responsible for the mass destruction, on a scale unmatched by any other European country, of the old formal gardens in the Renaissance, Mannerist, Baroque and Rococo styles....The loss was total.'[54] In Sotherton, Mr Rushworth's mania for the 'improvement' of his estate echoes the fact that Lancelot Brown earned his distinctive nickname for his repeated belief that any landscape had 'capabilities of improvement', but also the belief (or suspicion) that the function of the landscape gardener was that of *correcting* the defects of nature in what amounted to a *discourse of power*, of control and mastery. Carole Fabricant, seeing in this a model for some eighteenth-century gender-theories, suggests that 'There is little doubt who was the master, who the obedient and dismissive servant – though admittedly a servant well cared for, lavishly fed, and dressed in the finest money could buy....Contemporary treatises on gardening all agree that the landscape designer should not only use nature intelligently but *make her better*.'[55] This same connection, between landscaping and gender-theory, is made in a celebrated passage from *Northanger Abbey*:

In the present instance, [Catherine] confessed and lamented her want of knowledge, declared that she would give any thing in the world to be able to draw; and a lecture on the picturesque immediately followed, in which [Henry's] instructions were so clear that she soon began to see beauty in every thing admired by him, and her attention was so earnest that he became perfectly satisfied of her having a great deal of natural taste. He talked of fore-grounds, distances, and second distances – side-screens and perspectives; – lights and shades; – and Catherine was so hopeful a scholar, that when they gained the top of Beechen Cliff, she voluntarily rejected the whole city of Bath, as unworthy to make part of a landscape. Delighted with her progress, and fearful of wearying her with too much wisdom at once, Henry suffered the subject to decline, and by an early transition from a piece of rocky fragment and the withered oak which he had placed near its summit, to oaks in general, to forests, the inclosure of them, waste lands, crown lands and government, he shortly found himself arrived at politics; and from politics, it was an easy step to silence. (NA, 111)

This 'silence' on the subject of politics registers more properly as a *silencing*, in which Henry, in his self-appointed role as Catherine's educator, draws back on realising that 'his short disquisition on the state of the nation' (NA, 111) has run the risk of transgressing accepted gender-roles, carrying Catherine (and Eleanor, who is also present) across into the masculine, public, political sphere. It is for this reason that he dismisses through ridicule and the force of authority Eleanor's astute (mis-)interpretation of Catherine's remark, ostensibly referring to a new Gothic novel, 'I have heard that something very shocking indeed, will soon come out in London' (NA, 112):

'And you, Miss Morland – my stupid sister has mistaken all your clearest expressions. You talked of expected horrors in London, and instead of instantly conceiving, as any rational creature would have done, that such words could relate only to a circulating library, she immediately pictured to herself a mob of three thousand men assembling in St. George's Fields; the Bank attacked; the Tower threatened, the streets of London flowing with blood, a detachment of the 12th Light Dragoons (the hopes of the nation), called up to quell the insurgents, and the gallant Capt. Frederick Tilney, in the moment of charging at the head of his troop, knocked off his horse by a brickbat from an upper window. Forgive her stupidity.' (NA, 113)

As a number of commentators have pointed out, *every one* of the events which Henry dismisses here had actually taken place in London during the 1780s and 1790s.[56] It was an age of widespread popular demonstration, frequently spilling over into the violence of riot and looting, and often violently suppressed by the military, from the Gordon Riots of 1780 through to the mass meetings of the London Corresponding Society in the 1790s, to the Peterloo Massacre of 1819.

Naturally, in that great period of the formation of British identity, the patriotic significance of garden theory was very prominent. Linda Colley writes:

> By the time of Waterloo, a generation of patrician Britons had grown up for whom Continental Europe was more a cockpit for battle, and a landscape of revolutionary subversion, than a fashionable playground and cultural shrine. Out of necessity, therefore, as well as for reasons of prudence and patriotic choice, members of the ruling order were encouraged to seek out new forms of cultural expression that were unquestionably British.[57]

In the front rank of these cultural forms was the garden. Horace Walpole's *The History of Modern Taste in Gardening* (1780), amongst the most influential of all the eighteenth-century works of English garden theory, provides a clear example of the English (or perhaps more properly *British*) nationalist agenda which underpinned the idea of the garden: it was, he wrote elsewhere, 'an Art totally New,...Original, and indisputably English!'[58] Habitually, Walpole validates the landscape garden/Britishness by favourable contrast with the French:

> When a Frenchman reads of the garden of Eden, I do not doubt but he concludes it was something approaching to Versailles, with clipt hedges, berceaus, and trellis-work. If his devotion humbles him so far as to allow that, considering who designed it, there might be a labyrinth full of Æsop's fables, yet he does not conceive that four of the largest rivers in the world were half so magnificent as an hundred fountains full of statues by Girardon.[59]

So ingrained was the *History*'s anti-French animus that, when it was published as a parallel English–French text in 1785, one particularly extreme footnote was diplomatically expunged. John Dixon Hunt explains the *History*'s ideological subtext thus:

> Since the main European contender for preeminence in garden design was France, Walpole directed his fiercest attacks at what he considered its formal absurdities. But his deeper agenda was that the 'English Taste in Gardening' was a direct result of the growth of English political liberties, whereas French gardening demonstrated the unhappy rigours of absolutism....The fundamental assumption of a link between the English landscape garden and the British Constitution, which others had implied before him, underlies all of Walpole's discussion.[60]

As Walpole knew, the British could marshal the most powerful support in vindication of their gardens, and consequently their polity. John Milton, in his role as public relations man for the Protestant God, images forth in Book IV of *Paradise Lost* an Eden which strikingly anticipates the English landscape garden, as if God Himself had been employing Capability Brown to carry out His handiwork:

> Eden, where delicious Paradise,
> Now nearer crown with her enclosure green,
> As with a rural mound, the champaign head
> Of a steep wilderness, whose hairy sides
> With thicket overgrown, grotesque and wild,...
> Flowers worthy of Paradise, which not nice art
> In beds and curious knots, but nature boon
> Poured forth profuse on hill and dale and plain,
> Both where the morning sun first warmly smote
> The open field, and where the unpierced shade
> Embrowned the noontide bowers, thus was this place,
> A happy rural seat of various view[61]

Following the work of Edward Malins and then of Alistair Duckworth, *Mansfield Park* is usually read as Austen's contribution to a tradition of anti-improvement literature which took its lead from the hostility to Capability Brown articulated in the works of Richard Paine Knight and Sir Uvedale Price, and which was also to include Thomas Love Peacock's satirical *Headlong Hall*, published two years after *Mansfield Park* in 1816.[62] The reality seems to me more complex, with *Mansfield Park*, typically, registering an ideological ambivalence towards improvement rather than a downright hostility. It is not improvement itself, but abusive *over*-improvement that Austen targets, and she was not alone in this. Walpole, for one, acknowledges that 'every genius has his apes', and worries that 'in some lights the reformation seems to have been pushed too far...by the undertaker in fashion'.[63] The problem with over-improvement, *Mansfield Park* suggests, was that it could become anti-nationalist. Sotherton's avenue of oaks ('It is oak entirely', says Maria proprietorially) (MP, 83) is to be cut down, much to Fanny's dismay:

> 'Cut down an avenue! What a pity! Does it not make you think of Cowper? "Ye fallen avenues, once more I mourn your fate unmerited." '
>
> [Edmund] smiled as he answered, 'I am afraid the avenue stands a bad chance, Fanny.' (MP, 56)

This directly echoes one of Walpole's concerns about abusive improvements:

> Though an avenue crossing a park or separating a lawn, and intercepting views from the seat to which it leads, are capital faults, yet a great avenue, cut through the woods, perhaps before entering a park, has a noble air, and...announces the habitation of some man of distinction.[64]

The oaks are obviously significant here, having as they do a major place in English national symbology. In Simon Schama's words:

> It is one of the most familiar and cherished tableaux in all English history: the golden girl beneath the oak, about to inaugurate the nation's great age. But the supporting role taken by the tree is crucial to the mythical effect. So much of English history is oaken. Ancient Britons were thought to have worshipped them; righteous outlaws are sheltered by them; kings on the run hide in them; hearts of oak go to sea and win empires. It would only be in the next [i.e., seventeenth] century – in, for example, John Evelyn's *Sylva* (1664) that ancient trees would be explicitly seen as symbols of national durability. But the Harfield oak – knotty and gnarled, storm-struck but standing – is Elizabeth's first loyal supporter. It was, in effect, England bringing the strength and weight of its tradition to the proclamation of a momentous rebirth.[65]

But Humphry Repton, whom Rushworth wants to employ to improve Sotherton, was less of a radical in garden aesthetics than Brown, less willing to overhaul extant features of landscape and architecture in order to impose a theorised vision of naturalness. He was, indeed, openly critical, if not of Brown himself, then certainly of his disciples: 'Brown copied Nature, his illiterate followers copied him', he wrote.[66] And after all, Pemberley, the most idealised of all Austen's great houses, is recognisably Reptonian in its design, and when Mary Crawford suggests that 'Every generation has its improvements' (MP, 86), she is transposing garden design onto a social vision which, given the horrible dysfunctionality of the Bertram family, the novel's resolution must surely endorse: England *needs* improving.

VI.   SOTHERTON, STERNE AND SLAVERY

Sotherton's formal grounds are bounded by iron palisades, as well as by the ha-ha or sunken fence which, according to Walpole's famous formulation, was the most significant element in the liberatory aesthetic of the English landscape garden:

> I call a sunk fence the leading step, for these reasons. No sooner was this simple enchantment made, than leveling, mowing, and rolling followed. The contiguous ground of the park without the sunk fence was to be harmonized with the lawn within; and the garden in its turn was to be set free from its prim regularity, that it might assort with the wilder country without.... [Kemp] leaped the fence, and saw that all nature was a garden.[67]

In violation of the expansive principles of landcape gardening, Sotherton rather seems a space of enclosure and entrapment, of locked doors and gates whose purpose seems to be to safeguard against *exit*, for this signifies escape into the 'prohibited' (MP, 99), transgressive spaces outside. It is Fanny, refusing to budge, who warns of the physical and symbolic dangers of transgressing boundaries: 'You will hurt yourself, Miss Bertram...you will certainly hurt yourself against those spikes – you will tear your gown – you will be in danger of slipping into the ha-ha – you had better not go' (MP, 99–100). As I suggested in Chapter 1, Elizabeth Bennet's transgressing of spatial boundaries leads to a muddy if not actually a torn gown, but also to a heightened sense of sexual desirability; Catherine Morland's leads to knowledge. Fanny's warning against such transgression is, frankly, accusatory and whining ('You will...you will...you will...you will...you had better not'), each clause adding to the dangers of action, each clause underpinning Fanny's 'dynamics of fear' and her stasis.

Inside, Sotherton is 'insufferably hot' (MP, 91). Maria, soon to become its mistress, already feels trapped: even Mr Rushworth recognises that Sotherton 'looked like a prison – quite a dismal old prison' (MP, 53), and Maria 'figuratively' recognises that the 'iron gate and ha-ha give me a feeling of hardship. I cannot get out, as the starling said' (MP, 99). The intertext here is Laurence Sterne's *A Sentimental Journey* (1768), where, in a celebrated passage, Yorick, Sterne's travelling 'Man of Feeling', on seeing and hearing a caged starling, muses on the nature of freedom and slavery. This passage from Sterne offers significant foreshadowings of many of *Mansfield Park*'s dominant themes. It comes in the context of Yorick's visit to Paris, where he discovers that he is wanted for questioning by the Lieutenant de Police for being without a passport. As a citizen of an enemy country during wartime (he exclaims that 'it never entered my mind that we were at war with France' – this section of the book is set during the Seven Years War, most likely drawing on Sterne's own visit to Paris in 1762[68]) Yorick is threatened with imprisonment in the Bastille, which fate he attempts to rationalise optimistically – the Bastille is merely a 'house you can't get out of…not an evil to be despised'.[69] Sterne's intertext thus simultaneously provides a powerful symbolic referent of imprisonment for Sotherton (it is the Bastille; Maria will be robbed of her liberty in 'the house [she] can't get out of'), and contributes to the novel's overarching concerns with the relationship between the house, the landscape and the nation (like both the Bastille and the French formal garden, it is a violation of the libertarian principles which characterise Britishness), and a reminder of the deep background of the Napoleonic Wars informing *Mansfield Park* at every point – it is set during the climactic years of the final Franco-British war of the long eighteenth century.

Furthermore, and crucially, in acting as a corrective to Yorick's misguided optimism, the passage also draws readers back to the underpinning status of slavery in the novel, as that which provides the financial security which guarantees the Bertrams' social status:

> The bird flew to the place where I was attempting his deliverance, and thrusting his head through the trellis, press'd his breast against it, as if impatient – I fear, poor creature, said I, I cannot set thee at liberty – 'No,' said the starling – 'I can't get out – I can't get out,' said the starling.
>
> I vow, I never had my affections more tenderly awaken'd; or do I remember an incident in my life, where the dissipated spirits, to which reason had been a bubble, were so suddenly call'd home. Mechanical as the notes were, yet so true in tune to nature were they chanted, that in one moment they overthrew all my systematic reasonings upon the Bastile; and I heavily walk'd up stairs, unsaying every word I had said in going down them.
>
> Disguise thyself as thou wilt, still, Slavery! said I – still thou art a bitter draught! and though thousands in all ages have been made to drink of thee, thou art no less bitter on that account. – 'Tis thou, thrice sweet gracious goddess, addressing myself to LIBERTY, whom all in public or private worship, whose taste is grateful, and ever will be so, till NATURE herself shall change –[70]

Slavery had already figured as a narrative presence in *Tristram Shandy*: in Book IX, the following dialogue occurs between Corporal Trim and Uncle Toby:

When Tom, an' please your honour, got to the shop, there was nobody in it but a poor negro girl, with a bunch of white feathers slightly tied to the end of a long cane, flapping away flies – not killing them. – 'Tis a pretty picture! said my uncle Toby – she had suffered persecution, Trim, and had learnt mercy –...

A Negro has a soul? an' please your honour, said the Corporal (doubtingly).

I am not much versed, Corporal, quoth my uncle Toby, in things of that kind; but I suppose, God would not leave him without one, any more than thee or me –

– It would be putting one sadly over the head of another, quoth the Corporal.

It would so; said my uncle Toby. Why then, an' please your honour, is a black wench to be used worse than a white one?

I can give no reason, said my uncle Toby –

– Only, cried the Corporal, shaking his head, because she had no one to stand up for her –

– 'Tis that very thing, Trim, quoth my uncle Toby, – which recommends her to protection – and her brethren with her; 'tis the fortune of war which has put the whip into our hands *now* – where it may be hereafter, heaven knows! – but be it where it will, the brave, Trim! will not use it unkindly.

God forbid, said the Corporal.

Amen, responded my uncle Toby, laying his hand upon his heart![71]

This passage won the praise of Thomas Clarkson, who wrote in his *History of the Abolition of the Slave-Trade* (1808): 'Sterne, in his account of the Negro girl in his Life of Tristram Shandy, took decidedly the part of the oppressed Africans. The pathetic, witty and sentimental manner, in which he handled this subject, occasioned many to remember it, and procured a certain portion of feeling in their favour.'[72] Austen, as we have seen, read Clarkson enthusiastically during the years of *Mansfield Park*'s composition.

The slave-trade itself is discussed only once in *Mansfield Park*, and then in a reported conversation which primarily records the silence with which the subject is greeted:

'Your uncle [says Edmund] is disposed to be pleased with you in every respect; and I only wish you would talk to him more. – You are one of those who are too silent in the evening circle.'

'But I do talk to him more than I used [says Fanny]. Am sure I do. Did you not hear me ask him about the slave-trade last night?'

'I did – and was in hopes the question would be followed up by others. It would have pleased your uncle to be inquired of farther.'

'And I longed to do it – but there was such a dead silence! And while my cousins were sitting by without speaking a word, or seeming at all interested in the subject, I did not like – I thought it would appear as if I wanted to set myself off at their expense, by shewing a curiosity and pleasure in his information which he must wish his own daughters to feel.' (MP, 198)

Edward Said has read this passage as a powerful example of imperial false consciousness, of the denial required to maintain the necessary fiction that the inhabitants of Mansfield Park and their counterparts in Regency England were living a (the?) civilised life, when in fact that civilisation is economically founded on oppression and slavery.[73] But, as Katie Trumpener has pointed out, read more closely the passage can be understood solely as a critique of the Bertram girls, Maria and Julia: it is they who shut their ears to the subject of the slave-trade, a subject which Fanny, Edmund and even Sir Thomas seem keen to discuss. However we read this passage, it seems to me unlikely that either Austen or her novel are in denial and thus complicit in the imperial slave-trade through their silence. Rather, this is a subject of great subtlety and complexity whose implications *Mansfield Park* seems unable fully to assimilate.

The iniquities of slavery had become further focused in Sterne's mind while writing *A Sentimental Journey* through his correspondence with Ignatius Sancho, a slave who had become butler to the Duke of Montagu, who bequeathed him an annuity with which he opened a chandler's or grocer's shop in Westminster. Sancho came to a degree of cultural prominence in the mid-eighteenth century as a failed actor (he played the lead in Othello, and in a production of Aphra Behn's *Oroonoko*, but was hampered by a speech impediment), minor man of letters, and most visibly as the subject of a celebrated portrait by Gainsborough. Sancho represents, in Markman Ellis's words, 'the most complete assimilation of an African writer into British culture of the period'.[74] Sancho initially wrote to Sterne to express his gratitude for the abolitionist sentiments of *Tristram Shandy*, and for those expressed in the sermon 'Job's Account of the Shortness and Troubles of Life, considered' (1760): 'Consider slavery – what it is, – how bitter a draught, and how many millions have been made to drink of it.'[75] 'Now,' writes Sterne's biographer Ian Campbell Ross, 'Sancho asked Sterne if he might not give "one half hour's attention" to the African slave trade with the West Indies: "That subject, handled in your striking manner, would ease the yoke (perhaps) of many."'[76] Sterne's caged starling is, in part, the product of his correspondence with Sancho: Ellis suggests that 'the starling is made a metonymic emblem of African slavery.... The incarceration of this bird in the cage and its knowledge of the four words "I can't get out" make it a witty, though again perilously risky, pun on African slavery in the colonies.'[77]

Moving beyond its direct concerns with slavery, Sterne's captive starling caught the late eighteenth-century aesthetic imagination, inspiring numerous artistic representations. More generally, as Lorenz Eitner comments, the image of the caged bird had a resonant symbolic meaning in eighteenth-century painting, as 'a stock accessory in scenes of sentimental love, flirtation, or seduction, and a favourite of French painters of erotic genre.... [I]t suggested...the bitter-sweetness of erotic genre. The charming prisoner is the hostage of love.'[78] Austen, of course, internalises the polyvalent ideological signification of the caged starling: macrocosmically, it carries us out to England in 1814, while microcosmically it is a figure for Maria Bertram's doomed dynastic marriage as a form of entrapment in which she will become both unwilling erotic object and pampered prisoner: a caged bird. That is to say, she is herself a symbolic victim of the institution which underpins her family's wealth and status, slavery.[79]

Crossing the ha-ha thus leads not only to the transgressive space beyond the confines of Sotherton, where her desire can be actualised, but also in that transgression and actualisation – as the very name ha-ha suggests, in a manner of which Austen was surely conscious – to public ridicule and shame. Better to stay put, says Fanny; better not to risk 'slipping into the ha-ha' and ending up (literally and figuratively) a fallen woman – as Maria does, living out her days unforgiven in another prison, that compounded of her own 'guilt and misery' and of Mrs Norris's constant companionship.

Mr Rushworth cannot find the key: the key to the gate out of Sotherton and the key which will legitimately free Maria. It requires no great imagination to read the symbolism operative here: locks and keys, penetration and loss of virginity. The very fact of the land outside's being a 'prohibited' space denies it to Rushworth, for it is particularly the space of Henry and Maria's forbidden desire, *sexual* space. And, as noted in Chapter 1, Rushworth's fondness for theatrical costume, and particularly for the pink satin which Mrs Norris is careful to conceal from Sir Thomas on his return (lest he begin to entertain serious doubts about his prospective son-in-law), bespeaks his effeminacy, as well as his idiocy (does he actually have learning difficulties?). The 'spikes' on which Maria may 'tear [her] gown' are phallic, and they are also dangerous, signifying her preference for the prohibited (squeezing through the spikes with a lover) over the sanctioned (waiting for a husband's eventual arrival with the key – which, it is implied, he will be unable to use), means that Maria, according to Fanny's unforgiving doctrine, 'will certainly hurt [herself]', and ruin both her gown and her reputation. Fanny stays put.

5

Emma

I. ENGLAND

Historically, *Emma* has not wanted admirers, and has been judged by many to be Austen's most successful novel: 'Easily the most brilliant novel of the period, and one of the most brilliant of all novels' according to Marilyn Butler, it showcases, in Claudia Johnson's words, an Austen comfortably 'at the height of her powers'.[1] Certainly, the novel seems to resolve the contradictions which had so riven *Mansfield Park* – conflicts of property and propriety, of individual and national identity – though it does so at great cost. '3 or 4 families in a Country Village,' Austen once wrote, 'is the very thing to work on' (L, 275), and *Emma* makes good on this assertion by rejecting and wherever possible ignoring the world beyond the tiny confines of Highbury and Hartfield. It is, according to Nicola Watson, essentially a late-flowering anti-Jacobin novel of the 1810s;[2] without doubt, it is by far the most insular and centripetal – indeed, the most claustrophobic – of all Austen's novels. All of Austen's other novels, to varying degrees, posit a world just beyond their frame, a world of struggle, debate, war, ideas, whereas *Emma* comes closest of all to fulfilling the 'little Englandism' which even now seems to be Austen's major attraction for many of her readers.

In narrative terms, it is of course the tininess of Highbury's parameters which allows Emma Woodhouse herself to exercise such control, and crucially to impose upon this world her own fictions, versions of reality which seek, often successfully, to deny credence to outside events. This is why events – arrivals, gossip – hit the novel like earthquakes, because normally *nothing ever happens*:

'Cannot you imagine, Mr Knightley,' says Emma of Frank Churchill, 'what a *sensation* his coming will produce? There will be but one subject throughout the parishes of Donwell and Highbury; but one interest – one object of curiosity; it will be all Mr Frank Churchill; we shall think and speak of nobody else' (E, 149).

Highbury, firstly, is, as Roger Sales has demonstrated, away from channels of communication, not on a main coaching route and so relatively difficult to get to: when Mr Elton leaves Highbury, 'a trunk, directed to *The Rev. Philip Elton, White Hart, Bath*, was to be seen under the operation of being lifted into the butcher's cart, which was to convey it to where the coaches past' (E, 186).[3] Consequently, channels of communication are also relatively complicated, as the post needs to come in a similarly circuitous fashion: looking out at Highbury main street from Ford's, Emma expects to see 'a stray letter-boy on an obstinate mule' (E, 233). It is not however as *completely* isolated as the narrative, echoing Emma's own perspective, would want to have it: Mr Knightley tells Mrs Weston that 'there is nobody hereabouts to attach [Emma]', and that she remains unattached precisely because 'she goes so seldom from home' (E, 41). She has never been to London, 'only sixteen miles off' (E, 7), and never seen the sea. Her father's antisocial tendencies provide her with a further excuse not to stray from the domain over which she can exercise control: 'The relative seclusion of Highbury means that connections between power and mobility are particularly apparent.'[4] Mr Woodhouse himself, 'fond of society in his own way' (E, 20) but 'hating change of every kind' (E, 7), and who therefore considers Mrs Weston's removal to Randalls, 'only half a mile from them' as 'a black morning's work for her' (E, 6) and has not even visited his near-neighbour Mr Knightley's home at Donwell 'for two years' (E, 356), has his whims indulged by his daughter. What the novel attempts to do is to interpret a geographical index as a moral one, and thus when Emma, for once, finds herself beyond the confines of her narrow environment at Box Hill, she loses her bearings completely, goes morally beyond the pale. Colluding in Mr Woodhouse's hatred of change would seem to be the novel's ostensible way of denying its greater political context, a denial which, even in Highbury, ultimately proves impossible, and the novel ends on a hopeful note, with Emma and Mr Knightley planning 'the fortnight's absence in a tour to the sea-side' (E, 483).

The novel's insular Englishness is most powerfully adumbrated through its clash of competing masculinities in the representative characters of Mr Knightley (and to a lesser extent his brother John) and of Frank Churchill (and to a lesser extent Mr Elton). Mr Knightley unquestionably embodies an ideal of unaffected, plain-spoken Englishness which the novel endorses at every point. He has a 'downright, decided, commanding sort of manner'; there is 'nothing of ceremony about him' (E, 34, 57). This is most obviously epitomised in his relationship with his brother John:

> John Knightley made his appearance, and 'How d'ye do, George?' and 'John, how are you?' succeeded *in the true English style*, burying under a calmness that seemed all but indifference, the real attachment which would have led either of them, if requisite, to do every thing for the good of the other. (E, 99–100 – emphasis mine)

The novel goes to meticulous lengths to embed Mr Knightley as deeply as possible within his community. His estate, Donwell Abbey, is both a working farm and his seat as local upholder of the law, which tasks are for him indivisible:

> As a magistrate, he had generally some point of law to consult John about, or at least some curious anecdote to give; and as a farmer, as keeping in hand the home-farm at Donwell, he had to tell what every field was to bear next year, and to give all such local information as could not fail of being interesting to a brother whose home it had equally been the longest part of his life, and whose attachments were strong. The plan of a drain, the change of a fence, the felling of a tree, and the destination of every acre for wheat, turnips, or spring corn, was entered into with as much equality of interest by John, as his cooler manners rendered possible; and if his willing brother ever left him anything to inquire about, his inquiries even approached a tone of eagerness. (E, 100)

Even more than Darcy's Pemberley, it is Mr Knightley's Donwell Abbey which encapsulates in bricks and mortar an ideological ideal of identity politics and nationhood; as such, it is worth quoting the novel's description of the house at length:

> [Emma] felt all the honest pride and complacency which her alliance with the present and future proprietor could fairly warrant, as she viewed the respectable size and style of the building, its suitable, becoming, characteristic situation, low and sheltered – its ample gardens stretching down to meadows washed by a stream, of which the Abbey, with all the

old neglect of prospect, had scarcely a sight – and its abundance of timber in rows and avenues, which neither fashion nor extravagance had rooted up. – The house was larger than Hartfield, and totally unlike it, covering a good deal of ground, rambling and irregular, with many comfortable and one or two handsome rooms. – It was just what it ought to be, and it looked what it was – and Emma felt an increasing respect for it, as the residence of a family of such true gentility, untainted in blood and understanding.... The considerable slope, at nearly the foot of which the Abbey stood, gradually acquired a steeper form beyond its grounds; and at half a mile distant was a bank of considerable abruptness and grandeur, well clothed with wood; – and at the bottom of this bank, favourably placed and sheltered, rose the Abbey-Mill Farm, with meadows in front, and the river making a close and handsome curve around it. (E, 358, 360)

Though Austen herself was at best ambivalent about 'improvements', as previous chapters have discussed, the subject of landscape and garden theory was throughout the eighteenth century and beyond profoundly imbricated with theories of national identity. Donwell is so essentially a part of its landscape that it has no need of landscaping improvement, its grounds displaying instead 'all the old neglect of prospect', containing an avenue of limes which 'led to nothing' (E, 360) and therefore in the terms of contemporary landscape theory, of '[d]isputable ... taste' (E, 360). And so much the better for it, as the description of the house closes with Austen's most rapturous paean to Englishness:

It was a sweet view – sweet to the eye and mind. English verdure, English culture, English comfort, seen under a sun bright, without being oppressive. (E, 360)

Like Elizabeth Bennet's visit to Pemberley, Donwell has Emma speculating on her future relationship with its proprietor, speculations which fill her with 'honest pride' at the idea of the true-born Englishman, in contrast to the slippery deviousness of the continental-style Frank Churchill. Nevertheless, there is also an unarguably dynastic element to the marriage. While the Woodhouses are 'the younger branch of a very ancient family', the fortune which devolves to Emma is largely in capital:

The landed property of Hartfield certainly was inconsiderable, being but a sort of notch of the Donwell Abbey estate, to which all the rest of

Highbury belonged; but their fortune, from other sources, was such as
to make them scarcely secondary to Donwell Abbey itself, in every other
kind of consequence.   (E, 136)

Emma and Mr Knightley's marriage, then, is clearly a politic one
for both, adding the hard cash of Hartfield to the land of Donwell.

In direct contrast to Mr Knightley's uncomplicated English
masculinity, Frank Churchill embodies a masculinity which is
simultaneously and inextricably dandified and continental, and
thus, for Mr Knightley at least, effeminate: Frank's handwriting is
'too small – wants strength. It is like a woman's writing' (E, 297).
He may not, in fact, have travelled the sixteen miles to London simply
to get his hair cut, after all, but this is not the point – the point is
that this is the kind of thing Frank might plausibly do. In Douglas
McGrath's 1996 film adaptation, which starred Gwyneth Paltrow
as an impossibly delicate Emma, Frank Churchill was played by
Ewan McGregor with a hairstyle so preposterous that it threatened
seditiously to overwhelm the entire film, in what is a surely inten-
tional spin on a tendency in modern Hollywood identified by the
film writer Joe Queenan, 'the inadvertent but irremediable sabotaging
of a major motion picture by a disruptive hairstyle'.[5] As a type of
dandy he is the subject of an implied critique by his association with
the immorality of the Prince Regent. He is also tainted by overtones
of Frenchness. His name, Frank, is both an ironic pun (he is *not* frank,
but devious) and of course associates him with France. Mr Knightley
dismisses Frank's fondness for resorts and watering-places as a sure
sign of his 'proud, luxurious, and selfish' character:

'He cannot want money – he cannot want leisure. We know, on the
contrary, that he has so much of both, that he is glad to get rid of them at
the idlest haunts in the kingdom. We hear of him for ever at some watering-
place or other. A little while ago, he was at Weymouth.'   (E, 146)

Furthermore, as Sales has suggested, Frank's fondness for such resorts
also taints him with Frenchified overtones, as these 'were amongst the
favoured refuges for French émigrés during the Revolutionary and
Napoleonic Wars'.[6] Mr Knightley, implacably English, sees through
him, and sees him for the shady continental that he affects to be:

'No, Emma, your amiable young man can be amiable only in French,
not in English. He may be very "aimable", have very good manners, and

be very agreeable; but he can have no English delicacy towards the feelings of other people; nothing really amiable about him.'   (E, 149)

II. IRELAND

Frank and Jane Fairfax together burst Highbury's bubble of self-containment, he by providing a tempting but ultimately rejected glimpse of the world beyond its confines, she in her status as a victim of the Napoleonic Wars whose presence the novel works to deny. This is Jane's history, effaced from most accounts of the novel as it is *almost* effaced from the novel itself:

> Jane Fairfax was an orphan, the only child of Mrs Bates's youngest daughter.
> The marriage of Lieut. Fairfax of the — regiment of infantry, and Miss Jane Bates, had had its day of fame and pleasure, hope and interest; but nothing now remained of it, save the melancholy remembrance of him dying in action abroad – of his widow sinking under consumption and grief soon afterwards – and this girl....
> But the compassionate feelings of a friend of her father gave a change to her destiny. This was Colonel Campbell, who had very highly regarded Fairfax, as an excellent officer and most deserving young man; and farther, had been indebted to him, for such attentions, during a severe camp-fever, as he believed had saved his life.... He was a married man, with only one living child, a girl about Jane's age; and Jane became their guest, paying them long visits and growing a favourite with all; and before she was nine years old, his daughter's great fondness for her, and his own wish of being a real friend, united to produce an offer from Colonel Campbell of undertaking the whole charge of her education. It was accepted; and from that period Jane had belonged to Colonel Campbell's family, and had lived with them entirely, only visiting her grandmother from time to time.   (E, 163–4)

It is a tragic story, and one which Emma's subject-position of pampered comfort, sustained as it is by a concerted denial of all the implications of Jane's history – the history, that is, which conspires to make Jane an orphan, the history of Europe at the beginning of the nineteenth century – finds unassimilable. Instead, she reduces Jane's history to rumour and sleazy innuendo, the imagined affair with Mr Dixon of Baly-craig, the married Anglo-Irish landowner.

In 1795, Austen herself became acquainted, and perhaps romantically entangled, with a member of the Anglo-Irish Ascendancy, Tom Lefroy of County Longford, whom she referred to as 'my Irish friend' (L, 1). They met and danced at a number of balls, which had Austen telling Cassandra to 'Imagine to yourself everything most profligate and shocking in the way of dancing and sitting down together' (L, 1), and notes that 'he is so excessively laughed at about me at Ashe, that he is ashamed of coming to Steventon' (L, 1). The truth is that we have virtually no hard information about any relationship between Austen and Lefroy, which has given biographers room for a rich seam of speculation. The received account of this has Lefroy's family taking fright at his potential marriage to an impecunious clergyman's daughter, and thus forcibly removing him to London 'in virtual disgrace, never allowed to return', and from there to Dublin, where he soon married an heiress from Wexford, the sister of a college friend, but kept a corner of his heart free for Jane Austen until his dying day.[7] Perhaps more reliably, Claire Tomalin suggests that Lefroy may have been 'sent away by the Hampshire Lefroys to protect Jane from his philandering', citing a letter from the Lefroy family which says that Mrs Lefroy blamed him 'because he had behaved so ill to Jane'.[8] Whatever the exact nature of the relationship, it is certain that Austen's Irish charmer Tom Lefroy was an extraordinarily formidable man, 'the Right Honourable Thomas Langlois Lefroy, three times Gold Medallist at Dublin University, Doctor of Law, King's Counsel, Member of Parliament for Dublin University, Privy Councillor, sometime Baron of the Exchequer and Lord Chief Justice of Ireland'.[9] Writing from my own perspective, what seems most significant now about Lefroy is not his dancing feet but his consistently hardline reactionary politics. Graduating from Trinity College Dublin in 1795, he was brought back out of retirement, as it were, in 1798 to debate in the college Historical Society with Robert Emmet, the doomed Irish patriot and rebel leader.[10] He was also a fierce opponent of Daniel O'Connell, of Catholic emancipation, of the Reform Act, and of the repeal of the Corn Laws. In 1822, as First Sergeant of the Munster Circuit Court, he was heavily involved in putting down civil unrest through an intensive programme of executions. In 1872, three years after his death, the London *Times* wrote of Lefroy that 'unconsciously perhaps to himself, he thought the Irish race barbarian and savage'.[11] While the prospect of Jane Austen living in Longford, visiting and discussing fiction with her neighbour Maria Edgeworth, is certainly an appealing one, I would have to say that, contrary to the sentimental accounts of many biographers, I am very glad indeed that Jane Austen did not marry Thomas Lefroy. He sounds like an appalling man. It is, I think, indicative of the status of Austen's novels as themselves icons of Little Englandism, with the lack of sympathy or understanding for other nations and identities within these islands that this implies, that Lefroy should be so sentimentalised within Austen's own story.

Jane Fairfax's aunt, the babbling Miss Bates, famously talks interminable nonsense. But, as John Wiltshire has quite correctly suggested, most readers mimic her audience and simply switch off when she begins to speak, allowing their eyes to glide across the page.[12] Read with attention, her nonsense, like that of Thady Quirk, the outrageously unreliable narrator of Edgeworth's *Castle Rackrent* (1800), and any number of other Irish literary narrators and characters, is in fact meaningful, a form of encoded signification. A seeming parapraxis, a slip of the tongue, has Miss Bates commenting on recent political events, the Union of England and Ireland in 1801 (the event which predicates *Castle Rackrent*): 'the Campbells are going to Ireland...which must make it very strange to be in different kingdoms, I was going to say, but however different countries' (E, 159). The novel, ostensibly in political denial, suddenly explodes out into a new world of meaning.

Nor are these concerns with Ireland confined to *Emma*. As Katie Trumpener has suggested, the passage in *Mansfield Park* where Mary Crawford attempts unsuccessfully to hire a cart at harvest time in order to transport her harp to Mansfield is rich in its implications:

> 'The hire of a cart at any time [says Edmund], might not be so easy as you suppose; our farmers are not in the habit of letting them out; but in harvest it must be quite out of their power to spare a horse.'
>
> 'I shall understand all your ways in time [says Mary]; but coming down with the true London maxim, that every thing is to be got with money, I was a little embarrassed at first by the sturdy independence of your country customs. However, I am to have my harp fetched to-morrow. Henry, who is good nature itself, has offered to fetch it in his barouche. Will it not be honourably conveyed?'
>
> Edmund spoke of the harp as his favourite instrument, and hoped to be soon allowed to hear her. Fanny had never heard the harp at all, and wished for it very much. (MP, 58–9)

This of course carries the primary significance of a disdainful metropolitan disregard for the rural economy, but it also partakes of an unmistakable national symbolism. Trumpener writes: 'As a bardic instrument, the cherished vehicle of Irish, Welsh and Scottish nationalism, and then as the emblem of a nationalist republicanism, the harp stands for an art that honors the organic relationship between a people, their land, and their culture.'[13] The Crawfords, we know, have experience of the Irish: Henry entertains Julia Bertram with 'Irish anecdotes' which he gets from 'an old Irish groom of my uncle's', who, in classic Irish narratorial fashion, and like Miss Bates, tells 'ridiculous stories' (MP, 99).

III. GAMES

The hermetic quality in *Emma* is frequently symbolically articulated through the use of games: closed, lawful, self-referential systems which simultaneously operate as metaphors for Highbury itself, and the version of England presupposed here, while also breaking down this stability and undermining the imposed fixity of meaning. Within the overarching confines of its marriage plot, Nancy Armstrong has commented on the ways in which *Emma* develops 'an intricately precise language for sexual relationships'.[14] This language, other critics have suggested, is simultaneously both a language of money and of games. While Mark Schorer, and later Edward D. Copeland, have noted the novel's use of a verbal pattern of economic exchange and material value, commentators such as Alistair Duckworth, Alex Page, Joseph Litvak and J. M. Q. Davies have all focused on the language and imagery of games in the novel – motifs which, Davies argues, 'occur with sufficient frequency to suggest that they were consciously intended as a structuring device'.[15]

Both the Emma–Harriet–Mr Elton and the Emma–Frank affairs are conducted through word-games – 'enigmas, charades, or conundrums' (E, 70), verbal dares, riddles, a form of Scrabble. These word-games permit an imaginary verbal reality, highly codified and structured – the participants engage in role-playing, taking on fictional roles according to Emma's rules – and thus at the opposite pole of signification to Miss Bates's seemingly uncontrollable, anarchic babble. To this extent, Emma's word-games act as metonyms for her narrative as whole: she conceives of them as riddles to which the answer is always, to her, perfectly transparent. Like Mr Weston's conundrum, in which 'M. and A. – Em-ma' are 'the two letters of the alphabet...that express perfection' (E, 371), Emma's 'imaginist' (E, 335) narrative figures reality in entirely self-referential terms: 'Myself creating what I saw', as the telling quotation from Cowper's *The Task* has it (E, 344).

This, however, operates in a far more nuanced and complex manner within the practice of the novel itself, which frequently conspires to subvert Emma's fictions of control. Mr Elton similarly considers 'Emma' to be the real answer to his charade of '*Courtship*' (E, 72), and Emma is horrified – while Harriet, with inadvertent accuracy, wonders whether Mr Elton's charade might not, in a concealed manner, signify 'a shark' (E, 73). Emma imagines herself mistress of the game, the one who knows all the answers, but Mr Elton takes her games for reality, considering the charade as an opportunity given by Emma to subvert the rules of decorum, to express sentiments that he could not, in the normal course of things as a 'respectable' gentleman, utter. At least, not when sober: rather 'too much of Mr Weston's good wine' (E, 129), however, and the language of love pours – rather like Miss Bates's speech – unstoppably out of him, a language which in a codified form he considers has already been there for Emma to read in his charade, has already been written down in the book of charades, its cover illustrated with 'cyphers' (E, 69), for Emma to de-cipher. Emma, however, dismisses Harriet's speculations as 'Mermaids and sharks! Nonsense!' (E, 73), and can only interpret Mr Elton's discourse as 'talking nonsense...Who could have seen through such thick-headed nonsense?' (E, 129, 134).

Significantly, Mr Elton's charade enacts in miniature the novel's ideological position, its retreat from a public, political world into an enclosed, domestic one:

> My first displays the wealth and pomp of kings,
> Lords of the earth! their luxury and ease.
> Another view of man my second brings,
> Behold him there, the monarch of the seas!
>
> But ah! united, what reverse we have!
> Man's boasted power and freedom, all are flown;
> Lord of the earth and sea, he bends a slave,
> And woman, lovely woman, reigns alone.

Thy ready wit the word will soon supply,
May its approval beam in that soft eye!   (E, 71)

Harriet wonders whether the answer to the riddle might be 'kingdom'
(E, 72). And the opening couplet of the first stanza can certainly be
read as an encoded critique of Regency decadence – 'the wealth
and pomp of kings...their luxury and ease' – which serves as a
counterbalance to the novel's enforced dedication:

TO
HIS ROYAL HIGHNESS
THE PRINCE REGENT,
THIS WORK IS,
BY HIS ROYAL HIGHNESS'S PERMISSION,
MOST RESPECTFULLY
DEDICATED,
BY HIS ROYAL HIGHNESS'S
DUTIFUL
AND OBEDIENT
HUMBLE SERVANT,
THE AUTHOR.

On 16 February 1813, Austen wrote a letter to Martha Lloyd, commenting specifically on the Prince Regent's treatment of his estranged
wife Caroline. Prince George and Princess Caroline were married,
without previously having met, in 1795, and separated after the birth
of their only child, Princess Charlotte, in 1796, after which George
went on a celebrated and public course of dissipation. They formally
separated in 1813, by which time, owing to the mental incapacitation
of George III, Prince George had been made Regent. The Regent, in a
spectacular case of the pot calling the kettle black, cited rumours of
sexual liaisons to accuse his wife of being an unfit mother, and thus
deny her access to Charlotte. When the Regent was finally crowned
George IV in 1820, Caroline returned from exile and demanded to
be made queen. She was immediately put on trial for adultery in
the House of Lords, with the legal possibility of receiving the death
sentence for treason. As Colley notes, this led to the creation of a
widespread popular activist movement comprised of tens of
thousands of women who saw in Caroline's case their own dis-
enfranchisement writ large. In the words of one contemporary ballad:

Attend ye virtuous British wives
Support your injured Queen,
Assert her rights, *they are your own*,
As plainly may be seen.[16]

Anticipating these feminist sentiments of 1820, Austen's position in 1813 is unambiguously partisan (she is commenting specifically here on a letter from Caroline to the Regent, which her supporters then published in the *Morning Chronicle*):

> I suppose all the world is sitting in Judgement upon the Princess of Wales's Letter. Poor Woman, I shall support her as long as I can, because she *is* a Woman, & because I hate her Husband – but I can hardly forgive her for calling herself 'attached & affectionate' to a man whom she must detest – ...I do not know what to do about it; – but if I must give up the Princess, I am resolved at least always to think that she would have been respectable, if the Prince had behaved tolerably by her at first.   (L, 208)

While Austen was no admirer of the Regent, J. E. Austen Leigh's *Memoir* records that 'the Prince was a great admirer of her novels; that he read them often, and kept a set in every one of his residences'. Austen was invited to visit Carlton House, the Regent's London residence, where she was shown around by his librarian, James Stanier Clarke, on 13 November 1815. While she was there, 'Mr Clarke declared himself commissioned to say that if Miss Austen had any other novel forthcoming she was at liberty to dedicate it to the Prince', which amounted to a command. 'Accordingly such a dedication was immediately prefixed to "Emma" which was at that time in the press.'[17] Thus, while Austen had no choice in the matter of the dedication, what we know from the letters of her distaste for the Regent would dictate that the dedication be read ironically (hardly an outlandish reading strategy for an Austen novel, after all), while the novel itself covertly – here and through its presentation of Frank as a Frenchified Regency dandy – registers this distaste.

More generally, Mr Elton's charade mimics *Emma*'s inwardness with its implied critique of martial and imperial concerns: 'Behold him there, the monarch of the seas! ...Lord of the earth and sea, he bends a slave, / And woman, lovely woman reigns alone.' Written and set during the last years of the Napoleonic Wars, British naval prowess, celebrated in *Mansfield Park* and triumphantly in *Persuasion*, is subordinated here to domestic concerns – the grand ideological master-narrative of the European political stage (a term whose imperialising and masculinist implications I intend quite deliberately) is subsumed more rigorously here than in any of Austen's other novels within the 'feminine' confines of the marriage plot, where 'woman, lovely woman, reigns alone'. What this *is*, in fact, is a domesticising (in-)version of James Thomson's 'Rule Britannia', whose mythic naval-imperial status derived from its origins as the triumphant conclusion to Thomson and fellow-Scot David Mallett's *Alfred. A Masque* (with music by the London composer Thomas Arne), a work whose provenance and first performance has been brilliantly contextualised by Simon Schama.[18] As a response to the Jacobite movements of the first half of the eighteenth century, which were to climax with the rising focused around the Young Pretender Charles Edward Stuart in 1745, Henry St John, Viscount Bolingbroke (who had been barred from the House of Lords as a consequence of his own flirtation with Jacobitism in 1714), had written *The Idea of a Patriot King* as a guidebook for the young Frederick, Prince of Wales, in 1738. The *Patriot King* had as its model for the ideal British monarch King Alfred, the 'Guardian of Liberty', popularly credited as the founder both of trial by jury and of the British navy. Anti-Jacobite Scots themselves, Thomson and Mallett (his name an Anglicisation of the Scots Malloch) produced *Alfred* as a de facto staging of the *Patriot King*. The masque was commissioned by Prince Frederick for performance at Cliveden, his Buckinghamshire estate, on 1 August 1740, the anniversary of the coming of the Hanoverian dynasty with the accession to the throne of George I, Frederick's grandfather, in 1714. Frederick had become Prince of Wales in 1729, but had quarrelled with his father George II soon afterwards, partly for domestic reasons, because of the perceived inadequacy of his allowance. Barred from George's court, Frederick was to become a persistent critic of corruption in his father's regime, focusing particularly on the king's relationship with his prime minister Robert Walpole and acting as a figurehead for the opposition which was finally to oust Walpole in 1742, after which Frederick was reconciled with his father. He died in 1751 of injuries sustained from being hit by a cricket ball. As Schama suggests, the Cliveden performance was a brilliantly orchestrated publicity stunt, 'an occasion designed to advertise publicly, especially in the gossip-greedy press, the credentials of the Prince and his supporters as True Patriots', marking out Frederick as Alfred's true heir, 'the epitome of the patriot prince, the guardian of liberty'.[19] In the masque, a hermit calls forth visions of future English kings, Edward III and William III, and prophesies to Alfred at the moment of his seeming defeat by the Danes a coming British empire based on naval power:

> Distant posterity: when guardian laws
> Are by the patriot in the glowing senate
> Won from corruption; when th'impatient arm
> Of liberty, invincible, shall scourge
> The tyrants of mankind – and when the deep,
> Through all her dwelling waves, shall proudly joy
> Beneath the boundless empire of thy sons.[20]

The masque closes on a moment of prophetic triumphalism, with 'Rule Britannia' itself, followed by an exhortation from the hermit:

> When Britain first, at heaven's command
> Arose from out the azure main;
> This was the charter of the land,
> And guardian Angels sung this strain:
> 'Rule Britannia, rule the waves;
> Britons never will be slaves.'...

> Alfred! Go forth! Lead on the radiant years...
> I see thy commerce, *Britain* grasp the world
> All nations serve thee, every foreign blood
> Subjected pays its tribute to the *Thames*...
> Britons proceed, the subject deep command
> Awe with your navies every hostile land
> Vain are their threats, their armies all in vain
> They rule the world who rule the main.[21]

IV.   FEMININITY AND THE ROMANTIC FRIENDSHIP

The consequences of this ideological dynamic in *Emma*'s inversion of 'Rule Britannia' are themselves potentially subversive, a slippage and even a reversal of accepted gender roles. Many of the men in the novel – though significantly *not* Mr Knightley – are imbued with feminine characteristics. As Chapter 1 suggested, Mr Woodhouse is perhaps best read as an old woman, the companion of Miss and

Mrs Bates, comfortably at the bottom of Austen's list of notably unimpressive patriarchs and surely *not* Emma's (or anybody's) father. (Mr Woodhouse is my own blind-spot, for here my professional critical detachment breaks down, in the teeth of my fully theorised awareness of the distinction between literature and life, into genuine hatred and fury. Decades of reading, studying, teaching and writing about Jane Austen have only served to strengthen my sense that, far from a cherishably comic character, Mr Woodhouse is a pampered, whingeing, cretinous leech – a one-man justification for the class war and literature's best advert for compulsory euthanasia. In fact, I'd happily kill him myself, given the chance.) Although Mr John Knightley assures Emma that Mr Elton, in the company of men, is capable of what he sees as a properly masculine rationalism, this is only ever reported: 'With men he can be rational and unaffected, but when he has ladies to please every feature works' (E, 133). Hairstyle boy Frank Churchill, we have seen, has dandyish qualities which set him in opposition to the 'unaffected' masculinity of the Knightleys.

LeRoy W. Smith, following Karen Horney, understands Emma herself as undertaking a 'flight from womanhood', an 'attempt to take refuge in a male role in order to escape the implications for her life of the view of woman's nature and role in a male-dominated society'.[22] While my concerns here are primarily cultural-historical rather than, like Smith's, psychoanalytic, it remains the case that Emma's 'androgyny' in her assumption of a traditionally male role of social control and economic power carries over into a sexual androgyny, since sexuality here is to be understood quite firmly within the context of power-relations. Edmund Wilson may have been the first of Austen's readers directly to note Emma's indifference to men and 'infatuations with women', and several critics have since attempted to read a lesbian Emma, 'latent' or otherwise.[23]

As Lilian Faderman has noted, the romantic friendship between young women, of the kind we see with Emma and Harriet, characterised by physical and emotional intimacy, was often used as a licit means of manifesting an otherwise inexpressible lesbian desire.[24] The first thing we discover about Harriet is that 'Emma...had long felt an interest in [her], on account of her beauty' (E, 22):

> She was a very pretty girl, and her beauty happened to be of the sort Emma particularly admired. She was short, plump and fair, with a fine

bloom, blue eyes, regular features, and a look of great sweetness; and
before the end of the evening, Emma was as much pleased with her
manners as her person, and quite determined to continue the acquaintance. (E, 23)

This is the most detailed passage of physical description in the
novel (and one of the most detailed in Austen), and its purpose is
to establish that Emma's admiration for Harriet is predicated in
the first instance on purely physical grounds: 'Why,' Alex Page
exclaims, 'Emma has fallen in love at first sight. . . . Harriet's beauty
does it, especially those "soft blue eyes", the seat of libidinal power
since time immemorial.' Well, perhaps. Page further notes that the
novel's opening description of Emma herself as 'handsome, clever
and rich' (E, 5) contains 'an unmistakably masculine component'.[25] Indeed, all three of these adjectives might more traditionally
be said to belong to the masculine sphere, and it is certainly the
case that Emma's 'handsome' appearance is contrasted with Harriet's
'beauty', 'fair[ness]', 'bloom' and 'sweetness', all of which 'graces'
(E, 23) are clearly gendered feminine.

But the relationship between Emma and Harriet is obviously
also, and simultaneously, a relationship of power as well as of eroticism. 'Harriet kissed [Emma's] hand in silent and submissive gratitude' (E, 342): almost invisible in the text, this gesture of eroticism
circumscribed by domination ('submissive gratitude') is emblematic
of the dynamics of Emma and Harriet's relationship. Emma states
often that, as a wealthy heiress, she simply has no need of the
marriage-market. She tells Harriet:

> 'I have none of the usual inducements to marry. Were I to fall in love,
> indeed, it would be a different thing! but I have never been in love; it is
> not my way, or my nature; and I do not think I ever shall. And without
> love, I am sure I should be a fool to change such a situation as mine.
> Fortune I do not want; employment I do not want: I believe few married
> women are half as much mistresses of their husband's house as I am of
> Hartfield; and never, never could I expect to be so truly beloved and
> important; so always first and right in any man's eyes as I am in my
> father's.' (E, 84)

This is not self-deception: it is clear-sightedness.

However, Emma's oft-stated resolution never to marry is contingent upon one important detail, that Mr Knightley similarly never
marries. She says to Mrs Weston:

'Mr Knightley! – Mr Knightley must not marry! – You would not have little Henry cut off from Donwell. I cannot at all consent to Mr Knightley's marrying; and I am sure it is not likely. I am amazed that you should think of such a thing!' (E, 224)

This outburst, which continues over the next few pages, obviously protesting too much, is Emma's response to Mrs Weston's having 'made a match between Mr Knightley and Jane Fairfax' (E, 224). (If Emma, narratively, has a fondness for playing God, then here Mrs Weston indulges in the impermissible activity of playing Emma.) Emma's concern for her nephew Henry's inheritance *is* obviously a deception, but not of the kind commonly accepted. Her horror at the prospect of Mr Knightley's marrying is not because, unbeknown to herself, she has been secretly in love with him all along but because a Mrs Knightley would immediately usurp her position as Highbury's first lady: 'she could not endure the idea of Jane Fairfax at Donwell Abbey. *A Mrs Knightley for them all to give way to! –* No, Mr Knightley must never marry. Little Henry must remain the heir of Donwell' (E, 228 – emphasis mine).

The real crisis arises when Harriet ceases simply to be herself a cypher, a mouthpiece and a vehicle for Emma's desires, and takes on a life of her own within the novel as an autonomously speaking subject, uttering, in Mikhail Bakhtin's phrase, '[her] own directly signifying discourse'.[26] And what Harriet's new-found 'licentious tongue' speaks is her desire for Mr Knightley. Turning Emma's own words back on her, Harriet says:

'I do not wonder, Miss Woodhouse...that you should feel a great difference between two, as to me or as to anybody. You must think one five million times more above me than the other. But I hope, Miss Woodhouse, that supposing – that if – strange as it may appear – . But you know they were your own words, that *more* wonderful things had happened, that matches of *greater* disparity had taken place than between Mr Frank Churchill and me; and, therefore, it seems as if such a thing even as this, may have occurred before and if I should be so very fortunate, beyond expression, as to – if Mr Knightley should really – if *he* does not mind the disparity, I hope, dear Miss Woodhouse, you will not set yourself against it, and try to put difficulties in the way. But you are too good for that, I am sure.' (E, 407)

The reason for the hesitant nature of this passage is obvious: Harriet is learning to speak. Emma has been noting with approval that

Mr Knightley has begun to take a fond interest in Harriet, taking this as a sign that her Pygmalion-enterprise has been a success; that she was right about Harriet all along. It is only when she re-reads Mr Knighley's fondness for Harriet as sexual desire (for Emma's mind is full of erotic fictions), and understands this as a real threat to her own position, that she decides to marry Mr Knightley: 'It darted through her, with the speed of an arrow, that Mr Knightley must marry no one but herself!' (E, 408).

Brian Wilkie has seen this realisation as a religious 'catastrophic conversion', a movement, by divine grace, from 'blindness' (E, 408, but recurring throughout the novel) to revelation: 'She saw it all with a clearness which had never blessed her before' (E, 408) – the scales have fallen from her eyes.[27] This rather hopeful (Wilkie calls it 'visionary') quality in the novel – an overwhelming redemption, irreducible to logic – requires serious questioning for two reasons (three, counting my own hostility to religious conversions). Firstly, a matter of phrasing: 'Mr Knightley must marry no one but herself' is something of a negative revelation, denying Mr Knightey to anyone else rather than affirming Emma's own love for him. Secondly, the metaphor, 'It darted through her with the speed of an arrow'. This image draws attention to itself by its very rarity: an open metaphor is a highly unusual thing in an Austen novel, and so is almost certainly used deliberately. While it *can* be understood in the conventional manner as a pre-Freudian representation of the workings of the subconscious mind, an overpowering sensation shortcutting consciousness and the possibility of verbal signification, this understanding lays bare its very conventionality. The fact remains that this rare and deliberate thing, an Austen metaphor, is a cliché: Cupid's Arrow.[28] With her social position, she believes, severely threatened, Emma salvages her status by assuming the only role 'superior' to that of a Miss Woodhouse, 'a Mrs Knightley for them all to give way to'.

V.   'KITTY, A FAIR BUT FROZEN MAID'

Returning to the charades, Emma's book of cyphers, far from being a version of controlled reality, offers Austen the opportunity for one of the most deliciously subversive moments in all her fiction.

Mr Woodhouse was almost as much interested in the business as the girls, and tried very often to recollect something worth putting in. 'So

many clever riddles there used to be when he was young – he wondered
he could not remember them! but he hoped he should in time.' And it
always ended in 'Kitty, a fair but frozen maid'.   (E, 70)

Although Mr Woodhouse can only remember the opening stanza,
the full text of 'Kitty, a Fair But Frozen Maid' runs as follows:

A RIDDLE
BY THE SAME, [i.e. By MR. GARRICK.]

Kitty, a fair but frozen maid,
Kindled a flame I still deplore;
The hood-winked boy I call'd in aid,
Much of his near approach afraid,
So fatal to my suit before.

At length, propitious to my pray'r,
The little urchin came;
At once he fought the midway air,
And soon he clear'd, with dextrous care,
The bitter relics of my flame.

To Kitty, Fanny now succeeds,
She kindles slow, but lasting fires:
With care my appetite she feeds;
Each day some willing victim bleeds,
To satisfy my strange desires.

Say, by what title or what name,
Must I this youth address?
Cupid and he are not the same,
Though both can raise, or quench a flame –
I'll kiss you if you guess.[29]

Usually attributed, as here, to David Garrick, the poem first
appeared in Part Four (1771) of the printer John Almon's six-part
miscellany, *New Foundling Hospital for Wit*. It is a veritable catalogue of bawdry, in which the speaker recounts his having
contracted syphilis ('a flame I yet deplore') from a prostitute, Kitty.
The second stanza describes a painful method of cure, while in
the third the speaker maintains that from now on he shall only
have sex with a virginal Fanny ('Fanny', as in Fanny Price, was
perhaps and certainly is now a slang word for vagina) – 'Each day
some willing victim bleeds / To satisfy my strange desires', a reference

to the belief that sex with virgins could cure syphilis. Both the riddle's solution, the chimney sweeper, and its prize, a kiss, are slang expressions for sexual intercourse. This is powerful stuff, clearly: what does it tell us about Mr Woodhouse? While it may simply indicate that he is an idiot, which we knew already, Jill Heydt-Stevenson offers a reading so outrageous in its implications that I simply have to quote it here, even though it conflicts completely with my own account of Mr Woodhouse:

> Through a series of covert allusions, Austen raises the ludicrous and hilarious possibility that the clearly asexual Mr Woodhouse might have been a libertine in his youth and now suffers from tertiary syphilis. For example, Emma's father, a hypochondriac, cannot bear to be cold and so prefers a fire, even in midsummer; the riddle's narrator, ill with venereal disease, also longs for fire to cure him. Both Mr Woodhouse and the narrator despise marriage and want to surround themselves with young virgins who will keep them 'well'. Further, it is also deliciously, though seditiously, funny that one of the repeated cures for venereal disease was a light diet mostly consisting of a thin gruel – Mr Woodhouse's favourite meal, and the only one he can 'with thorough self-approbation, recommend'.[30]

I wonder!

In her novels *Cecilia* and *Camilla*, Frances Burney created an all-encompassing social, economic, sexual and existential metaphor, the lottery. In *Camilla*, Burney has her heroine draw a winning ticket in a lottery, only to be forced to return the prize. In *Cecilia*, the businessman Mr Simpkins misconstrues Captain Aresby's remark on the emptiness of Vauxhall pleasure-gardens, 'nobody here! a blank *partout!*':

> 'if I understood right, you said something of a blank? pray, sir, if I may be so free, has there been anything in the nature of a raffle, or a lottery, in the garden? or the like of that?'[31]

Aresby has wandered into the build-up to the suicide of Cecilia's bankrupt guardian Mr Harrel. With some style, Mr Harrel invites all of his creditors to a fantastic *grande bouffe* at Vauxhall, at the climax of which he blows out his brains.

The heroine of Charlotte Smith's *Euphemia* (1790) exclaims that she has 'drawn a blank in the lottery of life'.[32] Harriet Smith, watching Mr Elton's trunk being loaded onto the butcher's cart, feels that 'every thing in this world, excepting that trunk and the direction, was consequently a blank' (E, 186). In *Pride and Prejudice*, Lydia Bennet seems to have drawn a similar blank in ending up with Wickham. During an evening at the Phillipses, 'Mrs Phillips protested that they would have a nice comfortable noisy game of lottery tickets' (PP, 74). While Wickham lies to Elizabeth about his and Darcy's relationship, Lydia plays the lottery avidly, and afterwards 'talked incessantly of lottery tickets, of the fish she had lost and the fish she had won' (PP, 84) (the OED defines 'fish' here as 'A small piece of bone or ivory, sometimes fish-shaped; used as a counter in games'). Elizabeth Bennet's own speech is shot though with the language of uncertainty, an unconscious signifier of the precariousness of her own social and economic security: 'dare', 'inconsistencies', 'unlucky', 'puzzle', 'venture', 'risk', 'chance', 'accident', 'forfeit', 'fortune', 'caprice and instability' are just a few examples of this. Even the novel's happy lovers, Jane and Bingley, have their falling in love described by Mrs Gardiner as 'hackneyed... doubtful...*indefinite*' (PP, 140), and represented by Elizabeth herself in terms of games of chance: 'these four evenings have enabled them to ascertain that they both like Vingt-un better than Commerce', to which Charlotte Lucas replies that, as far as she is concerned, 'Happiness in marriage is entirely a matter of chance' (PP, 22–3). 'Commerce' here unites in one word, like *Emma*'s 'fortune', economics and chance. That the Longbourn estate devolves onto Mr Collins is a matter of luck – that Mr Bennet has fathered no male children – which Austen metaphorically represents by making Mr Collins an avid games-player – he plays backgammon with Mr Bennet, is eager to learn whist at the Phillipses, passes his time playing quadrille at Rosings. And, of course, he wins: at Rosings we read of him 'thanking [Lady Catherine] for every fish he won, and apologising if he thought he won too many' (PP, 166). Elizabeth may criticise Charlotte's 'lack of 'principle and integrity' for marrying Mr Collins simply for 'security', but he is a lucky gambler, and Elizabeth's own language serves to highlight the fundamental *insecurity* of her own world.

It is Frank Churchill, however, and not Emma herself, who is *Emma*'s expert games-player. Four times in the novel, and by three different people (Emma, Frank himself, Mr Knightley), he is described as the 'child of good fortune' or the 'favourite of fortune' (E, 428, 443, 448) – with its cognate, 'fortunate', frequently reiterated to describe Frank – 'fortune' here combining the novel's twin interrelated interest in money and in games. Mr Knightley describes him to Emma in terms of a successful lottery-winner: 'He is a most fortunate man!...At three and twenty to have drawn such a prize!' (E, 428) Frank has chance on his side. It is for his propensity for, and skill at, games that Mr Knightley, the novel's straight-talker, distrusts Frank for 'manœuvring and finessing' (E, 146), and for having a 'mind full of intrigue...Mystery; Finesse – how they pervert the understanding!' (E, 446) To Mr Knightley, Frank has been '[p]laying a most dangerous game', a 'deeper game' hidden under the '[d]isingenuousness...[of] a child's play' (E, 445, 348) – and furthermore, in all probability, cheating: he twice suspects Frank of 'double dealing' (E, 343, 348). For Mr Knightley, the lesson that Emma should learn from her encounters with Frank is that games are to be played fairly: 'My Emma, does not every thing serve to prove more and more the beauty of truth and sincerity in all our dealings with each other?' (E, 446) – 'dealings' in this context having clear connotations of games-playing (specifically of card-playing), coming as it does at the very end of a speech *riddled* with the language of games. Furthermore, Mr Knightley's description of Frank as 'double dealing' (an accusation which he makes twice – which he doubles), echoes his initial assessment of Frank's character: 'His letters disgust me....It is on [Mrs Weston's] account that [Frank's] attention to Randalls is *doubly* due, and she must *doubly* feel the omission' (E, 149, emphasis mine). This 'double-doubling' is itself doubled by Mr Weston's account of Frank's impending return to Highbury: 'When Frank left us...it was quite uncertain when we might see him again, which makes this day's news doubly welcome' (E, 308). Frank's presence in the novel, either physically or discursively, is accompanied by the language of doubleness, of duplicity. Not so, of course, Mr Knightley – on the same page as his initial assessment of Frank's doubleness, Emma tells him: 'Your feelings are singular' (E, 149).

Frank's go at the word-game, which so excites Mr Knightley's suspicion, produces the word '*blunder*' (E, 348), a word which, as Joseph Wiesenfarth writes, 'runs like a discord throughout the novel'.[33] This word carries 'a meaning not...ostensible', signified only by 'a blush on Jane's cheek' (E, 348): a meaning which threatens to open up a whole new narrative within the novel, the truth of Frank and Jane's story, silenced because it is largely played out beyond the frame of Highbury, outside Emma's sphere of control. Emma is 'blinded' (E, 348) by this meaning, unable to see the significance, to decipher codes not of her own making: 'Never, for the twentieth part of a moment' (E, 350) has she suspected any attachment between Frank and Jane. Emma herself understands Jane as 'a riddle, quite a riddle' and a 'puzzle' (E, 285) but is convinced she has known the answer all along: 'there is a good deal of nonsense in it – but the part which is capable of being communicated, which is sense, is, that they are as far from any attachment or admiration for one another, as any two beings in the world can be' (E, 351). Simply perpetuating what she believes to be the 'superior intelligence' of her own fiction, Emma's attempt at a 'covert meaning' produces the word '*Dixon*' (E, 348), a reference to Emma's fiction about Jane's affair with the married Anglo-Irish landowner. There is no such attachment, however, and therefore '*Dixon*' is in this context a word which turns out to be both meaningless (it is strictly nonsense which Emma reads as sense, 'it all meant nothing') (E, 350), and as a proper noun, in contravention of the rules of the game. When Emma finally discovers the truth about Jane, she can only conclude that of 'a situation like Jane Fairfax's...one may almost say, that "the world is not their's, nor the world's law" ' (E, 400). That is, the very narrow confines of the world of Highbury, and the laws Emma attempts to impose upon it.

6

Persuasion

I. AFTER THE WAR

Persuasion is a post-war novel. In this, it differs quite explicitly from Austen's other completed works, all of which fall in their various ways under the shadow of the Franco-British wars of 1793–1815. Beginning in 'the summer of 1814' (P, 8) and continuing through 1815, the novel is both a reflection and a product of the social changes wrought by the Napoleonic Wars, changes which amounted, in Linda Colley's words, to 'nothing less than a redefinition of the nation.... [T]he post-Waterloo period...demonstrated...that in Great Britain, a nation forged more than anything else through military endeavour, the winning of radical constitutional and social change was also intimately bound up with the impact of war.'[1] These are changes which Austen characteristically articulates through the vehicle of property ownership and land-management. *Persuasion* is a novel of a different and developing conception of Britishness; it is, profoundly, the most modern of Austen's six canonical novels, one which shows the very beginnings of a new polity in anticipation of the 1832 Reform Act, and beyond that of the gradual widening of the franchise across the nineteenth and into the twentieth centuries. In a manner characteristic of Raymond Williams's sense of a 'long revolution', the production of modernity, *Persuasion* raises issues about the constitution of social organisation – the status of the aristocracy versus meritocratic conceptions of rank; the role of women; ideas of militarism and empire – with which we continue to wrestle.[2] Indeed, according to one of the most recent theorists of Britishness, the Scottish historian Richard Weight, it is *only* with the current generation that such issues may at last, definitively, have the chance of being resolved (though perhaps every generation since 1832 has thought this):

> Scotland, Wales and England had been locked together for four centuries in an uneasy relationship. From 1940 to 2000 they not only rediscovered their core national identities, they also re-imagined themselves, shedding many of the assumptions about class, race, gender, and religion which had once denied millions of people the right to belong to their nation. Many found these changes painful, some effected them unwillingly and some were still resisting them at the end of the century. But Britain did change dramatically in this period. And almost entirely for the better.[3]

The question, then, that *Persuasion* asks is by any standards a major one: Who owns Britain? Its answer is one which connects Austen to the main tradition of European thinking about national identity and nation-formation across the nineteenth century, when such concepts were being theorised in recognisably modern forms: as E. J. Hobsbawm suggests, it is 'the liberal bourgeoisies and their intellectuals' who 'impressed their character most firmly on the European nineteenth century, and especially on the period when the "principle of nationality" changed its map in the most dramatic way, namely the period from 1830 to 1880'.[4]

As previous chapters have suggested, Austen's use of the house as symbol for the State of the Nation was continually developing and being problematised right across the 1810s, from the first publication of *Sense and Sensibility* in 1811. That novel witnessed the devastating effects upon the all-female second branch of the Dashwood family of an aggressive patriarchy working through the dead hand of patrilineal inheritance which conspires to leave them without rights, homeless and impoverished, forced to fall upon the good nature of a distant male relative. This pattern, we saw, of disinheritance replicated itself across *all* of the novel's relationships. Such an iniquity occurs again in *Pride and Prejudice*, predicating the novel's action from the opening sentence – the Bennet girls are similarly disinherited and impoverished by a patrilineal order, the entail which devolves the Longbourn estate, on Mr Bennet's death, to the nearest male heir, Mr Collins. *Pride and Prejudice*, however, powerfully counteracts this gloomy view of the legal lot of women through fairytale magic, the presentation of Pemberley as a model of estate-management and therefore of an idealised British constitution. While the sour *Mansfield Park* denies or negates this idealism,

Emma rallies to present Donwell Abbey and its owner, Mr Knightley, quite explicitly as cherishable embodiments of Englishness, though at the cost of imbuing the narrative with a claustrophobia articulated, as in *Mansfield Park*, symbolically through insularity and incest, this time with distinctly Francophobic overtones. From the very opening chapter of *Persuasion*, such symbolic problems seem to have reached some kind of conclusion, with the aristocratic Sir Walter Elliot forced in the closing months of the Napoleonic Wars to move out of his ancestral home of Kellynch Hall because his lifestyle of unproductive extravagance can no longer be supported:

> 'What will he be doing, in fact [asks Lady Russell], but what very many of our first families have done, or ought to do?'...He was not only to quit his home, but to see it in the hands of others, a trial of fortitude, which stronger heads than Sir Walter's have found too much. – Kellynch-hall was to be let. (P, 12, 15)

Into Kellynch moves a naval family headed by Admiral Croft, a veteran of Trafalgar. By the novel's close, *everybody* lives in rented accommodation. The deployment of the house in Burkean fashion as a ready symbol for national stability is no longer, for Austen at least, a desirable option – if indeed it ever was.

II. 'A LEECH OR BLOODSUCKER'

A model of compression as ever, *Persuasion*'s opening chapter paints a damning portrait of Sir Walter Elliot as a human relic, the useless embodiment of a sterile aristocracy: self-regarding, unproductive, anachronistic:

> Sir Walter Elliot, of Kellynch-hall, in Somersetshire, was a man who, for his own amusement, never took up any book but the Baronetage; there he found occupation for an idle hour, and consolation in a distressed one; there his faculties were roused into admiration and respect, by contemplating the limited remnant of the earliest patents; there any unwelcome sensations, arising from domestic affairs, changed naturally into pity and contempt, as he turned over the almost endless creations of the last century – and there, if every other leaf were powerless, he could read his own history with an interest which never failed – this was the page at which the favourite volume always opened:

'ELLIOT OF KELLYNCH-HALL.

'Walter Elliot, born March 1, 1760, married, July 15, 1784, Elizabeth, daughter of James Stevenson, Esq. of South Park, in the county of Gloucester; by which lady (who died 1800) he has issue Elizabeth, born June 1, 1785; Anne, born August 9, 1787; a still-born son, Nov. 5, 1789; Mary, born Nov. 20, 1791.'

Precisely had the paragraph originally stood from the printer's hands; but Sir Walter had improved it by adding, for the information of himself and his family, these words, after the date of Mary's birth – 'married, Dec. 16, 1810, Charles, son and heir of Charles Musgrove, Esq. of Uppercross, in the county of Somerset,' – and by inserting most accurately the day of the month on which he had lost his wife. (P, 3)

Far from Sir Walter's 'consolation', what this passage from the *Baronetage* offers *readers* of *Persuasion* is more like a chronicle of loss, of the dead wife and of that far from incidental stillborn son – Sir Walter is not the first of Austen's patriarchs to be unable to produce a male heir, and therefore to risk the dissipation of his estate. That the stillborn son should date from the Revolutionary year of 1789 must also, given the degree of precision in everything Austen does in this passage, be a quite deliberate symbolic gesture here on the novel's opening page: a harbinger of the death of aristocracy.

This image links Austen to a major tradition of symbolic thinking about the demise of the aristocracy and the need for constitutional change which was articulated across the post-Revolutionary debates of the 1790s and beyond. In *The Rights of Man*, Thomas Paine wrote of primogeniture as a form of infanticide:

The nature and character of aristocracy shows itself to us in this law [of primogeniture]. It is a law against every law of nature, and Nature itself calls for its destruction. Establish family justice, and aristocracy falls. By the aristocratical law of primogenitureship, in a family of six children, five are exposed. Aristocracy never has more than *one* child. The rest are begotten to be devoured. They are thrown to the cannibal for prey, and the natural parent prepares the unnatural repast.[5]

Paine's image of aristocracy devouring its children draws on the Greek primal myth of Kronos, father of Zeus, devouring his own offspring: the cannibal god depicted definitively for Romanticism by Goya in 'Saturn Devouring His Children' (1821–3), one of the terrifying counter-Enlightenment nightmares that comprise his series of 'Black Paintings'.[6] The sleep of reason, Goya knew, produces monsters. Paine's vision in turn counters Edmund Burke's version of all hell being let loose in the French Revolution, which is played out allegorically as a classic Freudian drama, the desire of the son (that is, the people) to kill the father (the king) and gain sexual possession of the mother (the queen), which family romance produces a monstrous birth:

> [One] should approach the faults of the state as to the wounds of a father, with pious awe and trembling solicitude. By this wise prejudice we are taught to look with horror on those children of their country who are prompt rashly to hack that aged parent in pieces, and put him into the kettle of magicians, in hopes that by their poisonous weeds, and wild incantations, they may regenerate the paternal constitution, and renovate their father's life....
>
> But, when all the good arts had fallen into ruin, they proceeded, as your assembly does, upon the equality of men, and with as little judgement, and as little care for those things which make a republic tolerable or durable. But in this, as well as almost every instance, your new commonwealth is born, bred and fed, in those corruptions, which mark degenerated and worn out republics. Your child comes into the world with the symptoms of death.[7]

But what if that one male heir is already dead? In its concerns here, *Persuasion* has clear thematic links with the other great political novel of 1818, Mary Shelley's *Frankenstein*, another symbolic account of the deaths of women and children in childbirth and at the hands of a potentially unstoppably violent embodiment of social upheaval – the revolutionary Monster, the one man who is many men, the Body Politic whose demands for reform, to be afforded the Rights of Man, are ignored at society's peril. A year later, the Peterloo Massacre was to provoke such national outrage that the British government finally realised that they *could not* treat crowds calling for social and parliamentary reform with the same brutal high-handedness as they had the mass meetings of the London Corresponding Society in the 1790s, which Austen discussed *in the same volume* in 1818, in *Northanger Abbey*'s concerns with the military suppression of mass dissent on the streets of London, dismissed by Henry Tilney as foolish girlish fantasising but historically accurate nevertheless. However, in 1819, many in the crowd at St Peter's Fields were demobbed veterans of the Napoleonic Wars, furious that they had fought to save a nation which they returned to find as corruptly caste-ridden and unrepresentative as ever.

As P. B. Shelley famously wrote on hearing the news of Peterloo, 'Ye are many, they are few'.[8] The yoking together of *Northanger Abbey* and *Persuasion* in one volume may be the fortuitous product of Austen's untimely death, but *as a combination* they are worth taking seriously as they effectively bookend not only Austen's mature writing career, but also the Napoleonic Wars which were obliquely to shape that career, offering a fascinating study in contrasts, in the different political concerns and social organisations of the 1790s and the immediate post-war years.

Sir Walter, who produces nothing, not even heirs recognised by the patrilineal system which defines him, is unable to survive in the post-war order. He has run out of money:

> [Anne] knew, that when he now took up the Baronetage, it was to drive the heavy bills of his tradespeople, and the unwelcome hints of Mr Shephard, his agent, from his thoughts. The Kellynch property was good, but not equal to Sir Walter's apprehension of the state required in its possessor. While Lady Elliot lived, there had been method, moderation and economy, which had just kept him within his income; but with her had died all such right-mindedness, and from that period he had been constantly exceeding it. It had not been possible for him to spend less; he had done nothing but what Sir Walter Elliot was imperiously called on to do; but blameless as he was, he was not only growing dreadfully in debt, but was hearing of it so often, that it became vain to attempt concealing it longer, even partially, from his daughter. (P, 9)

This is a characteristic concern of modernising anti-aristocratic ideologies. A century and a quarter after the publication of *Persuasion*, George Orwell, the greatest and most sympathetic of all theorists of Englishness, could still have Sir Walter and his descendants in his sights in his classic statement of Second World War patriotism, 'The Lion and the Unicorn':

> For long past there had been in England an entirely functionless class living on money that was invested they hardly knew where, the 'idle rich', the people whose photographs you can look at in the *Tatler* and the *Bystander*, always supposing that you want to. The existence of these people is by any standard unjustifiable. They were simply parasites, less useful to society than his fleas are to a dog.[9]

Having no use-value, the aristocracy – though one should never underestimate the tenacity with which they held on to their status until well into the twentieth century – were rendered increasingly anachronistic by the prevailing post-Enlightenment utilitarian economy. This is especially the case when we remember that the situation of the apotheosis of aristocracy in the monarchy at the time of *Persuasion*'s publication was hardly a propitious one: George III had by this time become the 'old, mad, blind, despised and dying king' of Shelley's 'England in 1819', while his dandified son, the Prince Regent, was hardly a model for the nation.[10] Again, this was a British manifestation of a European phenomenon, in which the institution of the monarchy was divested of what remained of its divinity. Thus, as Hobsbawm notes, when in 1825 King Charles X of France revived the ancient ceremony of coronation, only 120 people turned up to be cured of scrofula, the King's Evil, which could be cured by the royal touch. At the last coronation in 1774, 2400 sufferers had presented themselves for cure.[11]

Sir Walter sets enormous store by his 'ancient and respectable family...mentioned in Dugdale' (P, 4). The implication here is obvious and powerful: Sir Walter is a relic, a 'trophy of time', in Graham Parry's phrase.[12] Sir William Dugdale, the great seventeenth-century antiquarian, published *The Baronetage of England* in 1675–6, and it is this, alongside John Debrett's *The Baronetage of England* (1808), the work to which the opening chapter makes direct reference, which Sir Walter reads. Dugdale's *magnum opus*, the *Monasticon Anglicanum* (1655–73), was compiled in partial collaboration with Roger Dodsworth, who had died in 1654 but who returned to life in 1826 as the subject of a bizarre hoax perpetrated by the Tory journalist Theodore Hook, the editor of *John Bull* magazine, in which it was claimed that a frozen body, dug from an Alpine glacier, had thawed out, miraculously returned to life, and declared himself to be none other than Roger Dodsworth, returned to life after more than a century and a half in suspended animation.[13] Mary Shelley, with her interest in revivified bodies, used the hoax as the basis of her essay of the same year, 'Roger Dodsworth: The Reanimated Englishman'.[14] Like Roger Dodsworth, Sir Walter, 'mentioned in Dugdale', is frozen in time.

Not only is he frozen, though – Sir Walter is a kind of vampire. The first three decades of the nineteenth century saw a surge of interest in the vampire as a cultural phenomenon, in the poetry of Coleridge, Byron, Southey and Keats, amongst others; in fiction via Polidori's *The Vampyre* and Lady Caroline Lamb's *Glenarvon*; and on the stage in the works of Nodier, Planché and their followers.[15]

As Marx was to realise, vampirism provided a ready metaphor for the activities of an exploitative ruling class: bloodsuckers, leeches, parasites. The first extant use of the word 'vampire' in English dates from 1732, from an article in the *Gentleman's Magazine* whose writer clearly understood that he was dealing with a metaphor for exploitative political relations: 'These *Vampyres* are said to torment and kill the *Living* by *sucking out all their blood*; and a *ravenous Minister*...is compared to a *Leech* or *Bloodsucker*, and carries his Oppressions beyond the Grave, by anticipating the *publick Revenues*, and entailing a perpetuity of *Taxes*, which must gradually drain the Body Politick of its Blood and Spirits.'[16] As Count Dracula knew, vampires, existing across vast spans of time, are the very archetype of aristocracy, as he is both an individual and his own bloodline, his ancestors, and blood is his life: 'We Szekelys have a right to be proud, for in our veins flows the blood of many brave races who fought as the lion fights, for lordship.'[17]

By the time she wrote *Persuasion*, Austen had obviously caught up with the mainswell of British Romantic writing. While, as Chapter 2 argued, *Sense and Sensibility*'s literary aesthetics were if anything backward-looking, with Marianne Dashwood reading Thomson and Cowper – but also Scott – here the operative intertextual figures are Scott again and, significantly, the very modern Byron, the particular favourite of the wounded romantic Captain Benwick. In Lyme, Anne and Benwick 'walked together some time, talking as before of Mr. Scott and Lord Byron, and still as unable...as any other two readers, to think exactly alike of their merits' (P, 107). Benwick and Louisa Musgrove 'had fallen in love over poetry'; from their marriage, Anne believes, 'He would gain cheerfulness, and she would learn to be an enthusiast for Scott and Lord Byron' (P, 167). Byron was more deeply implicated than any other individual in the Romantic cult of vampirism. Indeed, the modern conception of the decadent, aristocratic vampire is drawn largely from Byron. His contemporaries, too, were given to describing him in vampiric terms. Ruthven Glenarvon, the thinly disguised Byron of Lady Caroline Lamb's sensational *Glenarvon* (1816), is a figure of supernatural evil, whose ancestor 'drank hot blood from the skull of his enemy and died'.[18] Three years later, the vampire-Byron reappeared as Lord Ruthven, malevolent anti-hero of John Polidori's *The Vampyre* (1819), its author's contribution to the famous storytelling session in the Villa Diodati, which also produced *Frankenstein*; *The Vampyre* draws on Byron's own contribution to the proceedings, a quasi-vampiric prose fragment.[19] Byron's poem 'The Giaour' features a celebrated curse:

> But first, on earth as Vampire sent,
> Thy corse shall from its tomb be rent;
> Then ghastly haunt thy native place.
> And suck the blood of all thy race[20]

Like the vampire, Sir Walter is not only frozen in time but eternally youthful because he incarnates aristocratic values. He is unchanging while all around him time moves on:

> He had been remarkably handsome in his youth and, at fifty-four, was still a very fine man. Few women could think more of their personal appearance than he did; nor could the valet of any new made lord be more delighted with the place he held in society. He considered the blessing of beauty as inferior only to the blessing of a baronetcy; and the Sir Walter Elliot, who united these gifts, was the constant object of his warmest respect and devotion. . . . [H]e could plainly see how old all the rest of his family and acquaintance were growing. Anne haggard, Mary coarse, every face in the neighbourhood worsting; and the rapid increase of the crow's foot about Lady Russell's temples had long been a distress to him. (P, 4, 6)

As a number of commentators have noted, time and its effects are a major theme in the novel, which ultimately enacts Anne's redemption of lost time.[21] The times they are a-changing, and the novel clearly favours those who show the marks of these changes. While Sir Walter himself is unchanging, recent history has inscribed itself on the faces of the Crofts, who take his place: Mrs Croft's 'reddened and weather-beaten complexion, the consequence of her having been almost as much at sea as her husband, made her seem to have lived some years longer in the world than her real eight and thirty' (P, 48). Sir Walter's dislike of the navy precisely reiterates the terms of his twin concerns with blood and beauty, which are to him the same concern:

> 'I have two strong grounds of objection to it. First, as being the means of bringing persons of obscure birth into undue distinction, and raising men to honours which their fathers and grandfathers never dreamt of; and secondly, as it cuts up a man's youth and vigour most horribly; a sailor grows old sooner than any other man; I have observed it all my

life. A man is in greater danger in the navy of being insulted by the rise of one whose father, his father might have disdained to speak to, and of becoming prematurely an object of disgust himself, than in any other line.' (P, 19)

As Mrs Clay, who has herself 'freckles, and a projecting tooth, and a clumsy wrist, which [Sir Walter] was continually making severe remarks upon in her absence' (P, 34),[22] intimates to Sir Walter, it is his very unproductiveness which maintains his perpetual youth. Furthermore, Mrs Clay suggests, this perpetual youth is bound up with a property-ownership which no longer obtains for Sir Walter:

'We are not all born to be handsome. The sea is no beautifier, certainly; sailors do grow old betimes; I have often observed it; they soon lose the look of youth. But then, is it not the same with many other professions, perhaps most other? Soldiers, in active service, are not at all better off: and even in the quieter professions, there is a toil and labour of the mind, if not of the body, which seldom leave a man's looks to the natural effect of time.... In fact, as I have long been convinced, though every profession is necessary and honourable in its turn, it is only the lot of those who are not obliged to follow any, who can live in a regular way, in the country, choosing their own hours, following their own pursuits, and *living on their own property* [italics mine], without the torment of trying for more; it is only their lot, I say, to hold the blessings of health and a good appearance to the utmost: I know no other set of men but what lose something of their personableness when they cease to be quite young.' (P, 20–1)

These concerns about an unproductive aristocracy and their assumptions of social superiority over relatively meritocratic mercantile and professional classes find articulation across a number of the period's political novels, not least Austen's own. In *Pride and Prejudice*, Darcy may begin by regretting Elizabeth's family connections with the Gardiners, who live within sight of their own warehouses in Cheapside, but the novel closes, as we have seen, not with Elizabeth and Darcy themselves but with an affirmation of the Gardiners' centrality to the world the Darcys inhabit, a world which is much the better for their presence. By the same token, Darcy begins the novel *already* in the company of Bingley, the scion of a wealthy northern industrial family. *Mansfield Park* shows Sir Thomas Bertram having to resort to two disastrous business ventures – the keeping of slaves on his sugar plantation in Antigua and the selling of his oldest daughter to the filthy rich Rushworths – in order to maintain his family's lifestyle and status. *Emma*'s Mr Knightley may be a landed gentleman, but that land is worked, and the high regard he has for his estate manager William Larkins is indicative of his recognition, not only of Larkins's high personal and professional qualities, but also of the extent to which his continued economic existence depends on Larkins. This is indicative, as are many of the other examples adduced here, of the ways in which the hegemonic power of the British ruling classes was perhaps forcibly redefined across a long eighteenth century to accommodate an awareness and increasingly a practical inclusion of agriculture (the details of estate management) and then commerce and industry.[23] Sir Walter ignores the dialectics of history at his peril.

But the novel of the 1810s which most powerfully explores these themes of the relationship between labour and status must surely be Frances Burney's *The Wanderer* (1814). Burney's focus on economic dependency across all of her novels amounts to a neurosis, albeit an understandable one for a professional woman writer.[24] *Cecilia* (1783), the novel from which Austen probably got the title for *Pride and Prejudice*, is subtitled 'Memoirs of an Heiress', and records, with an accountant's skill, the gradual dismantling of its heroine's fortune at the hands of her wastrel guardian Mr Harrel, who has amassed huge debts to finance his fashionable lifestyle. One of his creditors, the 'man of business', Mr Hobson, makes a number of speeches in which he articulates what is for Burney the central concern of her fictional world:

> 'As to his being a lord, ... I am one of them that lay no great stress upon that, unless he has got a good long purse of his own, and then, to be sure, lord's no bad thing. But as to the matter of saying Lord such a one, how d'ye do? and Lord such a one, what do you want? and such sort of compliments, why, in my mind, it's a mere nothing, in comparison of a good income. As to your son, ma'am, he did not go the right way to work. He should have begun with business and gone into pleasure afterwards'.[25]

For all their comic treatment, tradesmen in Burney's novels do tend to be associated with progress and modernity. In *The Wanderer*, Mr Tedman, the tradesman to whose daughters the heroine Juliet Granville, financially and socially adrift for most of the novel, teaches music, is favourably contrasted to most of the novels' representatives of the gentry and aristocracy: 'Mr. Tedman himself,' says Juliet, 'notwithstanding his deficiency in education and language, is, I believe, really good.'[26] Indeed, Juliet herself goes into business on a number of occasions throughout the novel, as a music-teacher or a mantua-maker, indicative of Burney's own conception, at least, of an integral relationship between heroine and tradesperson. In this former capacity it is *only* Mr Tedman who willingly pays her for her services. When Mr Giles Arbe entreats with Juliet's creditors on her behalf, Miss Bydel admonishes him: 'Why are you calling all the ladies to account for not paying this young music-mistress, just as if she were a butcher, or a baker; or some useful tradesman.' 'Well, so she is, Ma'am!' is Mr Arbe's reply.[27] Mr Arbe is the novel's vehicle for a powerful and consistent critique of the treatment of artisans and tradespeople, even criticising Juliet for allowing over-scrupulousness about the source of her own finances to prevent her from paying her own debts: 'Why now here's money enough! – Why should not all those poor people be paid?':[28]

> 'I am not for neglecting the farmers and trades-people [he says to Mrs Maple]; quite the contrary; for I think you should neither eat your meat, nor drink your beer, nor sit upon your chairs, nor wear your clothes, till you have rewarded the industrious people who provide them. Till then, in my mind, every body should bear to be hungry, and dry, and tired, and ragged! For what right have we to be fed, and covered, and seated, at other folks' cost? What title to gourmandize over the butcher's fat joints, and the baker's quartern loaves, if they who furnish them are left to gnaw bones, and live upon crumbs? We ought all of us to be ashamed of being warmed, and dizened in silks and satins, if the poor weavers who fabricate them, and all their wives and babies, are shivering in tatters; and to toss and tumble ourselves about, on coaches and arm-chairs, if the poor carpenters, and upholsterers, and joiners, who have had all the labour of constructing them, can't find a seat for their weary limbs!'[29]

These weary tradespeople are absent subjects of *Persuasion*'s opening chapter. Sir Walter can keep them at bay no longer.

'Vanity was the beginning and end of Sir Walter's Elliot's character; vanity of person and of situation' (P, 4). There is a hidden pun here, for Sir Walter's 'vanity' is both self-regarding and futile: he is vain and his life is *in* vain. To symbolise this, Austen surrounds Sir Walter with images of his own sterile self-duplication. Firstly, there is the Baronetage. As readers open *Persuasion* they read of a character opening a book, to read about himself – a book which, furthermore, he has amended in his own hand. This purely textual doubling is an image for Sir Walter himself – the Baronetage is his 'book of books' (P, 7), a tautology which, in Tony Tanner's words, 'signifies only itself'[30] – like, that is, Sir Walter himself, and like his later pronouncement that 'rank is rank' (P, 150). In the same way that the Baronetage offers for Sir Walter a reflection of himself, so too does his house, for he lives in a house of mirrors, amongst endless images of himself. When Admiral Croft moves into Kellynch, the first thing he does is to take Sir Walter's mirrors down: 'oh Lord! there was no getting away from oneself', he says, while 'looking with serious reflection' (P, 128). That Admiral Croft's reflection is serious while Sir Walter's is merely an empty signifier tells us much about the political world of *Persuasion*.

Another image of Sir Walter's self-duplication is his oldest daughter Elizabeth, who shares her father's agelessness:

> It sometimes happens that a woman is handsomer at twenty-nine than she was ten years before; and generally speaking, if there has been neither ill health nor anxiety, it is a time of life at which scarcely any charm is lost. It was so with Elizabeth; still the same handsome Miss Elliot that she had begun to be thirteen years ago; and Sir Walter might be excused, therefore, in forgetting her age, or, at least, be deemed only half a fool, for thinking himself and Elizabeth as blooming as ever, amid the wreck of the good looks of every body else.   (P, 6)

It is strongly implicit in the novel that, for all her pristine beauty – indeed, precisely *because* of it – Elizabeth will never marry. She and her father are each other's mirrors, their relationship one of mutual narcissism, for each looks at the other and sees themselves: she is 'very handsome, and very like himself' (P, 5). Thus here we have the last and most coldly sterile of all Austen's incestuous relationships, for such it surely is:

> Sir Walter's continuing in singleness requires explanation. – Be it known, then, that Sir Walter, like a good father, ... prided himself on remaining single for his dear daughter's sake. For one daughter, the eldest, he would really have given up any thing, which he had not been very tempted to do. Elizabeth had succeeded, at sixteen, to all that was possible, of her mother's rights and consequence.   (P, 5)[31]

They are a pair of Dorian Grays.

Indeed, Elizabeth's status in the novel as a form of sexual trophy is doubly incestuous, as Sir Walter initially plans to marry her off to his 'Heir presumptive, William Walter Elliot, Esq., great grandson of the second Sir Walter' (P, 4), though Mr Elliot rejects her and goes for money instead, 'uniting himself to a rich woman of inferior birth' (P, 8), who dies shortly afterwards. Mr Elliot is eventually unmasked by Mrs Smith as one 'who thinks only of himself', and who is therefore 'hollow' (P, 199) – a meaningless, insubstantial, 'artificial' (P, 208) reflection. He is also, like *Emma*'s Frank Churchill, double in the sense of behaving with 'duplicity' (P, 207) – as Anne comes to realise, he plays a 'double...game' (P, 250). The relationship between Sir Walter Elliot and Mr William Walter Elliot is symbolically adumbrated through nomenclature, as is the case throughout the novel, in which there are doublings and further redoublings of names: Sir Walter Elliot, Mr William Walter Elliot, little Walter Musgrove; Charles Musgrove, Charles Hayter, Charles Smith. To a large part, of course, these doublings represent the dynastic concerns of the Elliot men, which the novel rejects. In the same way, Sir Walter's Baronetage lists the wives of the 'ancient and respectable family' of the Elliots, 'all the Marys and Elizabeths they had married' (P, 4). Two of Sir Walter's daughters are, of course, called Mary and Elizabeth. Only the middle daughter, Anne, seemingly nameless in the annals of the Elliots, is able to escape this endless patriarchal loop and progress into modernity. She is *sui generis*, not simply another reflection of family history: 'she was only Anne' (P, 35).

III.   THE NAVY AND THE NEW ECONOMY

As Sir Walter debates on the appropriate kind of tenant for Kellynch, his agent Mr Shepherd says:

> 'I must take leave to observe, Sir Walter...that the present juncture is much in our favour. This peace will be turning all our rich Navy Officers ashore. They will all be wanting a home. Could not be a better time, Sir Walter, for having a choice of tenants, very responsible tenants. Many a noble fortune has been made during the war. If a rich Admiral were to come our way, Sir Walter – '   (P, 17)

Anne agrees, if not exactly with Mr Shepherd's purely economic rationale, then certainly with the suitability of his proposed class of tenant for Kellynch: 'The navy, I think, who have done so much for us, have at least an equal claim with any other set of men, for all the comforts and the privileges which any home can give. Sailors work hard enough for their comforts, we must allow' (P, 19). Much of the action of the novel takes place amongst newly demobbed sailors – returning national heroes looking for a place, a home, in the post-war economy.

The military analyst C. W. Pasley, whom Austen had read most avidly, we remember, whilst working on *Mansfield Park*, had suggested that the very fact that Britain had not yet been overwhelmed by France and its allies, who were able to command great numerical and economic superiority, was precisely because of the heroics of the Royal Navy: 'It appears to me, that this country is by no means in a state capable of resisting a powerful invasion; and that nothing but our naval superiority has saved us from being at this moment a province of France.'[32] Pasley was writing in 1808, with the outcome of the Napoleonic Wars still very much in doubt (he himself feared the worst). By this time, however, the cumulative aftermath of a series of spectacular naval victories climaxing with Trafalgar in 1805, had cemented the status of the navy in the national imagination. This, as Norman Davies suggests, led to a cult of celebrity amongst its most prominent commanders:

> Her admirals – Anson, Byng, Collingwood, Duncan, Hawke, Hood, Howe, Jervis, Rodney, and Vernon – had carried all before them in a series of wars, turning often distant spots like Quiberon Bay (1759), Cape St Vincent (1797) or Aboukir (1798) into household names. The supreme triumph came during the Napoleonic Wars off Cape Trafalgar (21 October 1795), where Vice-Admiral Horatio Nelson (1758–1805) crowned a scintillating career of skill and daring with the defeat of the combined fleets of France and Spain. After that, the world knew for certain that the Royal Navy was in a class of her own.[33]

Indeed, and as such, British naval superiority was to become the cornerstone of its imperial power: 'In the nineteenth century, it was absolute master of all the world's oceans.'[34]

By making Admiral Croft a veteran of Trafalgar, Austen is of course associating him intimately with Nelson, and thus with a triumphantly patriotic assertion of heroic national identity. Nelson, a peerless military commander, was also a self-publicist of genius (and, like Napoleon, one of the great short men of history), eager to construct for himself a cult of heroic individualism, and in so doing to tap into the powerful symbolic reserves of Romanticism. He was acutely aware, for example, of the symbolic importance of medals and uniforms, which he collected for himself and wore on every occasion. As Colley puts it, 'Splendidly, unabashedly and utterly successfully, Nelson did what the majority of the men who dominated Great Britain sought to do more elegantly and discreetly: use patriotic display to impress the public and cement their authority.'[35] Nelson's heroic death at Trafalgar, killed by a sneaky assassin's bullet (the downside of his fondness for pomp and uniform meant that he was always a visible target), further cemented his mythic status, ensuring that, in Simon Schama's words, 'his heroic death guaranteed life to Great Britain':

> Nelson virtually designed his own apotheosis – his translation to the immortals. The huge ceremony in January 1806 completely overshadowed William Pitt's funeral the following month and, for that matter, was on a scale that outdid royal ceremony. Like Winston Churchill's funeral a century and a half later, everything was designed to tap into deep patriotic emotion. The body, preserved in alcohol, was unloaded from the shattered hulk of the *Victory* at Greenwich, then borne to a lying-in-state, where the hero's coffin could be viewed by ordinary sailors and the people whose love he had cultivated and genuinely cared for. Black barges carried the bier downstream, like Arthur to Avalon, to a four-hour service at St Paul's, where royals were allowed by their own anachronistic protocol to attend only in their capacity as private individuals. But unlike Churchill, this was where Nelson stayed in the black marble sarcophagus originally meant for Cardinal Wolsey, buried right beneath the centre of the dome.

This is not to say that Nelson was some kind of nascent democrat or freethinker. Politically, as Schama notes, he was 'a dyed-in-the-wool reactionary', a hanger-and-flogger and a propper-up of corrupt autocracies. However, especially compared with the desperate King and Regent, Nelson was, quite self-consciously, a model of popular national heroism.[36] The canonisation of Nelson as national saint and saviour was completed by Arthur William Devis's celebrated canvas 'The Death of Nelson' (1805), which dispensed with military ostentation to present Nelson in beatific terms, dressed in white robes, haloed by the ship's lantern but also seemingly illuminated by an inner light. He looks, if anything, Christlike.[37] For Sir Walter Elliot, to stand in opposition to Admiral Croft,

Nelson's representative in the post-war order, is to stand in opposition to the nation.

Just as Anne 'was only Anne', the young Lieutenant Frederick Wentworth of 1806 'had nothing but himself to recommend him' (P, 26). Anne is dissuaded from marrying him then, largely by Lady Russell, as he has 'no hopes of attaining influence, but in the chances of a most uncertain profession, and no connexions to secure even his farther rise in that profession' (P, 26–7). Reiterating Sir Walter's views on the relationship between aristocracy and agelessness, the professions and ageing, Lady Russell fears that Anne's marriage to such a man will leave her 'sunk by him into a state of most wearing, anxious, youth-killing dependence!' (P, 27) Just four years earlier, in 1814, *Mansfield Park* had begun by seemingly vindicating such a position, with the disastrous marriage of Frances, the youngest Ward sister, to 'a Lieutenant of Marines, without education, fortune or connections' (MP, 3). The persuasion of the novel's title, however, echoes this passage from Richardson's *Sir Charles Grandison*, that novel which Austen knew more intimately than any other, and which here positions 'persuasion' as an instrument of power-relations and moral victimhood:

> But the entreaty of such friends as undoubtedly means one's good, dilates and disarms one's heart and makes me wish to oblige them; and so renders one miserable, whether we do or do not comply. Believe me ... there is great cruelty in persuasion, and still more to a soft, gentle temper than a stubborn one. Persuaders know not what they make such a person suffer.[38]

This suspicion of persuasion is reiterated in *Pride and Prejudice*, in an early dialogue between Elizabeth and Darcy. 'To yield readily – easily – to the *persuasion* of a friend is no merit with you,' says Elizabeth, to which Darcy replies, 'To yield without conviction is no compliment to the understanding of either' (PP, 50). In fact, *not* marrying Wentworth has had this effect of 'wearing, anxious, youth-killing dependence' on Anne, whose 'attachment and regrets had, for a long time, clouded every enjoyment of youth; and an early loss of bloom and spirits had been their lasting effect' (P, 28). This word, bloom, is reiterated throughout the novel, enriching a major thematic concern with looks and looking, part of which we have already examined. Indeed, A. Walton Litz, noting that the word recurs six times in the first volume alone, goes so far as to suggest that *Persuasion* is a novel *about* 'the loss and return of "bloom" '.[39] In a manner characteristic of its time, Litz's argument here elides the novel's political complexities (and for me at least, *Persuasion* is primarily a political novel) in favour of a reading predicated on individual relationships, but nevertheless this remark bespeaks a truth about the novel.

Wentworth, meanwhile, has had a good war:

> All his sanguine expectations, all his confidence, had been justified. His genius and ardour had seemed to foresee his prosperous path. He had, very soon after their engagement ceased, got employ: and all that he had told her would follow, had taken place. He had distinguished himself, and early gained the other step in rank – and must now, by successive captures, have made a handsome fortune. [Anne] had only navy lists and newspapers for her authority, but she could not doubt of his being rich. (P, 29–30)

While Anne has taken damagingly outmoded advice from aristocrats, Wentworth, meritocrat that he is, has made his fortune off the back of the new world order. The naval practice of earning prize money, a form of state-sanctioned piracy (legitimated by an Act of Parliament of 1649) in which a share of the spoils from enemy ships, merchant and military, was divided out amongst those who captured them, could be incredibly lucrative. P. K. Kemp, in his study of the practice, offers some spectacular examples of fortunes made in this way during the eighteenth-century wars. In the War of Jenkins's Ear (1739–42), Captain (later Admiral Lord) Anson of the *Centurion* led the capture of the Manila galleon the *Nuestra Senhora del Cavadonga*, whose cargo was worth over £751,000, of which Anson managed to secure for himself a three-eighth sum, or £281,625. By 1747, Anson was Commander of the Fleet in the first Battle of Cape Finisterre, from which he earned £62,991. In 1760, the captains of the two ships responsible for the capture of the Spanish vessel the *Hermione*, made a profit of £64,963 each, while *every one* of the ordinary seamen involved made £485. At age 18, William Parker was made captain of the frigate *Amazon*; 12 years later, in 1812, he was able to retire with a fortune of £40,000. Increasing British naval superiority ensured that vast sums were there to be made throughout the wars.[40] 'How fast I made money in her', Wentworth recalls of his second ship, the *Laconia* (P, 67). Charles Musgrove believes that Wentworth 'had not made less than twenty thousand pounds by the war' (P, 75), while his wife speculates on his ennoblement as a consequence: 'If he should rise to any great honours! If he should ever be made a baronet!' – though, ever Sir Walter's daughter, she snobbishly adds that 'It would be a new creation, however, and I never think much of your new creations' (P, 75).

IV. 'THE PEN HAS BEEN IN THEIR HANDS'

Persuasion's politics are also and crucially articulated through an ongoing debate on the gendered nature of authority, which finally, in a manner characteristic of Austen, resolves itself in a debate on the representation of women in writing, very much as it had done in *Persuasion*'s posthumous companion-piece of 1818, *Northanger Abbey* (another reason why they provide such a fascinating combination). Austen establishes at the very beginning of the novel, with Sir Walter and his 'book of books', which ratifies his status and in which he inscribes his history with his own hand, that written, textual authority is a function and a weapon of a patriarchal order.

In part, it is the function of Mrs Smith – very much a device, a narrative agent – to confirm this to Anne, as well as to provide yet another embodiment of a woman who has fallen foul economically of the world of men – her husband was swindled in a business venture by Mr Elliot; his death has left her disabled and unprovided-for.[41] She has letters from Mr Elliot to her husband, which she shows Anne, hoping that they will convince her of her relative's true character, that 'He is totally beyond the reach of any sentiment of justice or compassion...black at heart, hollow and black!' (P, 199) The testimony of the letters is irrefutable, but convinces Anne only of Mr Elliot's past character (which he himself has confessed was far from spotless): as to his present character, she is unconvinced. With the letters, Mrs Smith says, 'I have shewn you Mr Elliot as he was a dozen years ago, and I will shew you him as he is now. I cannot provide written proof again, but I can give as authentic oral testimony' (P, 204). Anne is initially unconvinced – 'your authority is deficient,' she says, 'this will not do' (P, 205) – but eventually concurs, concluding that 'Mr Elliot is evidently a disingenuous, artificial, worldly man, who has never any better principle to guide him than selfishness' (P, 208). Mrs Smith's 'authority' is not 'deficient' at all, but it *is* a distinctively female form of authority, having reached Mrs Smith via her own personal 'historian' (P, 205), Nurse Rooke, who is at the centre of a circle of women – nurses, housekeepers, maids – privy to inside information on the families for whom they work. Thus, what Mrs Smith calls (and Anne learns to call) 'history' is what we might otherwise term gossip – a form of communication which, as Patricia Meyer Spacks has contested, has traditionally been both radically undervalued and derided, not least because of its association with women.[42]

Anne's celebrated debate with Captain Harville on gender and authority has her reiterating the lessons she learns from her encounter with Mrs Smith:

> 'Well, Miss Elliot...we shall never agree I suppose on this point. No man and woman would, probably. But let me observe that all histories are against you, all stories, prose and verse. If I had such a memory as Benwick, I could bring you fifty quotations in a moment on my side the argument, and I do not think I ever opened a book in my life which had not something to say about women's inconstancy. Songs and proverbs, all talk of woman's fickleness. But perhaps, you will say, these books are all written by men.'
>
> 'Perhaps I shall. – Yes, yes, if you please, no reference to examples in books. Men have had every advantage over us in telling their own story. Education has been theirs in much higher a degree; the pen has been in their hands. I will not allow books to prove anything.'   (P, 234)

This is a triangulated debate: Wentworth, also in the room, is also Anne's audience and subject. Significantly, of course, he is *writing* while Anne and Harville argue, writing the extraordinary letter to Anne which articulates his undying love. The debate is briefly interrupted by a noise: 'it was nothing more than that his pen had fallen down' (P, 233). The pen is no longer in his hands, and in this gap in his writing, which is also an ideological fissure, Wentworth hears Anne's speech, her 'word [which] had no weight' (P, 5) at the novel's beginning: 'All the privilege I claim for my own sex (it is not a very enviable one, you need not covet it) is that of loving longest, when existence or when hope is gone' (P, 235). Wentworth's letter is a recognition of Anne's words and a writing of his own desire. Having dropped his pen, he takes it up again with difficulty: the result is 'hardly legible', because he 'can hardly write':

> I can listen no longer in silence. I must speak to you by such means as are within my reach. You pierce my soul. I am half agony, half hope. Tell me not that I am too late, that such precious feelings are gone for

ever. I offer myself to you with a heart even more your own, than when you almost broke it eight years and a half ago. Dare not say that man forgets sooner than woman, that his love has an earlier death. I have loved none but you. Unjust I may have been, weak and resentful I have been, but never inconstant. You alone have brought me to Bath. For you alone I think and plan. – Have you not seen this? Can you fail to have understood my wishes? I had not waited even these ten days, could I have read your feelings, as I think you must have penetrated mine. I can hardly write. I am every instant hearing something which overpowers me. You sink your voice, but I can distinguish the tones of that voice, when they would be lost on others. – Too good, too excellent creature! You do us justice indeed. You do believe that there is true attachment and constancy among men. Believe it to be most fervent, most undeviating in

F. W.

I must go, uncertain of my fate; but I shall return hither, or follow your party, as soon as possible. A word, a look will be enough to decide whether I enter your father's house this evening or never. (P, 237–8)

Austen's narrative style, powerful and flexible though it may be, is also primarily monologic: that beautifully measured combination of irony and free indirect speech which is instantly recognisable. As such, there are some registers which are outside of her normal range as an author. Thus, at critical moments in her narrative, where direct agency is required simply to arrive at a resolution, where the detachment of irony is inappropriate, Austen tends, as it were, to hand control of her narrative over to the characters most directly involved. This is 'writing to the moment', of course, a residual epistolarity which returns us to Austen's own origins as a novelist in the eighteenth century. Thus at these moments of crisis we are given letters as forms of a necessarily unmediated polyphony. Willoughby's letter to Marianne, a disavowal of love, in which the rake is emasculated, spoken through by Miss Grey, who controls his pen. Darcy's monumental letter to Elizabeth, its novel's *peripeteia*, effecting a total interpretive reversal of *Pride and Prejudice* which forces readers, in effect, to reread the events of the first half from a radically different perspective, Darcy's. The flurry of letters which closes *Mansfield Park*, bringing Fanny back from Portsmouth into the fold of the Bertrams, seemingly unable to function without her: 'There is no end to the evil let loose upon us.' Here the register, a fitting if fortuitous way for Austen to close her writing career, is unadorned desire, a high Romanticism signalled by the novel's recurring intertextual preoccupation with Byron, and one which should finally give the lie to Charlotte Brontë's infamous dismissal of Austen as a frigid writer, 'a very incomplete, and rather insensible (*not senseless*) woman' for whom 'the Passions are perfectly unknown'.[43] Ironically enough, Wentworth's letter sounds to me like nothing so much as the Brontës, most particularly perhaps the rhetoric of uncontrolled passion which so characterises *Wuthering Heights*: 'You pierce my soul.'

'Is the pen a metaphorical penis?'[44] This, famously, is the question which opens Sandra Gilbert and Susan Gubar's landmark work of feminist analysis, *The Madwoman in the Attic* – its own title, of course, from Charlotte Brontë. *Pride and Prejudice* has an interestingly phallic exchange between Darcy and Caroline Bingley, who says to him: 'I am afraid you do not like your pen. Let me mend it for you. I mend pens remarkably well', to which Darcy, aware of Caroline's designs on him, but not interested, replies, 'Thank you – but I always mend my own' (PP, 47).[45] While I am not necessarily suggesting that what we have here in *Persuasion* is an example of undiluted *écriture féminine*, Wentworth's letter is certainly the product of slippage, what happens when the pen of partriarchal authority falls from his hands. The letter which brings about *Persuasion*'s resolution is so powerful, in part, because it is *un*authorised, not the product of authority, caused by a parapraxis, a slip of the pen, and therefore, like the authority of gossip, all the more true because 'saying what should not be said' (P, 234).

Afterword

I. WHO OWNS JANE AUSTEN? (PART 2)

The 1990s unquestionably witnessed the 'embodiment' of Jane Austen. As well as the various and high-profile film and television adaptations and versions of her novels – some of which will be discussed later in this Afterword, but many of which, in keeping with my position that Austen now exists culturally in numerous versions, have been discussed alongside their novelistic originals – which sometimes notoriously focused on the bodies of Austen's characters, there were contributions to this phenomenon from within the academy. In 1992, John Wiltshire published *Jane Austen and the Body*, a landmark study which, for the first time, systematically explicated Austen's characteristic repertoire of often tiny, but only seemingly insignificant, looks and gestures, as well as attempting a proper medicalisation of her recurring concerns with sickness, weakness and hypochondria. Consequently, Wiltshire, rather brilliantly, concentrates on the meaning of the blush:

> The blush is not a straightforward phenomenon of the body, rather one of the acutest signs of the bodily enigma, and its deployment in Austen's narratives is governed by her awareness of its problematic nature, and of the possibility of exploiting this for dramatic purposes. ... The blush is no unequivocal guide to emotion, and may be misread – to ironic effect. Its phenomenology is puzzling and its signification is problematic, but it does, in all its varieties, represent clearly a form of the juncture between the body and culture, and functions as a miniaturised version of hysteria, the embodied correlate of a social effect.[1]

Of course, the provenance of Wiltshire's book can partly be explained in the context of the prevalence of 'body studies' as perhaps *the* 'hot' methodology of 1990s academic criticism: reviewing *Jane Austen and the Body*, Karina Williamson quotes Terry Eagleton's remark that 'there will soon be more bodies in contemporary criticism than on the fields of Waterloo'.[2] It is also, however, part of a phenomenon more specific to Austen herself, and as such dates back considerably earlier than the 1990s.

The fetishising of Austen and her heroines is itself nothing new: reviewing R. W. Chapman's edition of Austen's novels in 1924, E. M. Forster begins:

> I am a Jane Austenite, and therefore slightly imbecile about Jane Austen. My fatuous expression, and airs of personal immunity – how ill they set on the face of, say, a Stevensonian! But Jane Austen is so different. She is my favourite author! I read and re-read, the mouth open and the mind closed. Shut up in measureless content, I greet her by the name of the most kind hostess, while criticism slumbers. The Jane Austenite possesses little of the brightness he ascribes so freely to his idol. Like all regular church-goers, he scarcely notices what is being said.[3]

It is largely this fetishising, with the question of who thinks they 'own' Austen, and why, and how this relates to the embodiment and sexualisation of Austen that is to be my subject in this Afterword.

In October 1990, news broke that Andrew Davies was preparing a screenplay for a new BBC adaptation of *Pride and Prejudice*. This was to become the famous BBC adaptation of 1995, 'the "wet-T-shirt-Darcy"' version, as Linda Troost and Sayre Greenfield have dubbed it, in honour of the famous scene in which Darcy, played by Colin Firth, dives into a lake and emerges dripping wet.[4] This adaptation (though toned down considerably from Davies's original, rather more sexually explicit, proposed screenplay) and this scene in particular, occasioned a brief outbreak of 'Darcy-mania' in the British press. This 'wet-T-shirt Darcy' crudely but accurately posits and appeals to a predominantly female implied audience. Cheryl L. Nixon argues that 'the recent film adaptations of Austen are successful because they, quite literally, "flesh out" her male characters'.[5] Lisa Hopkins suggests that '[Davies's] *Pride and Prejudice*...is unashamed about appealing to women – and in particular about fetishizing and framing Darcy and offering him up to the female gaze.'[6] Notably, one such female gaze is that of Helen Fielding's Bridget Jones, who obsessively watches and re-watches the BBC *Pride and Prejudice* on video. *Bridget Jones: The Edge of Reason* (1999), a rewriting, sometimes scene-for-scene, of *Persuasion* (as its predecessor, the immensely successful *Bridget Jones's Diary*, was, rather more loosely, structured around *Pride and Prejudice*), has its heroine, a television journalist, interviewing Colin Firth (or perhaps interviewing 'Colin Firth'), who tells her, 'I think it was very important to Andrew Davies that Mr. Darcy had the most enormous sex drive.... At one point Andrew even wrote as a stage direction: "Imagine that Darcy has an erection." '[7] To further the intertextual playfulness, in which cultural products and media intermingle across centuries, and in which fiction and reality contaminate each other, in the film version of *Bridget Jones's Diary* (with a screenplay co-written by Andrew Davies), Mark Darcy was played by none other than Colin Firth, surrounded by a cast of Austen veterans including Hugh Grant and Gemma Jones (Edward Ferrars and Mrs Dashwood in the Lee–Thompson *Sense and Sensibility*), Crispin Bonham-Carter (Bingley to Firth's Darcy in *Pride and Prejudice*) and Embeth Davidtz (Mary Crawford in the Rozema *Mansfield Park*).

Jane Austen, as unquestionably a major canonical figure, has a status best described as extra-academic, widely read by a number of very different interpretive communities, all of whom, including academic readers, I would argue, offer a remarkably stable and secure Jane Austen. Furthermore, within the academy, Austen was made a significant figure for canon-formation (witness F. R. Leavis). We are dealing, unquestionably, with a 'great writer' whose meaning will not be violated – with a cultural touchstone, be that culture polite letters, 'hard-nosed' academia or a comfortingly conservative 'heritage' Englishness. 'Radical' readings of Austen, when (and this is also an important point) they are noticed at all, can take on a symbolic significance, seized upon, often in the press, as a spring-board for anti-theory rants or valedictory pieces for the study of literature proper. Very occasionally, as with Edward Said's work on slavery and *Mansfield Park* (the work, that is, of a prominent critic who is not an Austen scholar, pronouncing on Jane Austen), such 'radical' versions of Austen are overpraised for their originality, for their potential fundamentally to realign perspectives on Austen – see, for example, the reviews of Said's *Culture and Imperialism* in *The New York Times Book Review*, entitled 'Who Paid the Bills at Mansfield Park?'; in *Dissent* (a review by Irving Howe), in *The London Review of Books*; and, notably, John Leonard's review in *The Nation*, which opens: 'See Jane sit, in the poise and order of *Mansfield Park*, not much bothering her pretty head about the fact that this harmonious "social space", Sir Thomas Bertram's country estate, is sustained by slave labor on his sugar plantations in Antigua.'[8] Implicit here are two things: firstly, a suspicion that the world of Austen scholarship is a fundamentally conservative one, in need of an awakening to the rigours of contemporary critical practice; and secondly, what has become the received wisdom, received as 'fact', that we owe this *Mansfield Park*-slavery reading to Edward Said, whose perspective as an outsider to the enclosed, conservative world of Austen criticism allows a fresh, hitherto unknown, brilliant reading – a reading impossible from 'within' (though this ignores the fact that accounts of the underpinning status of slavery to Mansfield Park, and *Mansfield Park*, can be traced back at least as far as Avrom Fleishman's *A Reading of 'Mansfield Park'*, published in 1967).[9]

II. 'THE PASSIONS ARE PERFECTLY UNKNOWN TO HER...'

What this means is that Austen scholars can find themselves attacked from both sides, portrayed either as frothingly irresponsible barbarians or as critical dinosaurs.

It need not surprise us that Austen-inspired moral panics or media frenzies, such as that surrounding the 'wet T-shirt Darcy', should so frequently stem from the apparently outlandish conjoining of Jane Austen and sex. It seems that imagining a Jane Austen who wrote about sex is, even *pace* the 1990s 'embodiment' of Austen, a bit like imagining one's parents having sex. This version of a fundamentally desexualised Austen has its earliest and most powerful expression, of course, in Charlotte Brontë's famous letter to W. S. Williams in 1850:

> the Passions are perfectly unknown to her: she rejects even a speaking acquaintance with that stormy Sisterhood. ... [W]hat throbs fast and full, though hidden, what the blood rushes through, what is the unseen seat of Life and the sentient target of death – *this* Miss Austen ignores; she no more, with her mind's eye, beholds the heart of her race than each man, with bodily vision, sees the heart in his heaving breast.[10]

In essence, this notion of Austen and sex remained unchanged through most of the twentieth century, and is still, I would argue, the current non-academic version of Jane Austen. A memoir of one of Gertrude Stein's Montparnasse parties has its author overhearing 'a tweedy Englishman with a long ginger moustache' saying, 'You are talking of Jane Austen and sex, gentlemen? ... The subjects are mutually exclusive.'[11] Rare early-century denunciatory accounts of Austen, by H. W. Garrod and E. N. Hayes, both turn on what is considered to be the author's refusal to engage with sexuality.[12] Furthermore, as Claudia L. Johnson notes, Garrod's account of Austen implies, with some disgust, that men who read and enjoy her are likely to be effete or homosexual.[13] (Hopkins writes, with regard to the 1995 BBC *Pride and Prejudice*, that 'Colin Firth had never previously read Jane Austen because he thought her books would be "sissy" '.[14]) That Austen's male readership might be gay is also implicit, as Johnson suggests, in Kipling's famous story 'The Janeites', where a group of First World War enlisted artillerymen inscribe the names of Austen's characters on their weapons: Humberstall, who calls his gun De Bugg, is put on charges by the Sergeant Major for 'writin' obese [that is, obscene] words on His Majesty's property'.[15] 'De Bugg' is taken, that is, for an encoded or poorly literate invitation for buggery, symbolically displayed on a large gun.

By the mid-century, this reading of a non-sexual Austen had become allied to a more general sense of the limitation of her materials. In 1953, Dorothy Van Ghent wrote:

> It is the frequent response of readers who are making their first acquaintance with Jane Austen that her subject-matter is itself so limited – limited to the manners of a small section of the English country gentry who apparently have never been worried about sex, death, hunger or war, guilt or God – that it can offer no contiguity with modern interests. . . . It is wronging an Austen novel to expect of it what it makes no pretense to rival – the spiritual profundity of the very greatest novels. But if we expect artistic mastery of limited materials, we shall not be disappointed.[16]

Also, Walter Allen in 1958:

> The scope of [Austen's] art is not lessened by her ignoring the major events in the history of her time: the reality of her world would not have been in any way intensified had she dragged in references to the Napoleonic Wars or the French Revolution.[17]

Ian Watt, in an introduction to a volume of critical essays on Austen, summed up thus:

> The first and most enduring of the critical problems that Jane Austen's works raise is one of scale: does the patent restriction of her subject matter of itself exclude her from the rank of great novelists?[18]

Van Ghent, Allen and Watt are the authors of books which, alongside Leavis's *The Great Tradition* and Wayne Booth's *The Rhetoric of Fiction*, are amongst the most significant mid-century general studies of the novel: *The English Novel: Form and Function, The English Novel*, and *The Rise of the Novel*. Their remarks can certainly be taken as representative of the critical climate of their time.

This *stable* Austen, apolitical, asexual, ahistorical, has been challenged by virtually every Austen critic since about 1970, a period which, as the Introduction stressed, has notably witnessed a rise in both historicist and feminist criticism. Within Austen studies, the influential books by Fleishman, Alistair M. Duckworth and Marilyn Butler largely set the tone for subsequent criticism. Or at least for critical methodology: although many Austen critics, including this one, take issue, for example, with Butler's reading of a High Tory Austen, the historicist-feminist critical model has, to reiterate the Introduction once again, unquestionably been the dominant one in recent Austen studies. Nevertheless, outside the community of Austen scholarship, the 'stable' Austen remains, even within the academy, an orthodoxy. I offer three critical quotations, ranging from the 1970s to the 1990s, in an attempt to demonstrate this. The first is from George Steiner's *After Babel*:

> Entire spheres of human existence – political, social, erotic, subconscious – are absent. At the height of political and industrial revolution, in a decade of formidable philosophic activity, Miss Austen composes novels almost extraterritorial to history.[19]

This from Judith Woolf's study of Henry James:

> Where her immediate predecessors Fanny Burney and Maria Edgeworth felt free to draw upon a range of human experience wide enough to include blackmail, suicide, abduction, lesbianism and breast cancer, Jane Austen can admit no material more dangerous than accidents, elopements, misunderstandings and unfulfilled bad intentions. She submits ... completely to the tendency in the novel to seek the happy ending ... providing as she does a homogeneous moral universe in which we are unobtrusively guided to the correct solution to all moral problems.[20]

Finally, this, from Harold Bloom's mighty *The Western Canon*:

> it has become fashionable to talk about the socioeconomic realities that Jane Austen excludes, such as the West Indian slavery that is the ultimate

basis for the financial security most of her characters enjoy. But all achieved works are founded upon exclusions, and no one has demonstrated that increased consciousness of the relation between culture and imperialism is of the slightest benefit whatsoever in learning to read *Mansfield Park*. . . . Austen's is a great art founded upon exclusions.[21]

(Bloom has obviously been reading Edward Said.)

These views remain occasionally echoed within Austen scholarship. The stated aim of Roger Gard's *Jane Austen's Novels: The Art of Clarity* (1992) is 'to stem the tendency in criticism and scholarship . . . to take Jane Austen out of the common realm and into that of historical or theoretical specialisms alone'.[22] Gard cites both Duckworth and Butler as important examples of this 'tendency', and his book is further motivated by a more general 'anti-theoretical' animus. It is, then, an example of what Stanley Fish has dubbed 'anti-professionalism' in English studies.[23] Anti-professionalism, as Fish notes, unites both journalistic commentators and (in a combination that might have amused F. R. Leavis) academics from 'traditional' universities, who use it as a means of shoring up their own institutional-cultural power, denying validity to other forms of knowledge, and therefore to outsiders. Fish's target here is Walter Jackson Bate in particular, and more generally 'the high humanism of which the Harvard English department remains the institutional embodiment'.[24] Where Gale's work differs from most other instances of anti-professionalism is in its focus on the critics of a firmly canonical writer: as Fish notes, scorn is usually reserved for attempts to destabilise the canon: 'Lesbian Feminist Poetry in Texas'; 'The Trickster Figure in Chicano and Black Literature'.[25]

It is, to reiterate, far from unusual that Austen be used in this way, as a vehicle for articulating a wider scepticism about some of the current methodologies within English Studies: thus Austen becomes, in some hands, not so much a vehicle for nostalgia about a lost, 'innocent' (and more desirable) England, but about a lost, 'innocent' (and more desirable) *English Studies* – not only, in Troost and Greenfield's words, articulating a 'reaction against the perceived crassness of modern life',[26] but also against the perceived crassness of the modern academy.

Tony Tanner's *Jane Austen*, published in 1986 though mostly written much earlier, says this:

But we can say without any prejudicial implications that, among other things, Jane Austen is announcing her purposeful – deliberate – intention to 'abstain' from the whole realm of sexual feelings. Not that she is unaware of it, or too prudish to recognize it. She simply won't write about it.[27]

It is worth noting that phrase 'But we can say without any prejudicial implications'. On the rare occasions that Tanner does concede the possibility of a sexual Austen, his criticism is habitually couched in evasive or apologetic language: 'Without wishing to deviate into the follies of would-be psychosexual criticism...'; 'if that seems far-fetched and perverse, just let me suggest...'; 'it is perhaps not entirely irrelevant to note'; 'I think it can be justifiably (and not salaciously) suggested that...'; 'I am being deliberately crude about this because I think that...'.[28] But there, Tanner, a great (if orthodox) voice in Austen criticism, knows whom he's likely to offend by his unprejudiced, far-fetched, perverse, not irrelevant, unsalacious, crude suggestions.

Finally, D. A. Miller's *Narrative and its Discontents* (1981), a large part of which is devoted to Austen, figures sex as 'unspeakable' in her narratives, and simply reiterates Dorothy Van Ghent's conclusions:

> Three subjects that Jane Austen's novels do not treat...are the Napoleonic wars, the sex life of their characters, and the farm labor of the tenants who farm their estates....It is by no means a negligible fact that Jane Austen does not take up these subjects....Subjects like this have no place – not even the shadow of a place – in her novels.[29]

III. MASTURBATION, SODOMY AND LESBIANISM

I have dwelt at such length on these accounts of a stable Austen in order to show quite how pervasive an orthodoxy this is. But it is the *un*orthodox readings of Austen that attract attention and condemnation, that elicit responses which suggest that something genuinely has been transgressed. I want to cite two perhaps obvious examples.

The first is Eve Kosofsky Sedgwick's essay 'Jane Austen and the Masturbating Girl', first published in *Critical Inquiry* in 1991, since reprinted in the collection *Tendencies*. The essay offers a reading of a masturbatory, homoerotic scene in *Sense and Sensibility* which is genuinely 'far-fetched and perverse', emphatically untenable. Counterpointed with *Sense and Sensibility* here is *Onanism and*

Nervous Disorders in Two Little Girls, a medical treatise of dubious provenance (it could be a work of pornography masquerading as a medical treatise) ascribed to Demetrius Zambrusco and dated 1881. Such a reading is wilfully unhistorical, working on the implication that discourses of sexual deviancy remained fixed from the 1790s to the 1880s, flying in the face of its own argument that the Zambrusco text is informed by fundamentally late-Victorian discourses of addiction. Sedgwick acknowledges an 'anachronistic gap' here, but ignores it.[30]

Perversity, though, is precisely Sedgwick's point. The beginning of her essay recounts the scandalous reception of the original MLA conference paper upon which it is based:

> The phrase itself is already evidence. Roger Kimball in his treatise on educational 'corruption', *Tenured Radicals*, cites the title 'Jane Austen and the Masturbating Girl' from an MLA convention program as if he were Perry Mason, the six words a smoking gun. The warm gun that, for the journalists who have adopted the phrase as an index of depravity in academe, is happiness, offering the squibby pop (fulmination? prurience? funniness?) that lets absolutely anyone, in the righteously exciting vicinity of the masturbating girl, feel a very pundit.
>
> There seems to be something self-evident – irresistibly so, to judge from its gleeful propagation – about use of the phrase, 'Jane Austen and the Masturbating Girl', as the QED of phobic narratives about the degeneracy of academic discourse in the humanities.[31]

This, of course, is precisely what Sedgwick intended, for the essay is really a noisy intervention by a starry American academic into what is again understood here as the cosy critical backwater of Jane Austen studies: most Austen criticism, Sedgwick asserts, is characterised by 'banality and timidity'.[32] The phrase 'Jane Austen and the Masturbating Girl' is figured as oxymoronic, a scandalous yoking of some words which should never, ever belong in the same sentence. *Épater la bourgeoisie.*

Sedgwick's shock-tactic position, however, finds an echo in an aside offered by Terry Eagleton in his book *Heathcliff and the Great Hunger*. Eagleton, making a point about Maria Edgeworth, casts around for the most self-evidently absurd comparison (and by extension the most self-evidently absurd research topic) he can think of, and settles gleefully on this: 'William Carleton complained of the "flatness" of Edgeworth's Irish novels and regretted their absence of "heart-stirring lovemaking", which is rather like regretting the absence of sodomy in Jane Austen.'[33] Eagleton is a witty critic, and this is a funny joke; but such absurdity, no doubt, will already have taken into account Mary Crawford's notorious joke about buggery in the navy in *Mansfield Park* – a novel, we noted, containing several such sexual puns, and also suffused with the language of (venereal?) disease.

The importance of Said's and Sedgwick's work on Austen has little, of course, to do with intrinsic merit (in Sedgwick's case, it has *nothing* to do with intrinsic merit), but is rather a consequence of what David R. Shumway has identified as 'the star system in literary studies'.[34] One consequence of the 'star system' is that it allows certain individuals the cultural capital to pronounce authoritatively on subjects well outside of their normal academic competence, and, perhaps more importantly, it allows that their pronouncements be taken seriously. Stanley Fish, a major twinkler in the firmament of stars, has himself defended something very like the existence of a 'star system' on grounds of principle. Arguing against the idea that articles be submitted anonymously to the *PMLA*, Fish asserts:

> Ours is a hierarchical profession in which some are more responsible for its products than others; and since one of those products is the standard of merit by which our labours will, for a time, be judged, there will always be those whose words are meritorious (that is, important, worth listening to, authoritative, illuminating) simply by virtue of the position they occupy in the institution. ... [M]erit is inseparable from the structure of the profession and therefore the fact that someone occupies a certain position in that structure cannot be irrelevant to the assessment of what he or she produces.[35]

Thus, Camille Paglia is able to describe Austen as 'very conservative', and to talk of Austen's age as a period when 'there were no inconvenient racial problems of any kind. Everything is very homogeneous'.[36] The first of these assertions is highly debatable, though it has its proponents (notably Marilyn Butler); the second, in ways which I hardly need elucidate again, is simply wrong (either that, or this entire book is wrong) – though in fairness, Paglia is attempting to account for the appeal of Austen in the 1990s America of O. J. Simpson and Rodney King.

That Sedgwick's argument is spurious is not to say, however, that a masturbatory reading of Austen is inconceivable. Better turn, as I argued in Chapter 1, to *Northanger Abbey*, and to Catherine Morland's exploration, with 'a very tremulous hand' of 'the place in the middle', which 'secured in all probability a cavity of importance': 'her feelings at that moment were indescribable. Her heart fluttered, her knees trembled, her cheeks grew pale' (NA, 169). After all, we have already been told that the prospect of visiting Northanger has 'wound up Catherine's feelings to the highest point of extasy' (NA, 140).

If this sounds a little like Morris Zapp – well, that's no bad thing. Zapp, we remember, is David Lodge's outrageous American Austen scholar, who, in *Changing Places*, concludes a seminar on *Persuasion* in which he suggests, 'gesturing freely with his cigar', that 'Readers of Jane Austen...should not be misled by the absence of overt reference to physical sexuality in her fiction into supposing that she was indifferent or even hostile to it' by reading a passage from that novel and pronouncing 'If that isn't an *orgasm*, what is it?'[37] Zapp is, after all, unquestionably a brilliant academic (Stanley Fish, incidentally, is often thought to be the real-life model for Zapp), and provides, as the Introduction suggested, a fictional mouthpiece for some of Lodge's more outlandish theories on Austen (Lodge is himself an Austen critic of some distinction). The advantage of this tactic is obvious, deflecting the inevitable hostility that such pronouncements, if made within the context of 'serious' academic discourse, would attract.

Finally, I want to glance at Terry Castle's 'Sister–Sister', a review essay on Deirdre Le Faye's magisterial revised edition of Austen's letters, which appeared in the *London Review of Books* in August 1995, and more particularly at the furore which ensued. What is most striking about Castle's piece is its considered mildness, its lack of stridency or flamboyant claims, its determination to eschew what it terms 'the vulgar case for Austen's homoeroticism'.[38] The substance of Castle's claim is expressed thus: 'Sororal or pseudo-sororal attachments are arguably the most immediately gratifying human connections in Austen's imaginative universe. . . . Reading Austen's letters to Cassandra, one cannot help but sense the primitive adhesiveness – and underlying eros – of the sister–sister bond.'[39] Furthermore, broadly speaking, the yoking together of Austen and lesbianism is nothing new – a lesbian Emma Wood-house was first read by Edmund Wilson in *The New Yorker* in 1945, and most notably by Marvin Mudrick in 1952.[40] More specifically, Castle's essay follows more than a decade of feminist research on the so-called 'romantic friendship', notably Janet Todd's *Women's Friendship in Literature* and Lilian Faderman's *Surpassing the Love of Men*.[41]

However, the cover of the *LRB* bore the classic Janeite-baiting headline 'Was Jane Austen Gay?' (which it later admitted had nothing to do with Castle herself), and all hell was let loose. For several months, the *LRB*'s letters-page ran an ongoing correspondence, sometimes vitriolic, sometimes ingenious. Marianne Macdonald, an arts reporter with the *Independent* newspaper (who makes habitual reference to 'Mr Castle') writes, 'Terry Castle must have a gruesome imagination', and considers the piece to have been argued 'in what may be a typically masculine fashion'.[42] Amongst the many, many letters on the subject, Brian Southam finds Castle's argument 'meagre and curiously unconvincing', though in fairness admits that 'it has to be taken seriously'.[43] Claudia Johnson weighs in with a letter in which she 'hope[s] the public will forgive me for protracting the debate long enough, I hope, to clarify it', before commencing what is in effect a dry run of her piece in *The Cambridge Companion to Jane Austen*.[44] Nothing is clarified: Brian Southam, Keith Walker, Kathy O'Shaughnessy, Loraine Fletcher, Phil Edwards and others all write in refuting Johnson's letter. During all of this Terry Castle herself is a regular correspondent, understandably claiming that 'My comments have been grotesquely, indeed almost comically, distorted', while also making the following, important point:

> What is disconcerting about the press reaction to my review is that so many people, apparently, still consider the mere suggestion that someone like Austen might have had homosexual feelings such an appalling slur that any hope of a sensitive debate on the matter becomes impossible. It is neither a crime nor a sin to love – in whatever way one is able – a person of one's own sex.[45]

Of course, interest in Jane Austen was heightened at the time by the spate of television and film versions of her novels. *People* magazine nominated Austen as 'one of the most intriguing people of 1995';[46] 'Currently, it seems,' Martin Amis wrote in the *New Yorker* in January 1996, 'Jane Austen is hotter than Quentin Tarantino.'[47] (And, in the wake of the huge success of *Pulp Fiction* in 1995, Tarantino was then very hot indeed.) Austen, in fact, was one of the bestselling authors of the mid-1990s: *Pride and Prejudice* sold 177,000 copies in 1995 alone, obviously a direct consequence of the BBC production of that year.[48] 1996 saw the publication of the first of Stephanie Barron's intriguing series of 'Jane Austen mysteries', *Jane and the Unpleasantness at Scargrave Manor* (Stephanie Barron is a pseudonym of Francine Matthews, author of the series of 'Meredith Folger' mysteries). *Jane and the Unpleasantness at Scargrave Manor* was followed by *Jane and the Man of the Cloth* (1997), *Jane and the Wandering Eye* (1998), *Jane and the Genius of the Place* (1999), *Jane and the Stillroom Maid* (2000), *Jane and the Prisoner of Wool House* (2003), and *Jane and the Ghosts of Netley* (forthcoming 2004). This project is not as bizarre as it sounds. Barron rather cleverly sets her mysteries during Austen's own 'mystery years' resident in Bath, 1801–6, years from which only five letters survive (three to her brother Frank, on their father's death, in January 1805, and two to Cassandra in April 1805). In essence, Barron is employing the same tactic as the majority of Austen's biographers do with these missing years – inscribing a narrative on fundamentally blank time. As David Nokes, one of her most recent biographers, admits, 'The truth is that we know virtually nothing about the state of Jane Austen's emotions during her years in Bath.'[49] Nokes, whose biography is itself quasi-novelistic, does nevertheless supply a narrative for these years. Though unlikely, then, it is not strictly impossible that Austen was indeed solving mysteries during these years.

At the beginning of the twentieth century, Henry James wrote of the 'body of publishers, editors, illustrators, [and] producers of the pleasant twaddle of magazines…[who found] their "dear", our dear, everybody's dear Jane so infinitely to their material purpose'.[50] At the end of the century, and on into the beginning of the twenty-first, it seems, little has changed. Jane Austen continues to fascinate so many of us, and to fascinate us in such different ways. On this, at least, we can surely all agree.

Notes

INTRODUCTION

1. H. G. Wells, *Experiment in Autobiography* (New York: Macmillan, 1934), p. 528.

2. David Lodge, *Changing Places* (London and Harmondsworth: Penguin, 1975), p. 15.

3. *Ibid.*, p. 215.

4. Avrom Fleishman, *A Reading of Mansfield Park* (Baltimore and London: Johns Hopkins Press, 1967).

5. Lodge, *Changing Places*, p. 44.

6. Lodge, *Nice Work* (Harmondsworth: Penguin, 1989), p. 325.

7. Marilyn Butler, *Jane Austen and the War of Ideas* (Oxford: Oxford University Press, 1975, rpt. with a new Introduction, 1987). Claudia L. Johnson, *Jane Austen: Women, Politics and the Novel* (Chicago and London: University of Chicago Press, 1988).

8. Margaret Kirkham, *Jane Austen, Feminism and Fiction* (Brighton: Harvester, 1983); Alison G. Sulloway, *Jane Austen and the Province of Womanhood* (Philadelphia: University of Pennsylvania Press, 1989); Deborah Kaplan, *Jane Austen Among Women* (Baltimore: Johns Hopkins Press, 1992).

9. Mary Evans, *Jane Austen and the State* (London: Tavistock, 1987).

10. Claudia L. Johnson, 'Austen Cults and Cultures', in Edward Copeland and Juliet McMaster (eds), *The Cambridge Companion to Jane Austen* (Cambridge: Cambridge University Press, 1997), pp. 211–26; John Wiltshire, *Recreating Jane Austen* (Cambridge: Cambridge University Press, 2001); Roger Sales, *Jane Austen and Representations of Regency England* (London: Routledge, 1996); Linda Troost and Sayre Greenfield (eds), *Jane Austen in Hollywood* (Lexington: University of Kentucky Press, 1998); Deirdre Lynch (ed.), *Janeites: Austen's Disciples and Devotees* (Princeton, NJ: Princeton University Press, 2000).

11. Mikhail Bakhtin, *The Dialogic Imagination: Four Essays*, ed. Michael Holquist, trans. Caryl Emerson and Michael Holquist (Austin: University of Texas Press, 1981).

12. The classic version of this thesis is to be found in Ian Watt, *The Rise of the Novel: Studies in Defoe, Richardson and Fielding* (London: Hogarth Press, 1987, first pub. 1957). For an influential updating of what is effectively the same thesis, see Michael McKeon, *The Origins of the English Novel* (London: Hutchinson Radius, 1988). There are many feminist histories of the novel adopting similar chronologies: see, for example, Ruth Perry, *Women, Letters and the Novel* (New York: AMS Press, 1980); Jane Spencer, *The Rise of the Woman Novelist: From Aphra Behn to Jane Austen* (Oxford: Blackwell, 1986); Dale Spender, *Mothers of the Novel: 100 good women writers before Jane Austen* (London: Pandora, 1986). One major dissenting voice needs to be noted: Margaret Anne Doody's *The True Story of the Novel* (London: Harper Collins, 1997) traces a history of the novel which is effectively as old as the history of letters. Self-consciously at odds with critical orthodoxy, which is always a good thing, Doody's work nevertheless strikes me as a beautiful folly, elegant and full of wonderful things, but fundamentally wrong.

13. Watt, *Rise of the Novel*, p. 208.

14. Henry Fielding, *Joseph Andrews and Shamela*, ed. Arthur Humphreys (London: Dent, 1973), p. 47.

15. Fielding, *The History of Tom Jones*, ed. R. P. C. Mutter (Harmondsworth: Penguin, 1966), p. 436.

16. Peter Garside, James Raven and Rainer Schöwerling (eds), *The English Novel 1770–1829: A Bibliographical Survey of Prose Fiction Published in the British Isles*, 2 vols (Oxford: Oxford University Press, 2000), 1: 308.

17. *Ibid.*, 1: 18.

18. Maria Edgeworth, *Belinda*, ed. Kathryn Kirkpatrick (Oxford: Oxford University Press, 1994), p. 3; Fanny [Frances] Burney, *Camilla; or, A Picture of Youth*, ed. Edward A. Bloom and Lillian D. Bloom (Oxford: Oxford University Press, 1972), pp. 2, 4. For an account of the significance of *Camilla*'s being termed a 'work', see Joyce Hemlow, 'Fanny Burney and the Courtesy Books', *PMLA*, 65 (1950), 739–61.

19. Garside, Raven and Schöwerling, *The English Novel*, 1: 87–8.

20. Lawrence Stone, *The Family, Sex and Marriage in England 1500–1800* (Harmondsworth: Penguin, 1979), p. 156.

21. Garside, Raven and Schöwerling, *The English Novel*, 1: 111.

22. Edward Copeland, *Women Writing About Money: Women's Fiction in England, 1790–1820* (Cambridge: Cambridge University Press, 1995), p. 6.

23. Lee Erickson, *The Economy of Literary Form: English Literature and the Industrialization of Publishing 1800–1850* (Baltimore and London: Johns Hopkins University Press, 1996), p. 131.

24. *Ibid.*, 129.

25. Ian Littlewood (ed.), *Jane Austen: Critical Assessments*, 4 vols (Mountfield: Helm Information, 1998), 1: 288.

26. Garside, Raven and Schöwerling, *The English Novel*, 1: 39–56; 2: 63–76.

27. Littlewood, *Critical Assessments*, 1: 423.

28. John Sutherland, *Victorian Novelists and Publishers* (London: Athlone Press, 1976).

29. Erickson, *Economy*, pp. 126–7.

30. Barbara M. Benedict, 'Sensibility by the Numbers: Austen's Work as Regency Popular Fiction', in Deirdre Lynch (ed.), *Janeites: Austen's Disciples and Devotees* (Princeton, NJ: Princeton University Press, 2000), p. 82.

31. Littlewood, *Critical Assessments*, 1: 263.

32. Fanny [Frances] Burney, *Cecilia; or, Memoirs of an Heiress*, ed. Judy Simons (London: Virago, 1986), p. 908.

33. Charlotte Smith, *The Old Manor House*, ed. Anne Henry Ehrenpreis with a new Introduction by Judith Phillips Stanton (Oxford: Oxford University Press, 1989), p. 265.

34. Benedict, 'Sensibility', p. 73.

35. Garside, Raven and Schöwerling, *The English Novel*, 2: 59.

36. George Savile, Marquis of Halifax, from 'The Lady's New Year's Gift: or, Advice to a Daughter', in Vivien Jones (ed.), *Women in the Eighteenth Century: Constructions of Femininity* (London: Routledge, 1990), p. 18.

37. Harriet Guest, *Small Change: Women, Learning, Patriotism, 1750–1810* (Chicago and London: University of Chicago Press, 2000).

38. Stone, *The Family*, p. 32.

39. *Ibid.*, p. 213.

40. David Spring, 'Interpreters of Jane Austen's Social World: Literary Critics and Historians', in Janet Todd (ed.), *Jane Austen: New Perspectives* (New York and London: Holmes and Meier, 1983), pp. 53–72.

41. W. H. Auden, 'Letter to Lord Byron', in *Collected Poems* (London: Faber, 1976), p. 79.

42. It seems unlikely that Austen herself would have known, even subconsciously, the bawdy overtones of the name. The *OED* has the earliest use of 'Fanny' as a slang word for vagina as late as 1879. However, Alice Chandler, in her study of Austen's bawdry, maintains that

'Fanny' was also eighteenth-century slang: see Alice Chandler, ' "A Pair of Fine Eyes": Jane Austen's Treatment of Sex', *Studies in the Novel*, 7 (1975), 91–2.

43. Jill Heydt-Stevenson, ' "Slipping into the Ha-Ha": Bawdy Humor and Body Politics in Jane Austen's Novels', *Nineteenth-Century Literature*, 55: 3 (December 2000), 329.

44. Maria Edgeworth, *Belinda*, p. 7.

45. Copeland, *Women Writing About Money*, pp. 9, 35.

46. Nancy Armstrong, *Desire and Domestic Fiction: A Political History of the Novel* (Oxford University Press, 1987), p. 9.

47. *Ibid.*, pp. 19, 6–7.

48. *Ibid.*, p. 26.

49. Peter Laslett, *Family Life and Illicit Love in Earlier Generations* (Cambridge: Cambridge University Press, 1977), p. 213; Laslett, 'Age at Menarche in Europe since the Eighteenth Century', in Theodore K. Rabb and Robert I. Rotberg (eds), *The Family in History* (New York: Harper and Row, 1973). The figure of 18–20 is offered by Fay Weldon, *Letters to Alice, on first reading Jane Austen* (London: Coronet, 1984), p. 36, though no documentary evidence is given.

50. James Boswell, *Boswell's Life of Johnson*, 6 vols, ed. G. B. Hill, revised by L. H. Powell (Oxford: Clarendon Press, 1964), 5: 209.

51. Stone, *The Family*, p. 401.

52. *Ibid.*, pp. 40–2.

53. William Patrick Day, *In the Circles of Fear and Desire: A Study of Gothic Fantasy* (Chicago and London: University of Chicago Press, 1985), p. 80.

54. Diane Long Hoeveler, *Gothic Feminism: The Professionalization of Genders from Charlotte Smith to the Brontës* (Liverpool: Liverpool University Press, 1998).

55. Glenda A. Hudson, *Sibling Love and Incest in Jane Austen's Fiction* (Basingstoke: Macmillan – now Palgrave Macmillan, 1992, 2nd edn 1999), p. 2.

56. *Ibid*, pp. 6, 7.

57. For an opposing view to my own on this specific passage, see Kathleen Lundeen, 'A Modest Proposal? Paradise Found in Jane Austen's Betrothal Scenes', *RES*, 41 (1990), 65–75, who suggests that 'Had this scene even a whiff of romance about it, her emergence from fantasy to reality would have been suspect.'

58. D. A. Miller, *Narrative and its Discontents: Problems of Closure in the Traditional Novel* (Princeton, NJ: Princeton University Press, 1981), p. xi.

59. Raymond Williams, *The Long Revolution* (London: Hogarth Press, 1992), p. 87.

60. Northrop Frye, *Anatomy of Criticism: Four Essays* (Princeton, NJ: Princeton University Press, 1957), pp. 33–4.

61. M. H. Abrams, *A Glossary of Literary Terms*, third edn (New York: Rinehart and Winston, 1971), p. 91. Northrop Frye, quoted in Edward W. Copeland, 'Money in the Novels of Fanny Burney', *Studies in the Novel*, 8 (1977), 31.

62. Frank Rahill, *The World of Melodrama* (University Park: The Pennsylvania University Press, 1967), p. xvii; Copeland, 'Money in the Novels of Fanny Burney', p. 31.

63. Edgeworth, *Belinda*, p. 20.

64. *Ibid.*, pp. 477–8.

65. Emily Lawless, *Maria Edgeworth* (London: Macmillan, 1904), p. 99.

66. F. R. Leavis, *The Great Tradition* (Harmondsworth: Penguin, 1972), p. 9.

67. Winston S. Churchill, *The Second World War Volume 5: Closing the Ring* (New York: Houghton Mifflin, 1951), p. 425.

68. See Claudia L. Johnson, *Women, Politics and the Novel* (Chicago and London: University of Chicago Press, 1988), pp. 1–27, for an influential analysis of this.

69. John Barrell, *The Dark Side of the Landscape: The Rural Poor in English Painting 1730–1840* (Cambridge: Cambridge University Press, 1980), p. 5.

70. PP, p. 406.

71. Linda Colley, *Britons: Forging the Nation 1700–1837* (London: Vintage, 1996), p. 303.

72. C. W. Pasley, *Essay on the Military Policy and Institutions of the British Empire*, 4th edn (London: T. Egerton, 1813), p. 42.

73. Colley, *Britons*, p. 303

74. Katie Trumpener, *Bardic Nationalism: The Romantic Novel and the British Empire* (Princeton, NJ: Princeton University Press, 1997).

75. Fiona Stafford, *The Last of the Race: The Growth of a Myth from Milton to Darwin* (Oxford: Clarendon Press, 1994).

76. Norman Davies, *The Isles: A History* (Basingstoke: Macmillan – now Palgrave Macmillan, 1999).

77. Tom Nairn, *After Britain: New Labour and the Return of Scotland* (London: Granta, 2001), pp. 128, 154.

78. Richard Weight, *Patriots: National Identity in Britain 1940–2000* (London and Basingstoke: Pan Macmillan, 2002), pp. 707–8.

79. Davies, *The Isles*, p. 831.

80. John Wiltshire, *Jane Austen and the Body: The Picture of Health* (Cambridge: Cambridge University Press, 1992); Hudson, *Sibling Love and Incest*; Edward Neill, *The Politics of Jane Austen* (Basingtoke: Macmillan – now Palgrave Macmillan, 1999); Barbara K. Seeber, *General Consent in Jane Austen: A Study in Dialogism* (Montreal: McGill-Queen's University Press, 2000).

81. Roland Barthes, 'The Death of the Author', in David Lodge (ed.), *Modern Criticism and Theory: A Reader* (London: Longman, 1988).

82. Michel Foucault, 'What is an Author?', in Lodge, *ibid.*, p. 209.

83. Terry Eagleton, *Sweet Violence: The Idea of the Tragic* (Oxford: Blackwell, 2003), pp. x–xi.

CHAPTER 1: *NORTHANGER ABBEY*

1. See David Nokes, *Jane Austen: A Life* (London: Fourth Estate, 1997), p. 1.

2. William Austen-Leigh, *Jane Austen: A Family Record*, revised and enlarged by Deirdre Le Faye (London: British Library, 1989), p. 243.

3. Henry Austen, 'Biographical Notice of the Author', in J. E. Austen-Leigh *et al.*, *A Memoir of Jane Austen and Other Family Recollections*, ed. Kathryn Sutherland (Oxford: Oxford University Press, 2002), p. 141.

4. Chapman, however, continues 'But we may suspect that it has not materially affected the impression we should have received from a richer survival. ...It would not have suited Jane Austen's sense of propriety to charge her sister sixpence (or thereabouts) for opinions on religion or politics, on life or letters, which were known already, or would keep. But news would not wait, and news must always give satisfaction' (L, p. ix). This account of Chapman's seems, if anything, to *compound* the accusations of triviality.

5. Roger Sales, *Jane Austen and Representations of Regency England* (London: Routledge, 1996), p. 87.

6. William Shakespeare, *Hamlet*, ed. Harold Jenkins (London and New York: Methuen, 1982), III:ii: 115–19.

7. Jill Heydt-Stevenson, ' "Slipping into the Ha-Ha": Bawdy Humor and Body Politics in Jane Austen's Novels', *Nineteenth-Century Literature*, 55:3 (December 2000), 325.

8. Margaret Anne Doody, 'Jane Austen's Reading', in J. David Grey (ed.), *The Jane Austen Handbook* (London: Athlone Press, 1986), p. 349.

9. See James B. Twitchell, *Dreadful Pleasures: An Anatomy of Modern Horror* (Oxford: Oxford University Press, 1985), p. 10.

10. R. T. Jones, '*Sir Charles Grandison*: "A Gauntlet Thrown Out" ', in Valerie Grosvenor Myer (ed.), *Samuel Richardson: Passion and Prudence* (London: Vision, 1986), pp. 135–44.

11. J. E. Austen-Leigh, *A Memoir of Jane Austen*, p. 71.

12. *Jane Austen's 'Sir Charles Grandison'*, transcribed and ed. Brian Southam, Foreword by Lord David Cecil (Oxford: Clarendon Press, 1980), p. 39.

13. Linda Colley, *Britons: Forging the Nation 1707–1837* (London: Vintage, 1996), p. 2.

14. Marjorie Garber, *Vested Interests: Cross-Dressing and Cultural Anxiety* (London and New York: Routledge, 1992), p. 27.

15. *Ibid.*, p. 26.

16. Harriet Guest, *Small Change: Women, Learning, Patriotism, 1750–1810* (Chicago and London: University of Chicago Press, 2000), pp. 40, 37.

17. Samuel Richardson, *The History of Sir Charles Grandison*, ed. Jocelyn Harris (Oxford: Oxford University Press, 1986), 3: 247.

18. Richardson, *The History of Sir Charles Grandison; In a Series of Letters*, 7 vols (London: J. Nunn *et al.*, 1820) 7:Index (under the heading 'BARNEVELT, Miss: there is no pagination for the index).

19. See Fidelis Morgan, *The Well-Known Trouble-Maker: A Life of Charlotte Charke* (London: Faber 1988). Morgan's biography reproduces Charke's *Narrative* in full.

20. See Pat Rogers, 'The Breeches Part', in Paul-Gabriel Boucé (ed.), *Sexuality in eighteenth-century Britain* (Manchester: Manchester University Press, 1982), pp. 244–58.

21. Roger Fiske, *English Theatre Music in the Eighteenth Century* (Oxford: Oxford University Press, 1973), pp. 402–3.

22. Garber, *Vested Interests*, pp. 259–65.

23. Colley, *Britons*, p. 257.

24. Elizabeth Mavor, *The Ladies of Llangollen* (Harmondsworth: Penguin, 1973), pp. 73–4.

25. Edmund Burke, *Reflections on the Revolution in France*, ed. Conor Cruise O'Brien (Harmondsworth: Penguin, 1968), p. 164.

26. John Barrell, *Imagining the King's Death: Figurative Treason, Fantasies of Regicide 1793–1796* (Oxford: Oxford University Press, 2000), p. 16.

27. Claudia L. Johnson, *Equivocal Beings: Politics, Gender, and Sentimentality in the 1790s* (Chicago and London: University of Chicago Press, 1995), pp. 1–19. For a broader discussion of the concept of 'effeminacy' in British moral and political discourse across the eighteenth century, see G. J. Barker-Benfield, *The Culture of Sensibility: Sex and Society in Eighteenth-Century Britain* (Chicago and London: University of Chicago Press, 1992), pp. 104–53.

28. Johnson, *Equivocal Beings*, pp. 191–203.

29. Claudia L. Johnson, *Jane Austen: Women, Politics and the Novel* (Chicago and London: University of Chicago Press, 1988), p. 7.

30. Mary Wollstonecraft, *A Vindication of the Rights of Woman*, ed. Miriam Brody (Harmondsworth: Penguin, 1975), p. 7.

31. *Ibid.* For a detailed account of figurings of Wollstonecraft as an 'Amazon', which closes with a reading of *Belinda*, see Barker-Benfield, *Culture of Sensibility*, pp. 368–94.

32. Wollstonecraft, *Vindication*, p. 80.

33. Mary Wollstonecraft and William Godwin, '*A Short Residence in Sweden*' and '*Memoirs of the Author of "The Rights of Woman"*', ed. Richard Holmes (Harmondsworth: Penguin, 1987), p. 232.

34. Margaret Kirkham, *Jane Austen, Feminism and Fiction* (Brighton: Harvester, 1983), p. 48. Kirkham also discusses the indirect effect of this scandal on Austen's writing after this year, when it became commensurately more difficult to articulate even a modest radicalism.

35. Johnson, *Women, Politics and the Novel*, p. 16.

36. Richard Polwhele, 'The Unsex'd Females', in Vivien Jones (ed.), *Women in the Eighteenth Century: Constructions of Femininity* (London and New York: Routledge, 1991), pp. 186–91.

37. P, pp. 290–1. My emphasis.

38. Samuel Taylor Coleridge, *Letters of Samuel Taylor Coleridge*, ed. Ernest Hartley Coleridge (London: Heinemann, 1895), 1: 323.

39. Maria Edgeworth, *Belinda*, ed. Kathryn J. Kirkpatrick (Oxford: Oxford University Press, 1994), pp. 74–5.

40. *Ibid.*, p. 47.

41. *Ibid.*, pp. 230–1.

42. Fanny [Frances] Burney, *Camilla; or, A Picture of Youth*, ed. Edward A. Bloom and Lillian D. Bloom (Oxford: Oxford University Press, 1972), p. 18.

43. [Frances Burney], *Memoirs of Doctor Burney, arranged from his own manuscripts, from family papers, and from personal recollections. By his Daughter, Madame D'Arblay*, 3 vols (London: Edward Moxon, 1832), 3: 234.

44. John Wiltshire, *Jane Austen and the Body: 'The picture of health'* (Cambridge: Cambridge University Press, 1992), pp. 62–109.

45. John Wiltshire, *Recreating Jane Austen* (Cambridge: Cambridge University Press, 2001), p. 19.

46. P, pp. 306–12. Chapman cites Harvey Eagleson as his own source for this.

47. Ann Radcliffe, *The Romance of the Forest*, ed. Chloe Chard (Oxford: Oxford University Press, 1986), pp. 109–10.

48. Sigmund Freud, *Case Histories II: The 'Rat Man', Schreber, The 'Wolf Man', A case of Female Homosexuality*, The Penguin Freud Library, vol. 9, trans. James Strachey *et al.*, ed. Angela Richards (Harmondsworth: Penguin, 1979), p. 315.

49. Gaston Bachelard, *The Poetics of Space*, trans. Maria Jolas (New York: Orion, 1964), p. 85. Bachelard is also used to discuss *Northanger Abbey*, though to rather different ends, in Tony Tanner, *Jane Austen* (Basingstoke: Macmillan – now Palgrave Macmillan, 1986), p. 49.

50. I first heard this question asked by Jim S. Borck in a paper entitled 'Austen's Heroes and Heroines Unclothed', SCSECS Conference, Baton Rouge, Louisiana, 9–12 March 2000.

CHAPTER 2: *SENSE AND SENSIBILITY*

1. Tony Tanner, *Jane Austen* (Basingstoke: Macmillan – now Palgrave Macmillan, 1986), p. 75.

2. Barbara K. Seeber, *General Consent in Jane Austen: A Study in Dialogism* (Montreal: McGill-Queen's University Press, 2000), pp. 15, 68.

3. This is the title of Tanner's chapter on *Sense and Sensibility*, pp. 75–102.

4. For the most comprehensive discussion of the novel's 'forced' resolution, see John Odmark, *An Understanding of Jane Austen's Novels* (Oxford: Blackwell, 1981), pp. 7–10, 92–100.

5. A. Walton Litz, *Jane Austen: A Study of Her Artistic Development* (London: Chatto and Windus, 1965), p. 72.

6. D. W. Harding, 'Character and Caricature in Jane Austen', in B. C. Southam (ed.), *Critical Essays on Jane Austen* (London: Routledge and Kegan Paul, 1968), p. 102.

7. Marvin Mudrick, *Jane Austen: Irony as Defense and Discovery* (Princeton, NJ: Princeton University Press, 1952), p. 93; Andrew H. Wright, *Jane Austen's Novels: A Study in Structure* (London: Chatto and Windus, 1961), p. 95.

8. Patricia Meyer Spacks, 'The Difference it Makes', in Elizabeth Langland and Walter Grove (eds), *A Feminist Perspective on the Academy: the difference it makes* (Chicago and London: University of Chicago Press, 1981), p. 20; Eve Kosofsky Sedgwick, 'Jane Austen and the Masturbating Girl', *Critical Inquiry*, 17 (1991), 833. One of the few dissenting voices is that of Glenda A. Hudson, who believes the resolution to be 'psychologically and morally appropriate': Hudson, *Sibling Love and Incest in Jane Austen's Fiction* (Basingstoke: Macmillan – now Palgrave Macmillan, 1992), p. 81.

9. Tanner, *Jane Austen*, pp. 99–100.

10. Louis Menand, 'What Jane Austen Doesn't Tell Us', *New York Review of Books*, 1 February 1996, 13–15.

11. Seeber, *General Consent*, p. 30.

12. Claire Tomalin, *Jane Austen: A Life*, revised edn (Harmondsworth: Penguin, 2000), p. 222.

13. Between 1815 and 1822, Montolieu produced translations of all of Austen's published novels except *Northanger Abbey*. For a fascinating account of Montolieu and her translations of Austen, on which I draw here, see Valérie Cossy, 'Texts Misrepresented: Jane Austen in France and Isabelle de Montolieu', *The European English Messenger,* 6/2 (Autumn 1997), 45–7.

14. Garside, Raven and Schöwerling, *The English Novel 1770–1829*, I: 235–6.

15. Edgeworth, *Belinda*, p. 3.

16. Cheryl L. Nixon, 'Balancing the Courtship Hero: Masculine Emotional Display in Film Adaptations of Austen's Novels', in Linda Troost and Sayre Greenfield (eds), *Jane Austen in Hollywood* (Lexington: University of Kentucky Press, 1998), pp. 39–41.

17. Cossy, 'Texts Misrepresented', p. 47.

18. B. C. Southam, *Jane Austen's Literary Manuscripts* (Oxford: Clarendon Press, 1964), pp. 55–7.

19. Marilyn Butler, *Jane Austen and the War of Ideas* (Oxford: Oxford University Press, 1975), pp. 182–3.

20. Eliza Fenwick, *Secresy; or, The Ruin on the Rock*, ed. Janet Todd (London: Pandora, 1989), pp. 15, 223.

21. Maria Edgeworth, 'Letters of Julia and Caroline', in *Letters for Literary Ladies*, ed. Claire Connolly (London: Dent, 1993), pp. 40–1.

22. Roland Barthes, *Writing Degree Zero and Elements of Semiology*, trans. Annette Levers and Colin Smith (Boston: Beacon, 1970), pp. 67–8.

23. See Wayne C. Booth, *The Rhetoric of Fiction*, 2nd edn (Harmondsworth: Penguin, 1983); Mikhail Bakhtin, *The Dialogic Imagination: Four Essays*, ed. and trans Michael Holquist and Caryl Emerson (Austin and London: University of Texas Press, 1981), and *Problems of Dostoevsky's Poetics*, trans. Caryl Emerson (Manchester: Manchester University Press, 1984).

24. Edward S. Hermann and Noam Chomsky, *Manufacturing Consent: The Political Economy of the Mass Media* (London: Vintage, 1994). For accounts of the creation of consensus in the realist novel, see, for example, Elizabeth Deeds Ermarth, *Realism and Consensus in the English Novel: Time, Space and Narrative*, 2nd edn (Edinburgh: Edinburgh University Press, 1998); Nicola J. Watson, *Revolution and the Form of the British Novel 1790–1825:Intercepted Letters, Interrupted Seductions* (Oxford: Clarendon Press, 1994); Seeber, *General Consent in Jane Austen*.

25. See Watson, *Revolution*, for a powerful articulation of this argument.

26. Gilbert Ryle, 'Jane Austen and the Moralists', in Southam (ed.), *Critical Essays on Jane Austen*, pp. 108–9. For more versions of this argument, see Q. D. Leavis, '*Sense and Sensibility*', in *Collected Essays, Volume 1: The Englishness of the English Novel*, ed. G. Singh (Cambridge: Cambridge University Press, 1983), pp. 147–60; Norman Sherry, *Jane Austen* (London: Evans Brothers, 1966), p. 56; Marilyn Butler, *Jane Austen and the War of Ideas*, p. 183; and, most powerfully, Litz, *Jane Austen*, pp. 73, 112.

27. David Nokes, *Jane Austen: A Life* (London: Fourth Estate, 1997), p. 31.

28. Janet Todd, *Sensibility: An Introduction* (London and New York: Methuen, 1986), p. 129.

29. Fanny [Frances] Burney, *Cecilia; or, Memoirs of an Heiress* (London: Virago, 1986), pp. 272, 591.

30. D. Grant Campbell, 'Fashionable Suicide: Conspicuous Consumption and the Collapse of Credit in Frances Burney's *Cecilia*', *Studies in Eighteenth-Century Culture*, 20 (1990), 139–40.

31. G. J. Barker-Benfield, *The Culture of Sensibility: Sex and Society in Eighteenth-Century Britain* (Chicago and London: Chicago University Press, 1992), pp. xvii, 220.

32. *Ibid.*, p. 224.

33. *Ibid.*, p. 239.

34. Mudrick, *Jane Austen: Irony*, p. 74.

35. David Lodge, *The Language of Fiction* (London: Routledge and Kegan Paul, 1966), p. 94.

36. Jan S. Fergus, *Jane Austen and the Didactic Novel: 'Northanger Abbey', 'Sense and Sensibility', and 'Pride and Prejudice'* (Basingstoke: Macmillan – now Palgrave Macmillan, 1983), p. 42.

37. Claudia L. Johnson, *Jane Austen: Women, Politics and the Novel* (Chicago and London: University of Chicago Press, 1988), p. 55.

38. Butler, *War of Ideas*, p. 186.

39. Andrew Wilton, *The Swagger Portrait: Grand Manner Portraiture in Britain from Van Dyck to Augustus John 1630–1930* (London: Tate Gallery, 1992), p. 17.

40. Amy J. Pawl, ' "And What Other Name May I Claim?" Names and Their Owners in Frances Burney's *Evelina*', *Eighteenth-Century Fiction*, 3 (1991), 283–99.

41. Frances Burney, *Evelina*, ed. Stewart J. Cooke (New York: Norton, 1998), p. 317

42. *Ibid.*, p. 319.

43. *Ibid*. Emphasis mine.

44. *Ibid.*

45. Mary Shelley, 'Mathilda', in *The Mary Shelley Reader*, ed. Betty T. Bennett and Charles E. Robinson (Oxford: Oxford University Press, 1990), p. 179.

46. *Ibid.*, pp. 208, 210.

47. *Ibid.*, p. 244.

48. Mary Poovey, *The Proper Lady and the Woman Writer: Ideology as Style in the Works of Mary Wollstonecraft, Mary Shelley, and Jane Austen* (Chicago and London: University of Chicago Press, 1984), p. 192.

49. Susan Griffin, *Pornography and Silence* (London: The Women's Press, 1981), pp. 20–1.

50. Toril Moi, 'Feminist Literary Criticism', in Ann Jefferson and David Rovey (eds), *Modern Literary Theory: A Comparative Introduction* (London: Batsford, 1986), p. 213.

51. Julia Kristeva, 'On Chinese Women', in *The Kristeva Reader*, ed. Toril Moi (Oxford: Blackwell, 1986), pp. 141, 145–6.

52. Ernest Jones, *On The Nightmare* (London: Hogarth Press/Institute of Psychoanalysis, 1949), p. 125.

53. Matthew Lewis, *The Monk*, ed. Howard Anderson (Oxford: Oxford University Press, 1973), p. 385.

54. Susan Staves, 'British Seduced Maidens', *Eighteenth-Century Studies*, 14 (1980–1), 114. For a full-length account of this subject, see R. F. Brissenden, *Virtue in Distress: Studies in the Novel of Sentiment from Richardson to Sade* (Basingstoke: Macmillan, 1974).

55. Mary Wollstonecraft, *Mary and the Wrongs of Women*, ed. Gary Kelly (Oxford: Oxford University Press, 1976), pp. 157–8.

56. Claudia L. Johnson, 'A "Sweet Face as White as Death": Jane Austen and the Politics of Female Sensibility', *Novel*, 22 (1989), 162.

57. Mary Delariviere Manley, *The New Atalantis*, quoted in Jane Spencer, *The Rise of the Woman Novelist: From Aphra Behn to Jane Austen* (Oxford: Blackwell, 1986), p. 114.

58. See Staves, 'British Seduced Maidens', 113, for how radical writers attacked the conventions of sentimental fiction in such ways. Johnson suggests that Brandon's 'story about the poor Eliza reads like an embedded radical novel of the 1790s, arraigning the callousness of tyrannical patriarchs whose principal object in life is to repair the waning fortunes of dissipated estates': 'A "Sweet Face as White as Death"', p. 168.

59. Johnson, 'A "Sweet Face as White as Death"', p. 168.

60. Butler, *War of Ideas*, p. 189.

61. Jane West, *A Gossip's Story, and a Legendary Tale* (London: T. N. Longman, 1798), 2 vols [3rd edn], 1: 205.

62. *Ibid.*, 2: 207, 208.

63. *Ibid.*, 2: 212–13.

64. *Ibid.*, 2: 220–1.

65. 'Jane Austen adopted the stories of Eliza Brandon and her daughter Eliza Williams – the surname probably came from the runaway daughter in *Grandison* – with very little change from *Clarissa*.' Jocelyn Harris, *Jane Austen's Art of Memory* (Cambridge University Press, 1989), p. 58. Harris furthermore notes that Brandon is the probable surname of *Pamela*'s Mr B. (he lives in Brandon Hall), who has himself a mysterious illegitimate daughter. Harris uses these patterns of influence to suggest that Marianne has been 'seduced by proxy' (p. 59).

66. Fenwick, *Secresy*, p. 100.

67. *Ibid.*, p. 116.

68. *Ibid.*, p. 188.

69. *Ibid.*, pp. 173, 283.

70. Edgeworth, 'Julia and Caroline', pp. 47, 59, 62.

CHAPTER 3: *PRIDE AND PREJUDICE*

1. R. W. Chapman (PP, p. 416) identifies Meryton as occupying the same geographical space as Hemel Hempstead, which must be nice for the good people of that town.

2. Johnson, *Women, Politics and the Novel*, p. 93.

3. For a lengthy discussion of this subject, see Barker-Benfield, *The Culture of Sensibility*, pp. 1–36.

4. Raymond Williams, *The Country and the City* (London: Hogarth Press, 1993).

5. Edmund Burke, *Reflections on the Revolution in France*, ed. Conor Cruise O'Brien (Harmondsworth: Penguin, 1968), p. 119.

6. Edward Malins, *English Landscaping and Literature 1660–1840* (London: Oxford University Press, 1966), p. 110.

7. Samuel Richardson, *The History of Sir Charles Grandison*, ed. Jocelyn Harris (Oxford: Oxford University Press, 1986), 7:272–3.

8. John Dixon Hunt and Peter Willis (eds), *The Genius of the Place: The English Landscape Garden 1620–1820* (Cambridge, MA, and London: MIT Press, 2000), p. 372. I am indebted to my former student Jean O'Mahony for the phrase 'pornography of estate management' as a description of Pemberley – it seems to me precisely right (which is why I stole it).

9. Alistair M. Duckworth, *The Improvement of the Estate: A Study of Jane Austen's Novels* (Baltimore and London: Johns Hopkins Press, 1971), p. 123.

10. Southam, *Jane Austen's Literary Manuscripts*, p. 62.

11. Most notably in the classic account by Reuben A. Brower, 'Light, Bright and Sparkling: Irony and Fiction in *Pride and Prejudice*', in Ian Watt (ed.), *Jane Austen: A Collection of Critical Essays*, Twentieth-century Views series (Englewood Cliffs, NJ: Prentice-Hall, 1963), pp. 62–75. See also Sandra M. Gilbert and Susan Gubar, *The Madwoman in the Attic: The Woman Writer and the Nineteenth-century Literary Imagination* (New Haven, CT: Yale University Press, 1979), p. 154; Hudson, *Sibling Love and Incest*, p. 68.

12. Johnson, *Women, Politics and the Novel*, p. 89.

13. *Ibid.*, p. 77.

14. Judith Lowder Newton, *Women, Power and Subversion: Social Strategies in British Fiction, 1770–1860* (London and New York: Methuen, 1985), p. 62. Similarly, Johnson, *Women, Politics and the Novel*, p. 76, considers the novel 'almost shamelessly wish-fulfilling'.

15. Butler, *War of Ideas*, p. 214.

16. Mary Wollstonecraft, *A Vindication of the Rights of Woman*, ed. Miriam Brody (Harmondsworth: Penguin, 1975), pp. 79, 83.

17. Johnson, *Women, Politics and the Novel*, p. 73; Butler, *War of Ideas*, p. 218.

18. *Gentleman's Magazine*, 43 (1773), 603. See Staves, 'British Seduced Maidens', 109, for an account of this.

19. Lilian S. Robinson, 'Why Marry Mr Collins?', in *Sex, Class and Culture* (London and New York: Methuen, 1986), p. 178.

20. *Ibid.*, p. 178.

21. Dorothy Van Ghent, *The English Novel: Form and Function* (New York: Harper and Row, 1953, rpt 1961), p. 103.

22. Phil Silvers, with Robert Saffron, *The Man Who Was Bilko* (London and New York: W. H. Allen, 1974), pp. 85–6.

23. Alice Chandler, ' "A Pair of Fine Eyes": Jane Austen's Treatment of Sex', *Studies in the Novel*, 7 (1975), 103n12.

24. Brower, 'Light, Bright and Sparkling', p. 71.

25. Stuart M. Tave, *Some Words of Jane Austen* (Chicago and London: University of Chicago Press, 1973), pp. 117–20.

CHAPTER 4: *MANSFIELD PARK*

1. Margaret Kirkham, for example, has glossed the passage as 'Jane Austen...in a letter of 1813, speaks of having been in love with Thomas Clarkson's writings', which is true, but selective. Kirkham, *Jane Austen, Feminism and Fiction* (Brighton: Harvester, 1983), p. 117. One of the very few critics to discuss Pasley at all, albeit that it is very brief, is Roger Sales, *Jane Austen and Representations of Regency England* (London: Routledge, 1996), p. 113.

2. C. W. Pasley, *Essay on the Military Policy and Institutions of the British Empire*, 4th edn (London: T. Egerton, 1813), p. 3.

3. *Ibid.*, p. 11.

4. Raymond Williams, *The Country and the City*, pp. 108–19.

5. Tony Tanner, *Jane Austen* (Basingstoke and London: Macmillan – now Palgrave Macmillan, 1986), pp. 143–4.

6. See, for example, Kingsley Amis, 'What Became of Jane Austen?' in Ian Watt (ed.), *Jane Austen: A Collection of Critical Essays* (Englewood

Cliffs, NJ: Prentice-Hall, 1963), pp. 141–4; Marilyn Butler, *Jane Austen and the War of Ideas*, p. 249; Joseph M. Duffy, Jr, 'Moral Integrity and Moral Anarchy in *Mansfield Park*', *ELH*, 23 (1956), 71–91. Naturally, these opinions tend to belong to an earlier, evaluative phase in literary studies. While Amis objects to the novel on moral grounds, particularly with regard to its vindication of Fanny and Edmund, both of whom (especially Fanny) he considers unacceptable, Butler argues that the novel suffers from Austen's 'change of strategy in the middle', from 'a skilful dramatization of the conservative case' to 'a bold effort at sympathetic "inward" presentation of the central character', which leads however to 'artistic failure'. Duffy's criticisms go deeper, accusing Austen of 'a tactless display of sympathy and prejudice towards her characters' (p. 71); of allowing her novelistic structure to 'disintegrate' and end 'in ruins' (p. 71); of having 'insufficient courage in her heroine to permit her to manage her own affairs' (p. 90); and of being 'unable to objectify the problems she raised or... unable to deal candidly with their implications' (p. 90). Duffy concludes: 'Viewed from the standpoint of its defects, the novel reads as though an eighteenth-century deist – a reformed humorist – were telling a moralistic fairy tale into which had strayed with shattering effect a pair of Victorian worldlings' (p. 91).

7. See, for example, Butler, *War of Ideas*, pp. 219–49; Tanner, *Jane Austen*, pp. 142–75.

8. Claudia L. Johnson, *Jane Austen: Women, Politics and the Novel*, p. 96. See also, for example, Lloyd W. Brown, 'The Comic Conclusions of Jane Austen's Novels', *PMLA*, 84 (2) (1969), 1582–7; Margaret Kirkham, *Feminism and Fiction*, pp. 101–6; Johanna M. Smith, '"My only sister now": Incest in *Mansfield Park*', *Studies in the Novel*, 18 (1) (1987), 1–15. This rather broad grouping requires clarification. Brown believes that '*Mansfield Park*... is ironic rather than moralistic' (p. 1582), and that it contains 'a parody of a happy ending' (p. 1585). Kirkham argues that Austen's undermining of the 'saintly' heroine constitutes a part of 'her most ambitious and radical criticism of contemporary prejudice in society and literature' (p. 119). Smith, again attending to the novel's ending, considers it 'a dismal failure', but one which Austen 'intended' (p. 1).

9. Mary Evans, *Jane Austen and the State* (London and New York: Tavistock, 1987), p. 30. Writing later, however, Evans modifies her suggestion: 'In one sense we can read *Mansfield Park* as an essay in the failings of unthinking patriarchy, in another we can read it as a discussion of how to be properly patriarchal'. Evans, 'Henry Crawford and the "Sphere of Love" in *Mansfield Park*', in Nigel Wood (ed.), *Mansfield Park* (Buckingham: Open University Press, 1993), pp. 44–5.

10. Lionel Trilling, '*Mansfield Park*', in Watt, *Jane Austen*, p. 125.

11. See, for example, Kirkham, *Feminism and Fiction*, pp. 101–20; Brean S. Hammond, 'The Political Unconscious in *Mansfield Park*', in Wood, *Mansfield Park*, pp. 58–87.

12. Tanner, *Jane Austen*, p. 143.

13. Amis, 'What Became of Jane Austen?', p. 144.

14. R. S. Neale, 'Zapp Zapped: Property and Alienation in Mansfield Park', in *Writing Marxist History: British Society, Economy and Culture Since 1700* (Oxford: Blackwell, 1985), p. 103.

15. For the fullest reading of Fanny's tendency toward stasis, see Tanner, *Jane Austen*, pp. 142–75.

16. Barbara Bail Collins, 'Jane Austen's Victorian Novel', *Nineteenth-Century Fiction*, 4 (1949–50), 175–85.

17. Trilling, '*Mansfield Park*', p. 129; Butler, *War of Ideas*, p. 221.

18. Kirkham, *Feminism and Fiction*, p. 102.

19. Hammond, 'The Political Unconscious', p. 82.

20. See the chapter of that name in Michael Williams, *Jane Austen: Six Novels and Their Methods* (Basingstoke: Macmillan – now Palgrave Macmillan, 1986), pp. 81–116.

21. Patricia Meyer Spacks, 'Dynamics of Fear: Fanny Burney', in Leopold Damrosch (ed.), *Modern Essays in Eighteenth-century Literature* (Oxford: Oxford University Press, 1988), pp. 455–88.

22. Mary Poovey, *The Proper Lady and the Woman Writer: Ideology as Style in the Works of Mary Wollstonecraft, Mary Shelley, and Jane Austen* (Chicago and London: University of Chicago Press, 1984): see especially pp. 212–18 for her account of Fanny. For similar reading, see Butler, *War of Ideas*, 212–49; Johnson, *Women, Politics and the Novel*, pp. 95–6.

23. Trilling, '*Mansfield Park*'.

24. Oliver MacDonagh, *Jane Austen: Real and Imagined Worlds* (New Haven and London: Yale University Press, 1991), p. 11. MacDonagh qualifies this statement 'in terms of Jane Austen's narrow range'.

25. Charles E. Edge, '*Mansfield Park* and Ordination', *Nineteenth-Century Fiction*, 16 (1961–2), 269–74, argues that 'a complete change of subject – ordination' is misleading: 'ordination begins a new sentence, and does not refer to *Mansfield Park*'. A similar point is made by Hugh Brogan, *TLS*, 19 December 1968, p. 1440. This prompted a flurry of letters in the *TLS* from some of the most distinguished names in Austen studies, agreeing or disagreeing with Brogan, from B. C. Southam (2 January 1969, p. 22), Margaret Kirkham (9 January 1969, p. 39), Denis Donoghue (16 January 1969, p. 62)

and Mary Lascelles (30 January 1969, p. 111). For what is perhaps the definitive word on this, see Park Honan, 'Richardson's Influence on Jane Austen', in Valerie Grosvenor Myer (ed.), *Samuel Richardson: Passion and Prudence* (London: Vision, 1986), pp. 165–77. Honan notes that, in his edition of the *Letters*, R. W. Chapman 'adds a gratuitous "&" and changes her capitals and punctuation to pervert [Austen's] meaning', and that 'She only meant to thank her sister Cassandra for asking about ordination while at their brother James's rectory' (p. 169).

26. MacDonagh, *Real and Imagined Worlds*, p. 15.

27. Tanner, *Jane Austen*, p. 170.

28. MacDonagh, *Real and Imagined Worlds*, p. 16.

29. For an account of this, see Elisabeth Jay, *The Evangelical and Oxford Movements* (Cambridge: Cambridge University Press, 1983).

30. MacDonagh, *Real and Imagined Worlds*, p. 3.

31. Henry Austen, 'Memoir of Miss Austen', in Austen-Leigh *et al.*, *A Memoir of Jane Austen and Other Family Recollections*, pp. 141, 153–4. For a recent study that discusses Austen's religion with great (not to say excruciating) seriousness, see Michael Giffin, *Jane Austen and Religion: Salvation and Society in Georgian England* (Basingstoke: Palgrave Macmillan, 2002).

32. Peter Garside and Elizabeth McDonald, 'Evangelicalism and *Mansfield Park*', *Trivium*, 10 (1975), 39. For more accounts of Evangelicalism's influence on the novel, see, for example, Q. D. Leavis, 'A Critical Theory of Jane Austen's Writings', in *Collected Essays. Volume 1: The Englishness of the English Novel*, ed. G. Singh (Cambridge: Cambridge University Press, 1983); Avrom Fleishman, *A Reading of 'Mansfield Park*', pp. 119–22; Williams, *The Country and the City*, pp. 92–6; MacDonagh, *Real and Imagined Worlds*, p. 14. As Garside and McDonald note, Methodism and Evangelicalism, in spite of their doctrinal differences (the Evangelicals did not dissent from the Church of England), were frequently yoked together, with accusations of Methodism often used as a stick to beat the Evangelicals. They quote Lord Cochrane's opinion of Admiral Gambier, patron of both Charles and Henry Austen, as a 'canting and hypocritical Methodist', noting that Cochrane here is 'aristocratically blurring the definition between Methodist and Evangelical' (p. 36).

33. Fleishman, *A Reading*, p. 21.

34. See Linda Colley, *Britons*, pp. 338–84.

35. George Eliot, *Middlemarch*, ed. David Carroll (Oxford: Oxford University Press, 1986), p. 417.

36. Clarence L. Branton, 'The Ordinations in Jane Austen's Novels', *Nineteenth-Century Fiction*, 10 (1955–56), 159–65. MacDonagh, *Real and Imagined Worlds*, also queries the method of Edmund's ordination (p. 17).

37. Branton, 'The Ordinations', p. 157.

38. See, for example, Fleishman, *A Reading*, pp. 20–1; MacDonagh, *Real and Imagined Worlds*, p. 18; Hammond, 'The Political Unconscious', p. 86.

39. Lennard J. Davis, *Resisting Novels: Ideology and Fiction* (London: Methuen, 1987), p. 225. For a more historically specific analysis with a similar premise, though written from a formalist perspective, see Robert Kiely, *The Romantic Novel in England* (Cambridge, MA: Harvard University Press, 1972).

40. Neale, 'Zapp Zapped', p. 94.

41. David Lodge, *Language of Fiction* (London: Routledge and Kegan Paul, 1966), pp. 99–101.

42. Garside and McDonald, 'Evangelicalism', pp. 44–5.

43. Fleishman, *A Reading*, p. 45.

44. Lodge, *Language of Fiction*, p. 104.

45. C. S. Lewis, 'A Note on Jane Austen', in Watt, *Jane Austen*, p. 30; David Monaghan, 'Jane Austen and the Position of Women', in Monaghan (ed.), *Jane Austen in a Social Context* (Basingstoke: Macmillan – now Palgrave Macmillan, 1981), p. 109; MacDonagh, *Real and Imagined Worlds*, p. 7.

46. The novel's account of incest has occupied the attention of several critics. The fullest account is in Hudson, *Sibling Love and Incest*, pp. 35–50 and *passim*, but see also R. F. Brissenden, '*Mansfield Park*: Freedom and the Family', in John Halperin (ed.), *Jane Austen: Bicentenary Essays* (Cambridge: Cambridge University Press, 1975), pp. 156–71; Johanna M. Smith, ' "My only sister now": Incest in *Mansfield Park*', *Studies in the Novel*, 18:1 (1987), 1–15; Mary Evans, 'Henry Crawford and the "Sphere of Love" in *Mansfield Park*', in Wood (ed.), *Mansfield Park*, pp. 32–52.

47. Lawrence Stone, *The Family, Sex and Marriage in England* (Harmondsworth: Penguin, 1979).

48. Hudson, *Sibling Love and Incest*, p. 12.

49. *Ibid.*, p. 35.

50. Otto Kernberg, *Borderline Conditions and Pathological Narcissism* (New York: Jacob Aronson, 1975), p. 233.

51. Smith, 'My only sister now,' p. 8.

52. John Dixon Hint and Peter Willis (eds), *The Genius of the Place: The English Lansdscape Garden 1620–1820* (Cambridge, MA, and London: MIT Press, 1988), p. 15.

53. Alexander Pope, 'Epistle IV. To Richard Boyle, Earl of Burlington', *The Poems of Alexander Pope*, ed. John Butt (London: Methuen, 1968), pp. 590, 586.

54. Roy Strong, *The Renaissance Garden in England* (London: Thames and Hudson, 1998), p. 11.

55. Carole Fabricant, 'Binding and Dressing Nature's Loose Tresses: The Ideology of Augustan Landscape Design', *Studies in Eighteenth-Century Culture*, 8 (1979), 113, 125–6.

56. For the fullest account of this, see Warren Roberts, *Jane Austen and the French Revolution* (Basingstoke: Macmillan – now Palgrave Macmillan, 1979), pp. 22–31.

57. Colley, *Britons*, pp. 179–80.

58. Horace Walpole, *The History of the Modern Taste in Gardening*, Introduction by John Dixon Hunt (New York: Ursus, 1995), p. 7.

59. *Ibid.*, pp. 18–19.

60. *Ibid.*, p. 8.

61. John Milton, 'Paradise Lost' IV, *The Complete English Poems*, ed. Gordon Campbell (London: Everyman, 1990), pp. 225, 228.

62. Edward Malins, *English Landscaping and Literature 1660–1840* (London: Oxford University Press, 1966), pp. 129–39; Alistair M. Duckworth, *The Improvement of the Estate. A Study of Jane Austen's Novels* (Baltimore and London: Johns Hopkins Press, 1971), pp. 35–80.

63. Walpole, *History of the Modern Taste*, pp. 49–50.

64. *Ibid.*

65. Simon Schama, *A History of Britain Volume 3: At the Edge of the World? 3000 BC–AD 1603* (London: BBC, 2000), pp. 352–3.

66. Malins, *English Landscaping*, p. 125.

67. Walpole, *History of the Modern Taste*, pp. 42–3.

68. Laurence Sterne, *A Sentimental Journey and Journal to Eliza*, Afterword by Monroe Engel (New York: Signet, 1964), p. 79.

69. *Ibid.*, p. 82.

70. *Ibid.*, p. 83.

71. Laurence Sterne, *The Life and Opinions of Tristram Shandy*, ed. Ian Campbell Ross (Oxford: Oxford University Press, 1983), p. 493.

For accounts of Sterne and slavery, on which I draw here, see Markman Ellis, *The Politics of Sensibility: Race, gender and commerce in the sentimental novel* (Cambridge: Cambridge University Press, 1996), pp. 55–79; Ian Campbell Ross, *Laurence Sterne: A Life* (Oxford: Oxford University Press, 2001), pp. 349–52.

72. Thomas Clarkson, *The History of the Rise, Progress and Accomplishment of the Abolition of the African Slave-Trade by the British Parliament*, 2 vols (London: Longman, Hurst, Rees and Orme, 1808), 1: 60–1.

73. Edward Said, *Culture and Imperialism* (New York: Alfred A. Knopf, 1993), p. 96.

74. Ellis, *Politics of Sensibility*, p. 59.

75. Sterne, 'Job's Account of the Shortness and Troubles of Life, Considered', *The Writings of Laurence Sterne*, 5 vols (New York: AMS Press, 1970), 5: 169.

76. Ross, *Lawrence Sterne*, p. 349.

77. Ellis, *Politics of Sensibility*, p. 74.

78. Lorenz Eitner, 'Cages, Prisons and Captives in Eighteenth-Century Art', in Karl Kroeber and William Walling (eds), *Images of Romanticism: Verbal and Visual Affinities* (New Haven and London: Yale University Press, 1978), p. 16.

79. Thus Patricia Rozema's feminist *Mansfield Park* offers a relatively sympathetic Maria (Victoria Hamilton), well aware of her own entrapment, who repeats the starling's lines in mitigation of her own affair with Henry.

CHAPTER 5: *EMMA*

1. Butler, *War of Ideas*, p. 274; Johnson, *Women, Politics and the Novel*, p. 126.

2. Watson, *Revolution and the Form of the British Novel*, p. 93.

3. See Roger Sales, *Jane Austen and Representations of Regency England* (London: Routledge, 1996), pp. 155–68 for a compelling reading of 'The Road and the Post Office' in *Emma*.

4. *Ibid.*, p. 155.

5. Joe Queenan, 'Hair Force', in *Confessions of a Ciniplex Heckler: Celluloid Tirades and Escapades* (New York: Hyperion, 2000), p. 143.

6. Sales, *Representations*, p. 145. See pp. 139–55 for a more general account, on which I draw here.

7. David Nokes, *Jane Austen: A Life* (London: Fourth Estate, 1997), p. 160. For the most elaborate account woven around this flimsy material, see Nadia Radovici, *A Youthful Love: Jane Austen and Tom Lefroy?* (Braunton: Merlin, 1995), who reads *Northanger Abbey* and *Persuasion* as encoded accounts of Austen and Lefroy's romance.

8. Claire Tomalin, *Jane Austen: A Life* (Harmondsworth: Penguin, 2000), p. 121.

9. Lt Colonel J. A. P. Lefroy, 'Jane Austen's Irish Friend: Rt. Hon. Thomas Langlois Lefroy', *Proceedings of the Huguenot Society of London*, 23: 3 (1979), 148.

10. Patrick Geoghegan, *Robert Emmet: A Life* (Dublin: Gill and Macmillan, 2002), pp. 72–3. A bust of Lefroy now stands with those of Emmet and of Edmund Burke in the Long Room of TCD's library.

11. *The Times*, 26 January 1872.

12. John Wiltshire, *Recreating Jane Austen* (Cambridge: Cambridge University Press, 2001), p. 127.

13. Katie Trumpener, *Bardic Nationalism: The Romantic Novel and the British Empire* (Princeton, NJ: Princeton University Press, 1997), p. 19.

14. Nancy Armstrong, *Desire and Domestic Fiction: A Political History of the Novel* (Oxford: Oxford University Press, 1987), p. 136.

15. J. M. Q. Davies, '*Emma* as Charade and the Education of the Reader', in David Monaghan (ed.), '*Emma*': *Contemporary Critical Essays*, New Casebooks Series (Basingstoke: Macmillan – now Palgrave Macmillan, 1992), pp. 77–87. See also Mark Schorer, 'The Humiliation of Emma Woodhouse', in David Lodge (ed.), *Emma*, Casebook Series (Basingstoke: Macmillan – now Palgrave Macmillan, 1968), pp. 170–87; Alistair M. Duckworth, ' "Spillikins, paper ships, riddles, conundrums, and cards": games in Jane Austen's life and fiction', in John Halperin (ed.), *Jane Austen: Bicentenary Essays* (Cambridge: Cambridge University Press, 1975); Alex Page, ' "Straightforward Emotions and Zigzag Embarrassments" in Austen's *Emma*', in James Engell (ed.), *Johnson and his Age* (Cambridge, MA, and London: Harvard University Press, 1984), pp. 559–74; Joseph Litvak, 'Reading Characters: Self, Society and Text in *Emma*', *PMLA*, 100(5) (1985), 763–73.

16. Linda Colley, *Britons: Forging the Nation 1700–1837* (London: Vintage, 1996), pp. 279–82.

17. Austen-Leigh *et al.*, *A Memoir of Jane Austen and Other Family Recollections*, p. 92. Kathryn Sutherland notes that 'permission to dedicate [*Emma*] to the Prince Regent was something of a two-edged compliment. [Austen] hoped the knowledge might speed up production, but saw no evidence for this. On the other hand, she did become liable to costs which had to be paid out of her own pocket – an expensive red morocco presentation binding' (p. 242).

18. Simon Schama, *A History of Britain Volume 2: The British Wars 1603–1776* (London: BBC, 2001), pp. 394–8.

19. *Ibid.*, pp. 395, 396.

20. James Thomson, *The Works of James Thomson*, 2 vols (Dublin: J. Exshaw, R. James, and S. Price, 1751), 2: 168.

21. *Ibid.*, 2: 187–9.

22. LeRoy W. Smith, *Jane Austen and the Drama of Women* (Basingstoke: Macmillan – now Palgrave Macmillan, 1983), p. 188n7; see also pp. 130–5.

23. Edmund Wilson, 'A Long Talk About Jane Austen', in Watt (ed.), *Jane Austen*, p. 39. Emma is described as a 'latent lesbian' by David Lodge, *Jane Austen: Emma*, p. 22 – this in the context of the work of Marvin Mudrick. Alex Page, 'Straightforward Emotions', pp. 561–3, writes of Emma's 'androgyny' and her 'erotic feelings for Harriet'. Christine St. Peter, broadening her discussion to Austen as a whole, claims that 'while an Austen heroine needs a husband, a man is not enough. She also needs a woman. Integral to the securing of a suitable male is the search for a compatible woman'; this does not, however, says St. Peter, make Austen herself a 'crypto-lesbian'! See Christine St. Peter, 'Jane Austen's Creation of the Sister', *Philological Quarterly*, 66(4) (1987), 474–5. A similar notion, though with specific reference to sisterly relationships rather than female relationships in general, is offered by Hudson, *Sibling Love and Incest*, p. 63. In the mid-90s, such speculations were further complicated (or enriched) by the furore which followed Terry Castle's speculations in 'Sister-Sister' about the erotics of Austen's *own* relationship with Cassandra. Emma Tennant's sequel, *Emma in Love*, also presents a lesbian Emma.

24. Lilian Faderman, *Surpassing the Love of Men: Romantic Friendship and Love Between Women from the Renaissance to the Present* (London: The Women's Press, 1985). For an analysis of the Romantic friendship in fiction, see Janet Todd, *Women's Friendship in Literature* (New York: Columbia University Press, 1980).

25. Page, 'Straightforward Emotions', p. 561.

26. Mikhail Bakhtin, *Problems of Dostoevsky's Poetics*, ed. and trans. Caryl Emerson (Manchester: Manchester University Press, 1984), p. 7.

27. Brian Wilkie, 'Jane Austen: Amor and Amoralism', *JEGP*, 91(4) (1992), 542.

28. For a detailed discussion of this image, see Mark Parker, 'The End of *Emma*: Drawing the Boundaries of Class in Austen', *JEGP*, 91(3), (1992), 344–59.

29. R. W. Chapman reproduces this poem in full in the notes to his Oxford edition of *Emma* (pp. 490–1), though passes silently over its sexual content. For readings which do focus on the sexual element of the poem, on which I draw here, see Alice Chandler, ' "A Pair of Fine Eyes": Jane Austen's Treatment of Sex', *Studies in the Novel*, 7 (1975), 91–2; Jill Heydt-Stevenson, ' "Slipping into the Ha-Ha": Bawdy Humor and Body Politics in Jane Austen's Novels', pp. 316–23.

30. Heydt-Stevenson, *ibid.*, p. 320.

31. Frances Burney, *Cecilia, or Memoirs of an Heiress*, ed. Judy Simons (London: Virago, 1986), p. 398.

32. Edward W. Copeland, 'Money in the Novels of Fanny Burney', *Studies in the Novel*, 8 (1977), 25. For an excellent analysis of this passage in *Cecilia*, and of the novel's relationship to a late eighteenth-century credit economy, see D. Grant Campbell, 'Fashionable Suicide: Conspicuous Consumption and the Collapse of Credit in Frances Burney's *Cecilia*', *Studies in Eighteenth-Century Culture*, 20 (1990).

33. Joseph Wiesenfarth, '*Emma*: point counter point', in John Halperin (ed.), *Jane Austen: Bicentenary Essays* (Cambridge: Cambridge University Press, 1975), p. 210.

CHAPTER 6: *PERSUASION*

1. Linda Colley, *Britons: Forging the Nation 1707–1837* (London: Vintage, 1996), pp. 342, 383.

2. See Raymond Williams, *The Long Revolution* (London: Hogarth Press, 1992).

3. Richard Weight, *Patriots: National Identity in Britain 1940–2000* (London, Basingstoke and Oxford: Pan Macmillan, 2003), p. 1.

4. E. J. Hobsbawm, *Nations and Nationalism since 1780: Programme, Myth, Reality*, 2nd edn (Cambridge: Cambridge University Press, 1992), p. 23.

5. Thomas Paine, 'The Rights of Man', in *The Thomas Paine Reader*, ed. Michael Foot and Isaac Kramnick (Harmondsworth: Penguin, 1987), p. 228.

6. For an account of the cultural myth of Kronos/Saturn, and of this painting, see Marina Warner, *No Go the Bogeyman: Scaring, Lulling and Making Mock* (London: Chatto and Windus, 1998), pp. 48–77.

7. Edmund Burke, *Reflections on the Revolution in France*, ed. Conor Cruise O'Brien (Harmondsworth: Penguin, 1968), pp. 194, 299.

8. P. B. Shelley, 'The Mask of Anarchy', in Duncan Wu (ed.), *Romanticism: An Anthology* (Oxford: Blackwell, 1995), pp. 943–53.

9. George Orwell, 'The Lion and the Unicorn', in *The Penguin Essays of George Orwell* (Harmondsworth: Penguin, 1984), p. 157.

10. Wu, *Romanticism: An Anthology*, p. 876.

11. Hobsbawm, *Nations and Nationalism* pp. 22–3.

12. For Dugdale, see Graham Parry, *The Trophies of Time: English Antiquarians of the Seventeenth Century* (Oxford and New York: Oxford University Press, 1995), pp. 217–48.

13. For an account of this, see Charles E. Robinson, 'Mary Shelley and the Roger Dodsworth Hoax', *Keats–Shelley Journal*, 24 (1975), 20–8.

14. See Shelley, 'Roger Dodsworth: The Reanimated Englishman', in *Collected Tales and Stories*, ed. Charles E Robinson (Baltimore: Johns Hopkins Press, 1976).

15. For accounts of the vampire in Romanticism, see, for example, Christopher Frayling, *Vampyres: Lord Byron to Count Dracula* (London: Faber, 1992), Darryl Jones, *Horror: A Thematic History in Fiction and Film* (London: Arnold, 2002), pp. 71–99, James B. Twitchell, *The Living Dead: A Study of the Vampire in Romantic Literature* (Durham, NC: Duke University Press, 1981).

16. Frayling, *Vampyres*, p. 27.

17. Bram Stoker, *Dracula*, ed. Nina Auerbach and David J. Skal (New York and London: W. W. Norton, 1997), p. 33.

18. Lady Caroline Lamb, *Glenarvon*, ed. Frances Wilson (London: Dent, 1995), p. 123.

19. Both Polidori's 'The Vampyre' and Byron's 'Fragment of a Novel' are reprinted in *The Penguin Book of Vampire Stories*, ed. Alan Ryan (Harmondsworth: Penguin, 1988).

20. George Gordon, Lord Byron, *Selected Poetry*, ed. Jerome McGann (Oxford: Oxford University Press, 1997), 27.

21. For the best account of this theme in the novel, see Cheryl Anne Weissman, 'Doubleness and Refrain in Jane Austen's *Persuasion*', *Kenyon Review*, NS 10:4 (1988), 87–91.

22. In a letter to the *TLS*, 7 October 1983, Nora Crook points out that Gowland's Lotion, a compound of corrosive sublimate of mercury, which Mrs Clay finds efficacious, and which Sir Walter recommends to Anne, was used to treat the scarring caused by syphilis: 'I should recommend Gowland, the constant use of Gowland, during the spring months. Mrs Clay has been using it at my recommendation, and you

see what it has done for her. You see how it has carried away her freckles' (P, 146).

23. For a version of this argument, see, for example, Barrell, *The Dark Side of the Landscape*, pp. 8–9.

24. For the best analysis of this theme in Burney's writing, see Edward W. Copeland, 'Money in the Novels of Fanny Burney', *Studies in the Novel*, 8 (1977), 24–37.

25. Burney, *Cecilia*, pp. 710–11.

26. Burney, *The Wanderer; or, Female Difficulties*, ed. Margaret Anne Doody, Robert L. Mack and Peter Sabor with an Introduction by Margaret Anne Doody (Oxford: Oxford University Press, 1991), p. 303.

27. *Ibid.*, p. 323.

28. *Ibid.*, p. 329.

29. *Ibid.*, p. 324.

30. Tanner, *Jane Austen* p. 216.

31. There is a textual variant here. While Chapman's Oxford edition, which I use, reads 'his dear daughter's sake', D. W. Harding's Penguin edition has 'his dear daughters' sake', which (fractionally) diminishes the incestuous overtones here: Austen, *Persuasion*, ed. D. W. Harding (Harmondsworth: Penguin, 1965), p. 37.

32. C. W. Pasley, *Essay on the Military Policy and Institutions of the British Empire*, 4th edn (London: T. Egerton, 1813), p. 2.

33. Norman Davies, *The Isles: A History* (Basingstoke: Macmillan – now Palgrave Macmillan, 2000), p. 592.

34. *Ibid.*, p. 587.

35. Colley, *Britons*, p. 198.

36. Simon Schama, *A History of Britain, Volume Three: The Fate of Empire 1776–2000* (London: BBC, 2002), p. 113.

37. For an account of this painting, see Colley, *Britons*, p. 194.

38. Richardson, *Sir Charles Grandison*, 6: 16.

39. A. Walton Litz, '*Persuasion*: Forms of Estrangement', in John Halperin (ed.), *Jane Austen: Bicentenary Essays* (Cambridge: Cambridge University Press, 1975), p. 223.

40. P. K. Kemp, *Prize Money: A Survey of the History and Distribution of the Naval Prize Fund* (Aldershot: Wellington Press, 1946), pp. 9–23.

41. Mrs Smith's presence in the novel has tended to prove controversial. Marvin Mudrick, *Irony as Defense and Discovery*, p. 222, considered

that 'her presence is too useful, her story too pat'. Butler, *War of Ideas*, p. 280, believes the whole episode with Mrs Smith to be 'glaringly wrong . . . undermotivated and inconsistent'. John Odmark, *An Understanding of Jane Austen's Novels* (Oxford: Blackwell, 1981) sees her function as 'contrivance and coincidence' (p. 35), while Michael Williams, *Jane Austen: Six Novels and their Methods* (Basingstoke: Macmillan, 1986), p. 155 believes her to be 'clumsily jerked into the novel'. Conversely, Kirkham, surely correctly, reads her as part of 'an extended "sisterhood", not based on "blood" but on extra-familial ties between women', Margaret Kirkham, *Jane Austen, Feminism and Fiction* (Brighton: Harvester, 1983), p. 150.

42. Patricia Meyer Spacks, *Gossip* (New York: Alfred A. Knopf, 1985).

43. Brontë, *Critical Assessments*, 1: 428–9.

44. Sandra M. Gilbert, and Susan Gubar. *The Madwoman in the Attic: The Woman Writer and the Nineteenth-Century Literary Imagination* (New Haven and London: Yale University Press, 1979), p. 3.

45. For this reading, see Heydt-Stevenson, 'Slipping into the Ha-Ha', p. 309.

AFTERWORD

1. John Wiltshire, *Jane Austen and the Body: 'The Picture of Health'* (Cambridge: Cambridge University Press, 1992), pp. 18–19.

2. Karina Williamson, 'Body Language', *Essays In Criticism*, 44: 1 (January 1994), p. 52.

3. E. M. Forster, 'Jane Austen: 1. The Six Novels', *'Abinger Harvest' and 'England's Pleasant Land'*, ed. Elizabeth Heine, The Abinger Edition of E. M. Forster, vol. 10 (London: Andre Deutsch, 1996), p. 142.

4. Linda Troost and Sayre Greenfield, 'Introduction: Watching Ourselves Watching', in Troost and Greenfield (eds), *Jane Austen in Hollywood* (Lexington: University of Kentucky Press, 1998), p. 1.

5. Cheryl L. Nixon, 'Balancing the Courtship Hero: Masculine Emotional Display in Film Adaptations of Austen's Novels', in Troost and Greenfield, *ibid.*, p. 23.

6. Lisa Hopkins, 'Mr. Darcy's Body: Privileging the Female Gaze', in Troost and Greenfield, *ibid.*, p. 112.

7. Helen Fielding, *Bridget Jones: The Edge of Reason* (New York: Viking, 2000), p. 142.

8. John Leonard, 'Novel Colonies', *Nation* (22 March 1993), 383. See also Michael Gorra, 'Who Paid the Bills at Mansfield Park?', *New York*

Times Book Review, 28 February 1993, p. 11; Irving Howe, 'History and Literature: Edward Said's *Culture and Imperialism*', *Dissent*, 40 (Fall 1993), 557–9; W. J. T. Mitchell, 'In the Wilderness', *London Review of Books*, 8 April 1993. For a critical analysis of the responses to Said on Austen, see Susan Fraiman, 'Jane Austen and Edward Said: Gender, Culture and Imperialism', *Critical Inquiry*, 21 (Summer 1995), 805–21.

9. Avrom Fleishman, *A Reading of 'Mansfield Park'* (Baltimore and London: Johns Hopkins Press, 1967).

10. Brontë, *Critical Assessments*, 1: 428–9.

11. Jan S. Fergus, 'Sex and Social Life in Jane Austen's Novels', in David Monaghan (ed.), *Jane Austen in a Social Context* (London and Basingstoke: Macmillan – now Palgrave Macmillan, 1981), p. 66.

12. H. W. Garrod, 'Jane Austen: A Depreciation', in *Essays by Divers Hands: Transactions of the Royal Society of Literature*, 8 (Oxford, 1928); E. N. Hayes, '*Emma*: A Dissenting Voice', in David Lodge (ed.), *Jane Austen: 'Emma'*, Casebook Series (London and Basingstoke: Macmillan, 1968), pp. 74–8.

13. See Claudia L. Johnson, 'Austen Cults and Cultures', in Edward Copeland and Juliet McMaster (eds), *The Cambridge Companion to Jane Austen* (Cambridge: Cambridge University Press, 1997), pp. 211–26. For an excellent account of the problems faced by a modern academic up against the 'Jane Austen culture' of 'idolatrously committed Janeites', which includes a useful history of the rise of twentieth-century Janeism, see Claudia Johnson's 'Gender, Theory and Jane Austen Culture', in Nigel Wood (ed.), *Mansfield Park*, Theory in Practice Series (Buckingham: Open University Press, 1993), pp. 92–118.

14. Hopkins, 'Mr. Darcy's Body', p. 112.

15. Rudyard Kipling, 'The Janeites', *Collected Stories*, ed. Robert Gottlieb (London: Everyman, 1994), pp. 733–54. See Johnson, 'Austen Cults and Cultures', pp. 214–17, for this reading.

16. Dorothy Van Ghent, *The English Novel: Form and Function* (New York: Harper and Row, 1953, rpt 1961), p. 99.

17. Walter Allen, *The English Novel* (Harmondsworth: Penguin, 1958), p. 111.

18. Ian Watt (ed.), *Jane Austen: A Collection of Critical Essays*, Twentieth-Century Views Series (Englewood Cliffs, NJ: Prentice-Hall, 1963), p. 2.

19. George Steiner, *After Babel: Aspects of Language and Translation* (Oxford: Oxford University Press, 1975), p. 9.

20. Judith Woolf, *Henry James: The Major Novels* (Cambridge: Cambridge University Press, 1991), p. 9.

21. Harold Bloom, *The Western Canon: The Books and School of the Ages* (London: Macmillan – now Palgrave Macmillan, 1995), p. 257.

22. Roger Gard, *Jane Austen's Novels: The Art of Clarity* (New Haven and London: Yale University Press, 1992), p. 1.

23. See Stanley Fish, 'Profession Despise Thyself: Fear and Self-Loathing In Literary Studies', and 'Anti-Professionalism', in *Doing What Comes Naturally: Change, Rhetoric, and the Practice of Theory in Literary and Legal Studies* (Oxford: Clarendon Press, 1989), pp. 197–214, 241–56.

24. *Ibid.*, p. 208.

25. *Ibid.*, p. 197.

26. Troost and Greenfield, 'Watching Ourselves Watching', p. 4.

27. Tony Tanner, *Jane Austen* (London and Basingstoke: Macmillan – now Palgrave Macmillan, 1986), pp. 172–3.

28. *Ibid.*, pp. 9, 131, 181.

29. D. A. Miller, *Narrative and its Discontents: Problems of Closure in the Traditional Novel* (Princeton, NJ: Princeton University Press, 1981), pp. 4–5.

30. Eve Kosofsky Sedgwick, 'Jane Austen and the Masturbating Girl', *Tendencies* (London: Routledge, 1994), p. 115.

31. *Ibid*, p. 109.

32. Sedgwick, however, offers no evidence that she has actually read much Austen criticism: she cites only two works on Austen, one of which is Tanner's book – interestingly, Tanner is also one of the three Austen critics cited by Said, who reckons his chapter on *Mansfield Park* to be 'the best account of the novel'. (It isn't.) See Edward Said, *Culture and Imperialism* (New York: Alfred A. Knopf, 1993), p. 342 n. 36.

33. Terry Eagleton, *Heathcliff and the Great Hunger: Studies in Irish Culture* (London: Verso, 1995), p. 168.

34. See David R. Shumway, 'The Star System In Literary Studies', *PMLA* Special Edition (January 1997), 85–100.

35. Fish, 'No Bias, No Merit: The Case Against Blind Submission', In *Doing What Comes Naturally*, pp. 166–7.

36. Quoted in Devoney Looser, 'Feminist Implications of the Silver Screen Austen', in Troost and Greenfield, *Jane Austen in Hollywood*, p. 161.

37. David Lodge, *Changing Places*, p. 215.

38. Terry Castle, 'Sister–Sister', *London Review of Books*, 17: 15 (3 August 1995), 6.

39. *Ibid.*, p. 3.

40. See Edmund Wilson, 'A Long Talk About Jane Austen', reprinted in Watt (ed.), *Jane Austen*, pp. 35–40; Marvin Mudrick, *Jane Austen: Irony as Defense and Discovery* (Princeton, NJ: Princeton University Press, 1952).

41. Janet Todd, *Women's Friendship in Literature* (New York: Columbia University Press, 1980); Lilian Faderman, *Surpassing the Love of Men: Romantic Friendship and Love Between Women from the Renaissance to the Present* (London: The Women's Press, 1985).

42. *London Review of Books*, 17: 16 (24 August 1995), 4.

43. *Ibid.*, 17: 17 (7 September 1995), p. 4.

44. *Ibid.*, 17: 19 (5 October 1995), p. 4.

45. *Ibid.*, 17: 16, p. 4.

46. Quoted in Rachel M. Brownstein, 'Out of the Drawing Room, Onto the Lawn', in Troost and Greenfield, *Jane Austen in Hollywood*, p. 19.

47. Martin Amis, 'Jane's World', *The New Yorker*, 8 Jan 1996, p. 31.

48. Clive Bloom, *Bestsellers: Popular Fiction Since 1900* (Basingstoke: Palgrave Macmillan, 2002), p. 41.

49. David Nokes, *Jane Austen: A Life* (London: Fourth Estate, 1997), p. 264. Nokes's is one of (at least) three biographies of Austen published in 1997: the others are Valerie Grosvenor Myer, *Jane Austen: Obstinate Heart* (New York: Arcade, 1997), and Claire Tomalin, *Jane Austen* (Harmondsworth: Penguin, 1997).

50. Johnson, 'Austen Cults and Cultures', p. 211.

Bibliography

M. H. Abrams, *A Glossary of Literary Terms*, Third edn. New York: Rinehart and Winston, 1971.

Walter Allen, *The English Novel*. Harmondsworth: Penguin, 1958.

Kingsley Amis, 'What Became of Jane Austen?' in Ian Watt (ed.), *Jane Austen: A Collection of Critical Essays*, Twentieth-century Views series. Englewood Cliffs, NJ: Prentice-Hall, 1963.

Martin Amis, 'Jane's World', *The New Yorker*, 8 Jan 1996.

Nancy Armstrong, *Desire and Domestic Fiction: A Political History of the Novel*. Oxford: Oxford University Press, 1987.

W. H. Auden, *Collected Poems*. London: Faber, 1976.

Jane Austen, *Jane Austen's Letters*, collected and edited by Deirdre Le Faye. Oxford: Oxford University Press, 1995.

——, *Jane Austen's 'Sir Charles Grandison'*, Transcribed and ed. Brian Southam, Foreword by Lord David Cecil. Oxford: Clarendon Press, 1980.

——, *The Novels of Jane Austen*, ed. R. W. Chapman, 6 vols, 3rd edn. London: Oxford University Press, 1969.

J. E. Austen-Leigh *et al.*, *A Memoir of Jane Austen and Other Family Recollections*, ed. Kathryn Sutherland. Oxford: Oxford University Press, 2002.

William Austen-Leigh, *Jane Austen: A Family Record*, revised and enlarged by Deirdre Le Faye. London: British Library, 1989.

Gaston Bachelard, *The Poetics of Space*, trans. Maria Jolas. New York: Orion, 1964.

M. M. Bakhtin, *The Dialogic Imagination: Four Essays*, ed. Michael Holquist, trans. Caryl Emerson and Michael Holquist. Austin: University of Texas Press, 1981.

——, *Problems of Dostoevsky's Poetics*, trans. Caryl Emerson. Manchester: Manchester University Press, 1984.

G. J. Barker-Benfield, *The Culture of Sensibility: Sex and Society in Eighteenth-Century Britain*. Chicago and London: University of Chicago Press, 1992.

John Barrell, *The Dark Side of the Landscape: The Rural Poor in English Painting 1730–1840*. Cambridge: Cambridge University Press, 1980.

——, *Imagining the King's Death: Figurative Treason, Fantasies of Regicide 1793–1796*. Oxford: Oxford University Press, 2000.

Roland Barthes, *Writing Degree Zero and Elements of Semiology*, trans. Annette Levers and Colin Smith. Boston: Beacon, 1970.

Barbara M. Benedict, 'Sensibility by the Numbers: Austen's Work as Regency Popular Fiction', in Deirdre Lynch (ed.), *Janeites: Austen's Disciples and Devotees*. Princeton, NJ: Princeton University Press, 2000.

Clive Bloom, *Bestsellers: Popular Fiction Since 1900*. Basingstoke: Palgrave Macmillan, 2002.

Harold Bloom, *The Western Canon: The Books and School of the Ages*. London and Basingstoke: Macmillan – now Palgrave Macmillan, 1995.

Wayne C. Booth, *The Rhetoric of Fiction*, 2nd edn. Harmondsworth: Penguin, 1983.

James Boswell, *Boswell's Life of Johnson*, 6 vols, ed. G. B. Hill, revised by L. H. Powell. Oxford: Clarendon Press, 1964.

Clarence L. Branton, 'The Ordinations in Jane Austen's Novels', *Nineteenth-Century Fiction*, 10 (1955–56).

R. F. Brissenden, '*Mansfield Park*: Freedom and the Family', in John Halperin (ed.), *Jane Austen: Bicentenary Essays*. Cambridge: Cambridge University Press, 1975.

——, *Virtue in Distress: Studies in the Novel of Sentiment from Richardson to Sade*. Basingstoke: Macmillan, 1974.

Reuben A. Brower, 'Light, Bright and Sparkling: Irony and Fiction in *Pride and Prejudice*', in Ian Watt (ed.), *Jane Austen: A Collection of Critical Essays*, Twentieth-century Views series. Englewood Cliffs, NJ: Prentice-Hall, 1963.

Lloyd W. Brown, 'The Comic Conclusions of Jane Austen's Novels', *PMLA*, 84: 2 (1969).

Rachel M. Brownstein, 'Out of the Drawing Room, Onto the Lawn', in Linda Troost and Sayre Greenfield (eds), *Jane Austen in Hollywood*. Lexington: University of Kentucky Press, 1998.

Edmund Burke, *Reflections on the Revolution in France*, ed. Conor Cruise O'Brien. Harmondsworth: Penguin, 1968.

Fanny [Frances] Burney, *Camilla; or, A Picture of Youth*, ed. Edward A. Bloom and Lillian D. Bloom. Oxford: Oxford University Press, 1972.

——, *Cecilia; or, Memoirs of an Heiress*, ed. Judy Simons. London: Virago, 1986.

——, *Evelina*, ed. Stewart J. Cooke. New York: Norton, 1998.

——, *Memoirs of Doctor Burney, arranged from his own manuscripts, from family papers, and from personal recollections. By his Daughter, Madame D'Arblay*, 3 vols. London: Edward Moxon, 1832.

Marilyn Butler, *Jane Austen and the War of Ideas*. Oxford: Oxford University Press, 1975, rpt. with a new Introduction, 1987.

George Gordon, Lord Byron, *Selected Poetry*, ed. Jerome McGann. Oxford: Oxford University Press, 1997.

D. Grant Campbell, 'Fashionable Suicide: Conspicuous Consumption and the Collapse of Credit in Frances Burney's *Cecilia*', *Studies in Eighteenth-Century Culture*, 20 (1990).

Terry Castle, 'Sister–Sister', *London Review of Books*, 17: 15 (3 August 1995).

Alice Chandler, ' "A Pair of Fine Eyes": Jane Austen's Treatment of Sex', *Studies in the Novel*, 7 (1975).

Winston S. Churchill, *The Second World War Volume 5: Closing the Ring*. New York: Houghton Mifflin, 1951.

Thomas Clarkson, *The History of the Rise, Progress and Accomplishment of the Abolition of the African Slave-Trade by the British Parliament*, 2 vols. London: Longman, Hurst, Rees and Orme, 1808.

Samuel Taylor Coleridge, *Letters of Samuel Taylor Coleridge*, ed. Ernest Hartley Coleridge. London: Heinemann, 1895.

Linda Colley, *Britons: Forging the Nation 1700–1837*. London: Vintage, 1996.

Barbara Bail Collins, 'Jane Austen's Victorian Novel', *Nineteenth-Century Fiction*, 4 (1949–50).

Edward W. Copeland, 'Money in the Novels of Fanny Burney', *Studies in the Novel*, 8 (1977).

——, *Women Writing About Money: Women's Fiction in England, 1790–1820*. Cambridge: Cambridge University Press, 1995.

Valérie Cossy, 'Texts Misrepresented: Jane Austen in France and Isabelle de Montolieu', *The European English Messenger*, 6/2 (Autumn 1997).

J. M. Q. Davies, '*Emma* as Charade and the Education of the Reader', in David Monaghan (ed.), *'Emma': Contemporary Critical Essays*, New Casebooks Series. Basingstoke: Macmillan – now Palgrave Macmillan, 1992.

Norman Davies, *The Isles: A History*. Basingstoke: Macmillan – now Palgrave Macmillan, 1999.

Lennard J. Davis, *Resisting Novels: Ideology and Fiction*. London: Methuen, 1987.

William Patrick Day, *In the Circles of Fear and Desire: A Study of Gothic Fantasy*. Chicago and London: University of Chicago Press, 1985.

Margaret Anne Doody, *The True Story of the Novel*. London: HarperCollins, 1997.

Alistair M. Duckworth, *The Improvement of the Estate: A Study of Jane Austen's Novels*. Baltimore and London: Johns Hopkins Press, 1971.

——, ' "Spillikins, paper ships, riddles, conundrums, and cards": games in Jane Austen's life and fiction', in John Halperin (ed.), *Jane Austen: Bicentenary Essays*. Cambridge: Cambridge University Press, 1975.

Joseph M. Duffy, Jr, 'Moral Integrity and Moral Anarchy in *Mansfield Park*', *ELH*, 23 (1956).

Terry Eagleton, *Heathcliff and the Great Hunger: Studies In Irish Culture*. London: Verso, 1995.

——, *Sweet Violence: The Idea of the Tragic*. Oxford: Blackwell, 2003.

Charles E. Edge, '*Mansfield Park* and Ordination', *Nineteenth-Century Fiction*, 16 (1961–2).

Maria Edgeworth, *Belinda*, ed. Kathryn Kirkpatrick. Oxford: Oxford University Press, 1994.

——, *Letters for Literary Ladies*, ed. Claire Connolly. London: Dent, 1993.

Lorenz Eitner, 'Cages, Prisons and Captives in Eighteenth-Century Art', in Karl Kroeber and William Walling (eds), *Images of Romanticism: Verbal and Visual Affinities*. New Haven and London: Yale University Press, 1978.

Markman Ellis, *The Politics of Sensibility: Race, gender and commerce in the sentimental novel*. Cambridge: Cambridge University Press, 1996.

George Eliot, *Middlemarch*, ed. David Carroll. Oxford: Oxford University Press, 1986.

Lee Erickson, *The Economy of Literary Form: English Literature and the Industrialization of Publishing 1800–1850*. Baltimore and London: Johns Hopkins University Press, 1996.

Elizabeth Deeds Ermarth, *Realism and Consensus in the English Novel: Time, Space and Narrative*, 2nd edn. Edinburgh: Edinburgh University Press, 1998.

Mary Evans, 'Henry Crawford and the "Sphere of Love" in *Mansfield Park*', in Nigel Wood (ed.), *Mansfield Park*. Buckingham: Open University Press, 1993.

——, *Jane Austen and the State*. London: Tavistock, 1987.

Carole Fabricant, 'Binding and Dressing Nature's Loose Tresses: The Ideology of Augustan Landscape Design', *Studies in Eighteenth-Century Culture*, 8 (1979).

Lilian Faderman, *Surpassing the Love of Men: Romantic Friendship and Love Between Women from the Renaissance to the Present*. London: Women's Press, 1985.

Eliza Fenwick, *Secresy; or, The Ruin on the Rock*, ed. Janet Todd. London: Pandora, 1989.

Jan S. Fergus, *Jane Austen and the Didactic Novel: 'Northanger Abbey', 'Sense and Sensibility', and 'Pride and Prejudice'*. Basingstoke: Macmillan – now Palgrave Macmillan, 1983.

——, 'Sex and Social Life in Jane Austen's Novels', in David Monaghan (ed.), *Jane Austen in a Social Context* (London and Basingstoke: Macmillan – now Palgrave Macmillan, 1981).

Helen Fielding, *Bridget Jones: The Edge of Reason*. New York: Viking, 2000.

Henry Fielding, *The History of Tom Jones*, ed. R. P. C. Mutter. Harmondsworth: Penguin, 1966.

——, *Joseph Andrews and Shamela*, ed. Arthur Humphreys. London: Dent, 1973.

Stanley Fish, *Doing What Comes Naturally: Change, Rhetoric, and the Practice of Theory In Literary and Legal Studies*. Oxford: Clarendon Press, 1989.

Roger Fiske, *English Theatre Music in the Eighteenth Century*. Oxford: Oxford University Press, 1973.

Avrom Fleishman, *A Reading of Mansfield Park*. Baltimore and London: Johns Hopkins Press, 1967.

E. M. Forster, 'Jane Austen: 1. The Six Novels', *'Abinger Harvest' and 'England's Pleasant Land'*, ed. Elizabeth Heine, The Abinger Edition of E. M. Forster, vol. 10. London: Andre Deutsch, 1996.

Susan Fraiman, 'Jane Austen and Edward Said: Gender, Culture and Imperialism', *Critical Inquiry*, 21 (Summer 1995).

Christopher Frayling, *Vampyres: Lord Byron to Count Dracula*. London: Faber, 1992.

Sigmund Freud, *Case Histories II: The 'Rat Man', Schreber, The 'Wolf Man', A case of Female Homosexuality*, The Penguin Freud Library, vol. 9, trans. James Strachey *et al.*, ed. Angela Richards. Harmondsworth: Penguin, 1979.

Northrop Frye, *Anatomy of Criticism: Four Essays*. Princeton, NJ: Princeton University Press, 1957.

Marjorie Garber, *Vested Interests: Cross-Dressing and Cultural Anxiety*. London and New York: Routledge, 1992.

Roger Gard, *Jane Austen's Novels: The Art of Clarity*. New Haven and London: Yale University Press, 1992.

H. W. Garrod, 'Jane Austen: A Depreciation', in *Essays by Divers Hands: Transactions of the Royal Society of Literature*, 8 (Oxford, 1928).

Peter Garside and Elizabeth McDonald, 'Evangelicalism and *Mansfield Park*', *Trivium*, 10 (1975).

Peter Garside, James Raven and Rainer Schöwerling (eds), *The English Novel 1770–1829: A Bibliographical Survey of Prose Fiction Published in the British Isles*, 2 vols. Oxford: Oxford University Press, 2000.

Patrick Geoghegan, *Robert Emmet: A Life*. Dublin: Gill and Macmillan, 2002.

Michael Giffin, *Jane Austen and Religion: Salvation and Society in Georgian England*. Basingstoke: Palgrave Macmillan, 2002.

Sandra M. Gilbert and Susan Gubar, *The Madwoman in the Attic: The Woman Writer and the Nineteenth-century Literary Imagination*. New Haven, CT: Yale University Press, 1979.

Michael Gorra, 'Who Paid the Bills at Mansfield Park?', *New York Times Book Review*, 28 February 1993.

J. David Grey (ed.), *The Jane Austen Handbook*. London: Athlone Press, 1986.

Susan Griffin, *Pornography and Silence*. London: Women's Press, 1981.

Harriet Guest, *Small Change: Women, Learning, Patriotism, 1750–1810*. Chicago and London: University of Chicago Press, 2000.

John Halperin (ed.), *Jane Austen: Bicentenary Essays*. Cambridge: Cambridge University Press, 1975.

Brean S. Hammond, 'The Political Unconscious in *Mansfield Park*', in Nigel Wood (ed.), *Mansfield Park*. Buckingham: Open University Press, 1993.

D. W. Harding, 'Character and Caricature in Jane Austen', in B. C. Southam (ed.), *Critical Essays on Jane Austen*. London: Routledge and Kegan Paul, 1968.

Jocelyn Harris, *Jane Austen's Art of Memory*. Cambridge: Cambridge University Press, 1989.

E. N. Hayes, '*Emma*: A Dissenting Voice', in David Lodge (ed.), *Jane Austen: 'Emma'*, Casebook Series (London and Basingstoke: Macmillan, 1968).

Joyce Hemlow, 'Fanny Burney and the Courtesy Books', *PMLA*, 65 (1950).

Edward S. Hermann and Noam Chomsky, *Manufacturing Consent: The Political Economy of the Mass Media*. London: Vintage, 1994.

Jill Heydt-Stevenson, '"Slipping into the Ha-Ha": Bawdy Humor and Body Politics in Jane Austen's Novels', *Nineteenth-Century Literature*, 55:3 (December 2000).

E. J. Hobsbawm, *Nations and Nationalism since 1780: Programme, Myth, Reality*, 2nd edn. Cambridge: Cambridge University Press, 1992.

Diane Long Hoeveler, *Gothic Feminism: The Professionalization of Genders from Charlotte Smith to the Brontës*. Liverpool: Liverpool University Press, 1998.

Park Honan, 'Richardson's Influence on Jane Austen', in Valerie Grosvenor Myer (ed.), *Samuel Richardson: Passion and Prudence*. London: Vision, 1986.

Lisa Hopkins, 'Mr. Darcy's Body: Privileging the Female Gaze', in Linda Troost and Sayre Greenfield (eds), *Jane Austen in Hollywood*. Lexington: University of Kentucky Press, 1998.

Irving Howe, 'History and Literature: Edward Said's *Culture and Imperialism*', *Dissent*, 40 (Fall 1993).

Glenda A. Hudson, *Sibling Love and Incest in Jane Austen's Fiction*. Basingstoke: Macmillan – now Palgrave Macmillan, 1992, 2nd edn 1999.

John Dixon Hunt and Peter Willis (eds), *The Genius of the Place: The English Landscape Garden 1620–1820*. Cambridge, MA, and London: MIT Press, 2000.

Elisabeth Jay, *The Evangelical and Oxford Movements*. Cambridge: Cambridge University Press, 1983.

Ann Jefferson and David Rovey (eds), *Modern Literary Theory: A Comparative Introduction*. London: Batsford, 1986.

Claudia L. Johnson, 'Austen Cults and Cultures', in Edward Copeland and Juliet McMaster (eds), *The Cambridge Companion to Jane Austen*. Cambridge: Cambridge University Press, 1997.

——, *Equivocal Beings: Politics, Gender, and Sentimentality in the 1790s*. Chicago and London: University of Chicago Press, 1995.

——, 'Gender, Theory and Jane Austen Culture', in Nigel Wood (ed.), *Mansfield Park*, Theory in Practice Series (Buckingham: Open University Press, 1993).

——, *Jane Austen: Women, Politics and the Novel*. Chicago and London: University of Chicago Press, 1988.

——, 'A "Sweet Face as White as Death"': Jane Austen and the Politics of Female Sensibility', *Novel*, 22 (1989).

Darryl Jones, *Horror: A Thematic History in Fiction and Film*. London: Arnold, 2002.

Ernest Jones, *On The Nightmare*. London: Hogarth Press/Institute of Psychoanalysis, 1949.

R. T. Jones, 'Sir *Charles Grandison*: "A Gauntlet Thrown Out"', in Valerie Grosvenor Myer (ed.), *Samuel Richardson: Passion and Prudence* (London: Vision, 1986), pp. 135–44.

Vivien Jones (ed.), *Women in the Eighteenth Century: Constructions of Femininity*. London: Routledge, 1990.

Deborah Kaplan, *Jane Austen Among Women*. Baltimore: Johns Hopkins Press, 1992.

P. K. Kemp, *Prize Money: A Survey of the History and Distribution of the Naval Prize Fund*. Aldershot: The Wellington Press, 1946.

Otto Kernberg, *Borderline Conditions and Pathological Narcissism*. New York: Jacob Aronson, 1975.

Robert Kiely, *The Romantic Novel in England*. Cambridge, MA: Harvard University Press, 1972.

Rudyard Kipling, *Collected Stories*, ed. Robert Gottlieb. London: Everyman, 1994.

Margaret Kirkham, *Jane Austen, Feminism and Fiction*. Brighton: Harvester, 1983.

Julia Kristeva, *The Kristeva Reader*, ed. Toril Moi. Oxford: Blackwell, 1986.

Lady Caroline Lamb, *Glenarvon*, ed. Frances Wilson. London: Dent, 1995.

Peter Laslett, 'Age at Menarche in Europe since the Eighteenth Century', in Theodore K. Rabb and Robert I. Rotberg (eds), *The Family in History*. New York: Harper and Row, 1973.

——, *Family Life and Illicit Love in Earlier Generations*. Cambridge: Cambridge University Press, 1977.

Emily Lawless, *Maria Edgeworth*. London: Macmillan, 1904.

F. R. Leavis, *The Great Tradition*. Harmondsworth: Penguin, 1972.

Q. D. Leavis, *Collected Essays, Volume 1: The Englishness of the English Novel*, ed. G. Singh. Cambridge: Cambridge University Press, 1983.

Lt. Colonel J. A. P. Lefroy, 'Jane Austen's Irish Friend: Rt. Hon. Thomas Langlois Lefroy', *Proceedings of the Huguenot Society of London*, 23:3 (1979).

John Leonard, 'Novel Colonies', *Nation*, 22 March 1993.

C. S. Lewis, 'A Note on Jane Austen', in Ian Watt (ed.), *Jane Austen: A Collection of Critical Essays*, Twentieth-century Views series. Englewood Cliffs, NJ: Prentice-Hall, 1963.

Matthew Lewis, *The Monk*, ed. Howard Anderson. Oxford: Oxford University Press, 1973.

Ian Littlewood (ed.), *Jane Austen: Critical Assessments*, 4 vols. Mountfield: Helm Information, 1998.

Joseph Litvak, 'Reading Characters: Self, Society and Text in *Emma*', *PMLA*, 100: 5 (1985).

A. Walton Litz, *Jane Austen: A Study of Her Artistic Development*. London: Chatto and Windus, 1965.

——, '*Persuasion*: Forms of Estrangement', in John Halperin (ed.), *Jane Austen: Bicentenary Essays*. Cambridge: Cambridge University Press, 1975.

David Lodge, *Changing Places*. London and Harmondsworth: Penguin, 1975.

—— (ed.), *Emma*, Casebook Series. Basingstoke: Macmillan – now Palgrave Macmillan, 1968.

——, *The Language of Fiction*. London: Routledge and Kegan Paul, 1966.

—— (ed.), *Modern Criticism and Theory: A Reader*. London: Longman, 1988.

——, *Nice Work*. Harmondsworth: Penguin, 1989.

Deirdre Lynch (ed.), *Janeites: Austen's Disciples and Devotees*. Princeton, NJ: Princeton University Press, 2000.

Kathleen Lundeen, 'A Modest Proposal? Paradise Found in Jane Austen's Betrothal Scenes', *RES*, 41 (1990).

Oliver MacDonagh, *Jane Austen: Real and Imagined Worlds*. New Haven and London: Yale University Press, 1991.

Michael McKeon, *The Origins of the English Novel*. London: Hutchinson Radius, 1988.

Edward Malins, *English Landscaping and Literature 1660–1840*. London: Oxford University Press, 1966.

Elizabeth Mavor, *The Ladies of Llangollen*. Harmondsworth: Penguin, 1973.

Louis Menand, 'What Jane Austen Doesn't Tell Us', *New York Review of Books*, 1 February 1996.

D. A. Miller, *Narrative and its Discontents: Problems of Closure in the Traditional Novel*. Princeton, NJ: Princeton University Press, 1981.

John Milton, *The Complete English Poems*, ed. Gordon Campbell. London: Everyman, 1990.

W. J. T. Mitchell, 'In the Wilderness', *London Review of Books*, 8 April 1993.

David Monaghan (ed.), *'Emma': Contemporary Critical Essays*, New Case-books Series. Basingstoke: Macmillan – now Palgrave Macmillan, 1992.

—— (ed.), *Jane Austen in a Social Context*. Basingstoke: Macmillan – now Palgrave Macmillan, 1981.

Fidelis Morgan, *The Well-Known Trouble-Maker: A Life of Charlotte Charke*. London: Faber 1988.

Marvin Mudrick, *Jane Austen: Irony as Defense and Discovery*. Princeton, NJ: Princeton University Press, 1952.

Valerie Grosvenor Myer, *Jane Austen: Obstinate Heart*. New York: Arcade, 1997.

—— (ed.), *Samuel Richardson: Passion and Prudence*. London: Vision, 1986.

Tom Nairn, *After Britain: New Labour and the Return of Scotland*. London: Granta, 2001.

R. S. Neale, *Writing Marxist History: British Society, Economy and Culture Since 1700*. Oxford: Blackwell, 1985.

Edward Neill, *The Politics of Jane Austen*. Basingtoke: Macmillan – now Palgrave Macmillan, 1999.

Judith Lowder Newton, *Women, Power and Subversion: Social Strategies in British Fiction, 1770–1860*. London and New York: Methuen, 1985.

Cheryl L. Nixon, 'Balancing the Courtship Hero: Masculine Emotional Display in Film Adaptations of Austen's Novels', in Linda Troost and Sayre Greenfield (eds), *Jane Austen in Hollywood*. Lexington: University of Kentucky Press, 1998.

David Nokes, *Jane Austen: A Life*. London: Fourth Estate, 1997.

John Odmark, *An Understanding of Jane Austen's Novels*. Oxford: Blackwell, 1981.

George Orwell, *The Penguin Essays of George Orwell*. Harmondsworth: Penguin, 1984.

Alex Page, ' "Straightforward Emotions and Zigzag Embarrassments" in Austen's *Emma*', in James Engell (ed.), *Johnson and his Age*. Cambridge, MA, and London: Harvard University Press, 1984.

Thomas Paine, *The Thomas Paine Reader*, ed. Michael Foot and Isaac Kramnick. Harmondsworth: Penguin, 1987.

Mark Parker, 'The End of *Emma*: Drawing the Boundaries of Class in Austen', *JEGP*, 91: 3 (1992).

Graham Parry, *The Trophies of Time: English Antiquarians of the Seventeenth Century*. Oxford and New York: Oxford University Press, 1995.

C. W. Pasley, *Essay on the Military Policy and Institutions of the British Empire*, 4th edn. London: T. Egerton, 1813.

Amy J. Pawl, ' "And What Other Name May I Claim?" Names and Their Owners in Frances Burney's *Evelina*', *Eighteenth-Century Fiction*, 3 (1991).

Ruth Perry, *Women, Letters and the Novel*. New York: AMS Press, 1980.

Mary Poovey, *The Proper Lady and the Woman Writer: Ideology as Style in the Works of Mary Wollstonecraft, Mary Shelley, and Jane Austen*. Chicago and London: University of Chicago Press, 1984.

Alexander Pope, *The Poems of Alexander Pope*, ed. John Butt. London: Methuen, 1968.

Joe Queenan, *Confessions of a Ciniplex Heckler: Celluloid Tirades and Escapades*. New York: Hyperion, 2000.

Ann Radcliffe, *The Romance of the Forest*, ed. Chloe Chard. Oxford: Oxford University Press, 1986.

Nadia Radovici, *A Youthful Love: Jane Austen and Tom Lefroy?* Braunton: Merlin, 1995.

Frank Rahill, *The World of Melodrama*. University Park: The Pennsylvania University Press, 1967.

Samuel Richardson, *The History of Sir Charles Grandison*, ed. Jocelyn Harris. Oxford: Oxford University Press, 1986.

——, *The History of Sir Charles Grandison; In a Series of Letters*, 7 vols. London: J. Nunn *et al.*, 1820.

Warren Roberts, *Jane Austen and the French Revolution*. Basingstoke: Macmillan, 1979.

Charles E. Robinson, 'Mary Shelley and the Roger Dodsworth Hoax', *Keats–Shelley Journal*, 24 (1975).

Lilian S. Robinson, *Sex, Class and Culture*. London and New York: Methuen, 1986.

Pat Rogers, 'The Breeches Part', in Paul-Gabriel Boucé (ed.), *Sexuality in Eighteenth-century Britain*. Manchester: Manchester University Press, 1982.

Ian Campbell Ross, *Laurence Sterne: A Life*. Oxford: Oxford University Press, 2001.

Alan Ryan (ed.), *The Penguin Book of Vampire Stories*. Harmondsworth: Penguin, 1988.

Gilbert Ryle, 'Jane Austen and the Moralists', in B. C. Southam (ed.), *Critical Essays on Jane Austen*. London: Routledge and Kegan Paul, 1968.

Edward Said, *Culture and Imperialism*. New York: Alfred A. Knopf, 1993.

Christine St. Peter, 'Jane Austen's Creation of the Sister', *Philological Quarterly*, 66:4 (1987).

Roger Sales, *Jane Austen and Representations of Regency England*. London: Routledge, 1996.

Simon Schama, *A History of Britain Volume 1: At the Edge of the World? 3000 BC–AD 1603*. London: BBC, 2000.

——, *A History of Britain Volume 2: The British Wars 1603–1776*. London: BBC, 2001.

——, *A History of Britain Volume 3: The Fate of Empire 1776–2000*. London: BBC, 2002.

Mark Schorer, 'The Humiliation of Emma Woodhouse', in David Lodge (ed.), *Emma*, Casebook Series. Basingstoke: Macmillan – now Palgrave Macmillan, 1968.

Eve Kosofsky Sedgwick, 'Jane Austen and the Masturbating Girl', *Critical Inquiry*, 17 (1991).

Barbara K. Seeber, *General Consent in Jane Austen: A Study in Dialogism*. Montreal: McGill-Queen's University Press, 2000.

William Shakespeare, *Hamlet*, ed. Harold Jenkins. London and New York: Methuen, 1982.

Mary Shelley, *Collected Tales and Stories*, ed. Charles E. Robinson. Baltimore: Johns Hopkins Press, 1976.

——, *The Mary Shelley Reader*, ed. Betty T. Bennett and Charles E. Robinson. Oxford: Oxford University Press, 1990.

Norman Sherry, *Jane Austen*. London: Evans Brothers, 1966.

David R. Shumway, 'The Star System In Literary Studies', *PMLA* Special Edition (January 1997).

Phil Silvers, with Robert Saffron, *The Man Who Was Bilko*. London and New York: W. H. Allen, 1974.

Charlotte Smith, *The Old Manor House*, ed. Anne Henry Ehrenpreis with a new Introduction by Judith Phillips Stanton. Oxford: Oxford University Press, 1989.

Johanna M. Smith, ' "My only sister now": Incest in *Mansfield Park*', *Studies in the Novel*, 18: 1 (1987).

LeRoy W. Smith, *Jane Austen and the Drama of Women*. Basingstoke: Macmillan – now Palgrave Macmillan, 1983.

B. C. Southam, *Jane Austen's Literary Manuscripts*. Oxford: Clarendon Press, 1964.

Patricia Meyer Spacks, 'The Difference it Makes', in Elizabeth Langland and Walter Grove (eds), *A Feminist Perspective on the Academy: the difference it makes.* Chicago and London: University of Chicago Press, 1981.

——, 'Dynamics of Fear: Fanny Burney', in Leopold Damrosch (ed.), *Modern Essays in Eighteenth-century Literature.* Oxford: Oxford University Press, 1988.

——, *Gossip.* New York: Alfred A. Knopf, 1985.

Jane Spencer, *The Rise of the Woman Novelist: From Aphra Behn to Jane Austen.* Oxford: Blackwell, 1986.

Dale Spender, *Mothers of the Novel: 100 good women writers before Jane Austen.* London: Pandora, 1986.

David Spring, 'Interpreters of Jane Austen's Social World: Literary Critics and Historians', in Janet Todd (ed.), *Jane Austen: New Perspectives.* New York and London: Holmes and Meier, 1983.

Fiona Stafford, *The Last of the Race: The Growth of a Myth from Milton to Darwin.* Oxford: Clarendon Press, 1994.

Susan Staves, 'British Seduced Maidens', *Eighteenth-Century Studies*, 14 (1980–81).

George Steiner, *After Babel: Aspects of Language and Translation.* Oxford: Oxford University Press, 1975.

Laurence Sterne, *The Life and Opinions of Tristram Shandy*, ed. Ian Campbell Ross. Oxford: Oxford University Press, 1983.

——, *A Sentimental Journey and Journal to Eliza*, Afterword by Monroe Engel. New York: Signet, 1964.

——, *The Writings of Laurence Sterne*, 5 vols. New York: AMS Press, 1970.

Bram Stoker, *Dracula*, ed. Nina Auerbach and David J. Skal. New York and London: W. W. Norton, 1997.

Lawrence Stone, *The Family, Sex and Marriage in England 1500–1800.* Harmondsworth: Penguin, 1979.

Roy Strong, *The Renaissance Garden in England.* London: Thames and Hudson, 1998.

Alison G. Sulloway, *Jane Austen and the Province of Womanhood.* Philadelphia: University of Pennsylvania Press, 1989.

John Sutherland, *Victorian Novelists and Publishers.* London: Athlone Press, 1976.

Tony Tanner, *Jane Austen.* Basingstoke: Macmillan – now Palgrave Macmillan, 1986.

Stuart M. Tave, *Some Words of Jane Austen*. Chicago and London: University of Chicago Press, 1973.

James Thomson, *The Works of James Thomson*, 2 vols. Dublin: J. Exshaw, R. James, and S. Price, 1751.

Janet Todd, *Sensibility: An Introduction*. London and New York: Methuen, 1986.

——, *Women's Friendship in Literature*. New York: Columbia University Press, 1980.

Claire Tomalin, *Jane Austen: A Life*, revised edn. Harmondsworth: Penguin, 2000.

Lionel Trilling, '*Mansfield Park*', in Ian Watt (ed.), *Jane Austen: A Collection of Critical Essays*, Twentieth-century Views series. Englewood Cliffs, NJ: Prentice-Hall, 1963.

Linda Troost and Sayre Greenfield (eds), *Jane Austen in Hollywood*. Lexington: University of Kentucky Press, 1998.

Katie Trumpener, *Bardic Nationalism: The Romantic Novel and the British Empire*. Princeton, NJ: Princeton University Press, 1997.

James B. Twitchell, *Dreadful Pleasures: An Anatomy of Modern Horror*. Oxford: Oxford University Press, 1985.

——, *The Living Dead: A Study of the Vampire in Romantic Literature*. Durham, NC: Duke University Press, 1981.

Dorothy Van Ghent, *The English Novel: Form and Function*. New York: Harper and Row, 1953, rpt 1961.

Horace Walpole, *The History of the Modern Taste in Gardening*, Introduction by John Dixon Hunt. New York: Ursus, 1995.

Marina Warner, *No Go the Bogeyman: Scaring, Lulling and Making Mock*. London: Chatto and Windus, 1998.

Nicola J. Watson, *Revolution and the Form of the British Novel 1790–1825: Intercepted Letters, Interrupted Seductions*. Oxford: Clarendon Press, 1994.

Ian Watt (ed.), *Jane Austen: A Collection of Critical Essays*, Twentieth-century Views series. Englewood Cliffs, NJ: Prentice-Hall, 1963.

——, *The Rise of the Novel: Studies in Defoe, Richardson and Fielding*. London: Hogarth Press, 1987, first pub. 1957.

Richard Weight, *Patriots: National Identity in Britain 1940–2000*. London and Basingstoke: Pan Macmillan, 2002.

Cheryl Anne Weissman, 'Doubleness and Refrain in Jane Austen's *Persuasion*', *Kenyon Review*, NS 10: 4 (1988).

Fay Weldon, *Letters to Alice, on first reading Jane Austen*. London: Coronet, 1984.

H. G. Wells, *Experiment in Autobiography*. New York: Macmillan, 1934.

Jane West, *A Gossip's Story, and a Legendary Tale*, 2 vols. London: T. N. Longman, 1798 [3rd edn.].

Joseph Wiesenfarth, '*Emma*: point counter point', in John Halperin (ed.), *Jane Austen: Bicentenary Essays*. Cambridge: Cambridge University Press, 1975.

Brian Wilkie, 'Jane Austen: Amor and Amoralism', *JEGP*, 91:4 (1992).

Michael Williams, *Jane Austen: Six Novels and Their Methods*. Basingstoke: Macmillan – now Palgrave Macmillan, 1986.

Raymond Williams, *The Country and the City*. London: Hogarth Press, 1993.

——, *The Long Revolution*. London: Hogarth Press, 1992.

Karina Williamson, 'Body Language', *Essays In Criticism*, 44: 1 (January 1994).

Edmund Wilson, 'A Long Talk About Jane Austen', in Ian Watt (ed.), *Jane Austen: A Collection of Critical Essays*, Twentieth-century Views series. Englewood Cliffs, NJ: Prentice-Hall, 1963.

Andrew Wilton, *The Swagger Portrait: Grand Manner Portraiture in Britain from Van Dyck to Augustus John 1630–1930*. London: Tate Gallery, 1992.

John Wiltshire, *Jane Austen and the Body: The Picture of Health*. Cambridge: Cambridge University Press, 1992.

——, *Recreating Jane Austen*. Cambridge: Cambridge University Press, 2001.

Mary Wollstonecraft, *Mary and The Wrongs of Women*, ed. Gary Kelly. Oxford: Oxford University Press, 1976.

——, *A Vindication of the Rights of Woman*, ed. Miriam Brody. Harmondsworth: Penguin, 1975.

Mary Wollstonecraft and William Godwin, '*A Short Residence in Sweden*' and '*Memoirs of the Author of "The Rights of Woman"*', ed. Richard Holmes. Harmondsworth: Penguin, 1987.

Nigel Wood (ed.), *Mansfield Park*. Buckingham: Open University Press, 1993.

Judith Woolf, *Henry James: The Major Novels*. Cambridge: Cambridge University Press, 1991.

Andrew H. Wright, *Jane Austen's Novels: A Study in Structure*. London: Chatto and Windus, 1961.

Index